Around the AMERICAN TABLE

Around the AMERICAN TABLE

TREASURED RECIPES AND FOOD TRADITIONS

MICHAEL KRONDL

THE NEW YORK PUBLIC LIBRARY

Produced by Alison Brown Cerier Book Development, Inc.

ADAMS PUBLISHING
HOLBROOK, MASSACHUSETTS

Published by Adams Media Corporation
260 Center Street, Holbrook, MA 02343

ISBN: 1-55850-540-7

Printed in the United States of America.

J I H G F E D C B A

Library of Congress Cataloging-in-Publication Data
Krondl, Michael.
    Around the American table: treasured recipes and food traditions from the American cookery collections of the New York Public Library / Michael Krondl.
        p.   cm.
    "New York Public Library book."
    Includes bibliographical references and index.
    ISBN 1-55850-540-7   (hb)
    1. Cookery, American.   2. Food habits — United States — History.
3. United States — Social life and customs — History.   I. New York Public Library.   II. Title.
TX715.K8987   1995
641.5973 — dc20   95-38229
                                                                      CIP

The name "The New York Public Library" and the representation of the lion appearing in this Work are registered trademarks and the property of The New York Public Library, Astor, Lenox, and Tilden Foundations.

Produced by Alison Brown Cerier Book Development, Inc.

Book design: Javier A. Amador-Peña

This book is available at quantity discounts for bulk purchases.
For information, call 1-800-872-5627.

TO MY MOTHER AND FATHER

Contents

Preface

The culinary collection of The New York Public Library is a spectacular accumulation of material in a library world-renowned for its extensive collections. By itself, the subject of food and cookery comprises over 50,000 volumes. There are cookbooks, periodicals, prints, manuscripts, and menus. Some date back to the sixteenth century. Just the cookbooks alone number about 15,000.

This cookbook collection, perhaps the finest collection of historical cookbooks in the country, is part of a truly astonishing institution. The New York Public Library is considered one of the greatest libraries in the world and second in the United States only to the Library of Congress. Unique among the world's great libraries, NYPL through The Research Libraries—Center for Humanities, Social Science and Special Collections, The Library for the Performing Arts, The Schomburg Center for Research in Black Culture, and the soon-to-open Science, Industry and Business Library—makes its unique collections freely available to scholars, researchers, or anyone seeking information.

Cookbooks have been acquired comprehensively by the Research Libraries since the Library's founding in 1895—not only books from traditional publishers, but also those issued by individuals, by private clubs and charity organizations, and by fine presses in limited editions. The collection is international in scope, but regional American cooking has always been a primary focus of the acquisition process. There are over 3,000 American cookbooks. The majority are from the twentieth century, but there are over 300 from the nineteenth.

All the great American cookbook authors are represented. Many of the books are rare. The first cookbook ever written by an American, Amelia Simmons, is here in a 1796 printing, as well as the first Southern cookbook, Mary Randolph's *Virginia Housewife* in the 1824 edition. There is a copy of the first commercially published book by an African-American, Robert Roberts's *The House Servants' Directory, or a Monitor for Private Families* from 1827, a comprehensive guide for domestics which covers food service among other matters. Nineteenth-century Jewish-American cooking is presented in Esther Levy's *Jewish Cookery Book*, published in 1871, the first of its kind in the United States.

Given the extraordinary abundance of American cookbooks and their tremendous regional diversity, I decided to focus on the most significant regional styles during times when the culinary literature was most vibrant. Thus I looked to Virginia, in the early days of the Republic, as the finest early example of Southern cooking. The section on New Orleans concentrates on the late nineteenth century at a time when that uniquely American blend of French, Spanish, and African cooking that still flourishes today in Louisiana was being extensively documented for the first time. African-American cooks, who contributed much to American cooking, are the subject of a chapter set in the South in the era before many Blacks migrated north. The Pennsylvania Dutch are examined in their glory days in the years before the First World War. The industrial Midwest is seen through the cookbooks published by national food companies, which have influenced the way Americans have been eating for fifty years. And the Fifties, the era when the best and the worst America had to offer seemed to come together, could be seen most clearly under the California sun.

I chose recipes for several reasons. First, there were recipes I thought essential for historical reasons, recipes that form the foundation of our culinary heritage. I thought it important to include the first receipt for fried chicken (from *The Virginia Housewife*) as well as early versions of roast turkey, corn bread, macaroni and cheese, gumbo, chili, tomato ketchup, ice cream, apple pie, brownies, chocolate pudding, and chocolate chip cookies, to name just a few all-American foods. Secondly, I looked for dishes that told something about their place and time, such as the oyster-stuffed brisket of old Virginia, the breads of the nineteenth century, the distinctly French stewed ducks of Reconstruction-era Louisiana, the wedding-cake-like "Metropolitan Cake" of the Victorian era, even the cheese balls and cocktails of the suburban 1950s. Thirdly, there were recipes that have disappeared from our contemporary repertoire that I think merit rediscovery. Hannah Woolley's recipe for salmon salad with apples tastes like it came from some trendy contemporary restaurant. Mary Randolph's lemon ice cream is the epitome of simple elegance. Rufus Estes's grape-apple butter is just plain fabulous. And the anonymously penned recipe for apricot upside-down cake made with gingerbread from a pamphlet promoting molasses is pure genius.

I chose recipes that can be made in the modern kitchen—sometimes with the cooking method slightly modified, but with similar results. Most of the ingredients are available in any large supermarket, though for the occasional ingredient you may have to venture to a specialized market. I have not changed the recipes in any fundamental way, though in many of the earlier recipes, the instructions are so sketchy that another cook might have come up with a somewhat different dish. I had to gauge what was meant by a spoonful or a handful, to say nothing of "some." Neither measurements nor foods were as standardized as they are today. Most late nineteenth-century cookbooks, for example, assume that ten eggs weighed one pound (10 contemporary large eggs weigh 1¼ pounds), but in those days, when each egg was a slightly different size, that ratio was of limited use. However, I have cut down on the amount of fat called for, sometimes by more that half. Prior to the Second World War, most Americans were convinced that the more fat the better. Where I thought removing the fat would seriously alter the consistency of the dish, I left it alone.

Where I thought appropriate, I have suggested alternative ingredients. Ingredients in parentheses were part of the original recipes.

A number of ingredients have changed over the years, and if authenticity is important to you, you will want to keep the following changes in mind.

Flour, like all foods made in the days preceding industrialized agriculture, used to vary from region to region and even crop to crop. Thus a cook would have to adjust a recipe according to the qualities of her specific supply. Today, the closest you can come to nineteenth-century flour is an organically grown and unbleached variety, available in any health food store. Unbleached all-purpose flour is essential for any bread baking because the bleaching process breaks down gluten and thus makes it more difficult for a yeast dough to rise. In cakes and pies, bleached flour will yield a slightly more tender crumb.

Eggs in the nineteenth century seem to have been about the size of a "medium" egg today. However, I have changed all the ratios to conform to the modern convention of using large eggs whenever they are called for. Use only the standard "large" 2-ounce egg in all the recipes. A few recipes call for raw eggs, which can pose a health hazard should you eat an egg infected by salmonella bacteria. A recent study showed that about 1 in 10,000 eggs is infected. The only way to avoid this risk completely is to not eat raw or undercooked eggs.

Cornmeal is usually yellow today in the North and white in the South, though it is not at all clear that this was the case 150 years ago. So use what you have on hand.

Lard was invariably the cooking fat prior to the introduction of shortenings and vegetable oils around the turn of the century. Lard was generally homemade and had lots more flavor than the version you can buy today in supermarkets. In pie crusts, hydrogenated vegetable shortening has similar characteristics even if it does not taste as good. When frying, peanut oil has an almost meaty flavor that is not so different from lard. I have left the lard in the recipes, but included a substitute wherever possible. For more about early cooking fats, see page 62.

Suet, raw beef fat, was widely used to enrich savory stuffings as well as sweet puddings in the eighteenth and nineteenth centuries. It is usually used ground. Most butchers have a ready supply of suet on hand and should sell it to you at a nominal price. Have the butcher grind it for you or use a food processor.

Butter in most American cooking is usually salted. In the few instances where unsalted butter is called for, I have noted it; otherwise, use the lightly salted variety.

Beef today is probably as good as, if not better than, it ever was. It is vastly more tender than it was when cattle were driven to market on foot halfway across the country. Nineteenth-century beef was likely to have been leaner and in need of additional fat in cooking. Many cuts probably required longer cooking times as well.

Pork was very lean in Colonial times when pigs were allowed to roam the woods. It had a much gamier taste as well. After the United States became more densely settled, pigs began to get larger and fatter. Over the last twenty years this trend has reversed, and we now have pork that is much leaner than it was in our grandparents' time. It is trickier to cook lean meat because it dries out easily; in most cases, today's pork should not be cooked past medium well.

Chickens have undergone the greatest change, all for the worse. If you can, try to get free-range chicken; it is worth the price.

Cooking methods have changed even more than ingredients have over the last one hundred years. In the days when food was cooked over an open fire or in a wood-fired oven, everything had a little of that smokey taste. While this made breads and roasts more flavorful, it made cooking delicate pastries and custard more difficult. I have adapted all the recipes for the modern stove, but am mindful of the loss of flavor this occasionally entails.

This book owes its existence to the talent and experience of cooks and cookbook writers over the last 350 years, but it would not have been possible without the help of people very much alive today. I am grateful to the entire staff of The New York Public Library, but especially to Alison Ryley, whose knowledge of the culinary collection was invaluable, and to Karen Van Westering, Manager of Publications, whose support of the project and cookbook expertise have both been essential. Thanks are due also to Margaret Jones for assisting me with the bread recipes, Paul Barsky for his historical review, and all my friends who put up with peculiar menus and lectures when they were invited for dinner. I especially need to thank my editor, Alison Brown Cerier, for giving me enough rope to roam but reeling me back in time so I never had enough to hang myself. Thanks finally to Lucia DeRespinis, for everything.

Recipes by Course

The recipe name on the left was given by the original source. The name on the right is a descriptive contemporary title.

Fish

Seafood

Poultry

Vegetables

Vegetable Salads

Side Dishes

Breads

Cakes

Pies

Cookies and Candies

Breakfast

Cheese Omelet . . . . *(page 152)*

Crab Meat Delight . . . . Scrambled Eggs with
Crabmeat *(page 182)*

Buckwheat Cakes . . . . Yeast-Risen Buckwheat
Pancakes *(page 150)*

Rice Waffles . . . . Breakfast Waffles
with Rice *(page 165)*

Calas . . . . Rice Fritters *(page 189)*

Preserves and Condiments

Quince Marmalade . . . . *(page 216)*

Green Tomato Soy, or Sauce . . . . . Green Tomato and
Mustard Relish *(page 137)*

Tomata Catsup . . . . Tomato Ketchup *(page 80)*

Wild Grape Butter . . . . Apple Grape Butter *(page 195)*

Beverages

John Dabney's Mint Julep . . . . . . *(page 179)*

Gin Fizz . . . . Raspberry Gin Fizz *(page 303)*

Park Avenue Watermelon . . . . Watermelon Champagne
Cooler Cocktail *(page 302)*

Vegetable Cocktail . . . . *(page 304)*

Frog Lemonade . . . . Pineapple Lemonade *(page 125)*

Quick Chocolate . . . . New Mexican Hot
Chocolate *(page 262)*

Cooking by
the Book

Travelling in Europe and famished for the fare of his native land, Mark Twain made a list of foods he would like served as he got off the ship on his return. "I have selected a few dishes," he wrote in *A Tramp Abroad,* "and made out a bill of fare which will go home in the steamer that preceeds [sic] me, and be hot when I arrive—as follows." He then gave a list of some eighty dishes to be presented at his imaginary "modest, private affair." They included the bounty of the whole United States: from brook trout from the Sierra Nevadas and San Francisco mussels, to prairie hens from Illinois and black bass from the Mississippi, to Connecticut shad and canvas back duck from Baltimore. He listed foods that just didn't taste right in Europe: "American toast...American coffee...American butter...American roast beef." And he pined for Saratoga potatoes (potato chips), hot biscuits, roast turkey with cranberry sauce, buckwheat pancakes with maple syrup, terrapin (turtle) soup, corn on the cob, Boston baked beans, apple pie, pumpkin pie, and many more of the regional specialties renowned in nineteenth-century America. The food of his dreams was fresh, simply cooked, and plentiful; in a word, American. Or, at least, the American food of Mark Twain's time.

The broad outlines of our culinary heritage can be drawn quite succinctly. The first inhabitants arrived from Asia between fifteen and thirty thousand years ago, hunting and gathering their supper where they could find it. Most eventually settled down, cultivating corn, beans, squashes, and other foods, depending on the local climate. About four hundred years ago, Europeans arrived. Along the East Coast, most were English, and they cooked as they had in England, adding Native American foods and recipes. The Europeans forcibly brought Africans to North America, adding another set of ingredients and cooking techniques.

These influences came together to form a distinctly American way of cooking that prevailed from the late Colonial period through the mid-nineteenth century. Then the Industrial Revolution came and changed everything. People moved to the cities, started cooking with gas and electricity, and began to eat food that was partially or fully prepared outside the home by large industrial concerns. That process has accelerated as the twentieth century has progressed. A quick visit to any supermarket will confirm this: Simply count the number of processed items compared to those left in their natural state. Today it is hard to imagine that when Jefferson was president almost all food was "processed" on the farm and food stores as we know them did not exist.

But going beyond these broad outlines of our culinary past, what dishes were people actually cooking fifty, one hundred, two hundred, or even four hundred years ago? Food historians look to all kinds of sources to give them clues about the past. We have literature that, like Mark Twain's imagined little supper party, gives us an idea of the dishes people ate or wanted to eat. There are old inventories and shopping lists, menus for special occasions, accounts of what farmers planted, records of imports and exports. There are early drawings and later photographs. In the twentieth century we have television reports, magazine articles, restaurant reviews in newspapers, polls, and market studies. But none of these gives us the instructions necessary to prepare the food. They don't give us recipes. For that we need to turn to cookbooks.

Luckily we have old cookbooks, some that date as far back as ancient Rome. Cookbooks, though, are like postcards—they give us a particular view of a far-off place, with an element of fantasy and wishful thinking. Just as they do today, most people did not cook from cookbooks every day, but rather used them for special-occasion cooking. Imagine trying to extrapolate on the diet of the general population by studying such late twentieth-century bestsellers as Julia Child's *Mastering the Art of French Cooking* or Sheila Lukins and Julee Rosso's *Silver Palate* cookbooks. Old cookbooks do not tell us everything we might want to know about how people ate from day to day, but they provide the best information we have.

Over the centuries, cookbooks have been addressed to different kinds of audiences. The first cookbooks used in North America had been brought from England to colonies like Plymouth and Jamestown. Most of these seventeenth-century cookbooks were written by aristocratic ladies, like the *True Gentlewoman's Delight* penned by the Duchess of Kent, or by their chefs and stewards. Their audience was the minority who could read and could afford the fancy ingredients called for in the books. The recipe collections allowed the gentry to keep up with the Lord and Lady Joneses, even when they could not make it to court. The people who read the books, and most of the people who wrote them, did not do any hands-on cooking. The ladies and their senior servants might, however, read the recipes to their cooks, who could not read.

In their own modest way, the middle classes tried to keep up with the latest fashions in food. The Puritans who settled in Massachusetts, for example, were unusually literate, and we have no reason to think they didn't follow contemporary culinary literature. The average settler probably had no use for the latest dainties sought out in London, but cookbooks were consulted at the Governor's mansion and in the houses of rich merchants. We know there was a demand for English recipes in the colonies because once printing presses were set up here they started reprinting British cookbooks.

The settlers must have made accommodations for local ingredients. By the time the first American cookbook, *American Cookery* by Amelia Simmons, came out in 1799, the dishes it recorded—"pompkin pie," pickled watermelon rind, "cramberry sauce," and Indian pudding, among others—had been part of the American repertoire for years. Over twenty-five years earlier, Benjamin Franklin, representing the colonies in London, wrote home, asking for his favorite fruits as well as the buckwheat and cornmeal unavailable in England. In a response to a letter in the *London Gazetteer* that dared disparage cornmeal as "not affording an agreeable or easy digestible breakfast" he retorted:

> Pray let me, an American, inform the gentleman, who seems ignorant of the matter, that Indian corn, take it all in all, is one of the most agreeable and wholesome grains in the world; that its green leaves [ears?] roasted are a delicacy beyond expression; that samp, hominy, succatash, and nokehock [corn parched in hot ashes and pounded into meal], made of it, are so many pleasing varieties; that johny or hoecake, hot from the fire, is better than a Yorkshire muffin.

Although a distinctive way of American cooking was evolving, the cookbooks offered for sale in the early years of the Republic were essentially English. The relatively small literate audience for books of any kind must have felt little need for instructions on foods Americans ate every day and which their cooks already knew how to prepare—or at least the publishers thought so.

A gradual change took place as the nineteenth century progressed. Female literacy skyrocketed; at the time of the Revolution, it is estimated that about 40 percent of American women could read, and on the brink of the Civil War it may have been as high as 90 percent. Accordingly, the market for all books, but most especially cookbooks, targeted at women, increased dramatically. At the same time, many more families joined the middle class. Women were expected to keep up appearances, but without the kitchen staff that the affluent could afford. Insecure and lacking experience, they turned to cookbooks for guidance. The period after the Civil War saw an explosion of cookbooks— and it has yet to subside.

Cookbook authors began to change in the nineteenth century as well. Writing recipes used to be the purview of dedicated amateurs like Amelia Simmons or practiced professionals like Mary Randolph, the author of the first Southern cookery book, who sat down after a lifetime of practicing the culinary art to document her expertise. No one was able to make a living writing about food. Then along came Eliza Leslie and her colleagues. Miss Leslie made a profession of writing cookbooks, the most popular of which, *Miss Leslie's Complete Cookery,* first published in 1837, had gone through fifty-nine editions and several revisions before the beginning of the Civil War. Numerous other cookbooks attest to her popularity. Here were books aimed at a wide audience, and better representing the cooking style the average American middle-class family might strive for, at least when company called, than the books brought over by the first colonists. Once the Civil War was over, the field of cookery—along with most others—became increasingly professional, with culinary celebrities touring the country, writing columns for magazines, holding demonstrations, and, of course, writing cookbooks.

Until the late 1800s, cookbooks reflected established traditions, rarefied or perfected perhaps, but nevertheless stemming from the author's lifelong experience. Writers generally did not invent recipes for publication, or at least they did not boast of it. As the twentieth century approached, however, a new generation of cookery experts began to do just this, usually in the employ of food manufacturers. The food companies published cookbooks to teach the harried housewife how to make their new products part of her life—foods like Jell-O, baking powder, chocolate (until then consumed only as a drink), shredded wheat, and evaporated milk. While the older generation kept cooking as it always had, younger cooks grew up surrounded by advertisements convincing them to use a product like Crisco instead of lard. They gave up the fat their mothers had been using since the first pig encountered a cook and switched over to the new product. Guiding them along the way were books like *The Story of Crisco,* a comprehensive guide to American cooking—the Crisco way.

Though the dedicated amateurs never entirely disappeared, cookbook writing, like almost every other aspect of our lives, has been taken over by professionals. From the 1880s through the 1950s many cookbook writers received their credentials by attending academies of home economics, or domestic science, as it was once called. Today almost all cookbooks are written by people who make their living in the culinary field.

How have all these cookbooks influenced what we eat as a nation? Obviously some people do try to reproduce specific dishes from cookbooks and, if they like them, may make them part of their regular cooking. Nevertheless, the cook who becomes particularly adept at making, say, a Thai curry from a favorite cookbook is not likely to change the family's entire diet because of that one dish or cookbook. Even widely popular cookbooks tend to reflect current trends rather than originate new ones. Cooks were breaking eggs for omelets and frying chickens long before anyone thought to write down the recipes.

But we are fortunate that they *did* write the recipes down, because these records allow us to see the food we eat today in context. Cookbooks are a treasure trove of surprises and discoveries. In a book from 1824, we encounter macaroni and cheese, a dish that to us evokes the 1950s, alongside one for polenta, which we thought we discovered in the 1980s. We find that foods that were terribly fashionable in the 1990s, like crème brûlée, were familiar to the founders of our country. (The main difference is that they had the honesty to call the dish by its English name: burnt cream.) There are vegetables that were as commonplace in Thomas Jefferson's time as they are in ours but were often practically unknown to Americans in the interim. An author writing in 1949 remarked with surprise "that such delicacies as mushrooms, broccoli and endive, which have become commonplace on the American market only in the last decade, were no strangers to the presidential table in 1800."

Other dishes and, indeed, foods have practically disappeared. Hickory nuts, easily gathered by our rural ancestors, can't be

Digging into supper in the nineteenth century.

bought for love or money, and the haunting taste of black walnuts is all but unknown. Terrapin soup, favored by Mark Twain's contemporaries, is out of style not only because the terrapin turtle is now rare, but also because the idea of eating such foods has become unappealing.

However, taste is often cyclical. While we may chuckle at the all-white or all-pink tea parties that were the rage in the gay 1890s, we may be intrigued by a seventeenth-century recipe that counterpoints the rich taste of poached salmon with crisp, tart apples. Leafing through a nineteenth-century cookery book, you would be struck by the absence of vanilla and chocolate in desserts, but perhaps be inspired by the way lemon is used to great advantage, from lemon ice cream to lemon cookies to lemon rind in stuffings and even lemon-scented croquettes made with leftover poultry.

Indeed, even the most traditional recipes have been transformed over the years. Cuisine, like all aspects of culture, is in flux. Old-time inhabitants of New Orleans may be disturbed to learn that one hundred years ago, gumbo was different from the dish they are used to today. Southerners will argue what does and does not belong in a Brunswick stew, and Texans start brawls over chili, but ultimately a dish, or a recipe, is the product of an individual cook. While it is the result of generations of acquired knowledge, it is also brand new every time it is made. But that is what makes a good cook's recipe interesting—the little changes that give even the most conventional dish new life, the hints and suggestions from which even the most experienced chef can learn. Perhaps the most satisfying aspect of reading these repositories of our culinary past is the sense we get of communicating with our ancestral cooks, the creators of our heritage.

A meal planned around a few representative recipes can bring the past to life in the most immediate way possible—through smell, texture, and flavor. Thanksgiving, enriched by a few Pilgrim dishes, has new meaning. Consider a rambunctious Creole dinner for Mardi Gras, a hearty farmhouse breakfast for a frosty winter morning, a satisfying down-home Sunday dinner at the harvest. Indulge in the pomp and circumstance of a Victorian Christmas or the studied casualness of a fifties' cocktail party on the patio. Revive, if only just for an evening, the traditions of Southern hospitality....

Native Harvest

Cherokee Foodways and the
Coming of the Europeans

A sixteenth-century Powhattan village as depicted by eyewitness John White, a member of the Roanoke expedition.

The Carolinas, 1600

When the first group of European settlers arrived in 1585 on Roanoke Island, in present-day North Carolina, they found an established civilization cooking up foods they had been cultivating, hunting, and fishing for generations. The first description of American cookery and table manners comes from Thomas Harriot, who was sent by Sir Walter Raleigh to chronicle the expedition. "Their meate [food] is Mayz...of verye good taste, deers flesche, or some other beaste, and fishe," wrote Harriot after his first taste of hominy and American game. "They are very sober in their eatinge, and trinikinge, and consequently verye long lived because they doe not oppress nature."

These Indians were probably the Powhattan, a small tribe of Algonquian people closely related in language and customs to the Cherokee, the major civilization of the Appalachian interior. These tribes were agricultural people whose main crops of corn, beans, squashes, and sunflower seeds came from carefully cultivated and fertilized plots. While the women tended the fields and the earthenware cauldrons where supper was stewing, the men engaged in hunting, fishing, and war. "Their woemen know how to make earthen vessels with special Cunninge and that so large and fine, that our potters with [their] wheles can make noe better," noted Harriot.

Native Americans returning home with the harvest, a woodcut published in 1590.

Of course, climate and customs varied greatly throughout the Americas, and each culture had its own cuisine. Throughout the New World, though, the mainstay of all the agricultural nations was corn. For the Cherokee, corn was also at the center of a complex religious life. The Cherokee greeted each year's first corn on the cob with a great festival. People gathered from all over Appalachia for a solemn ceremony performed by the priests and other participants who had prepared themselves by prayer, fasting, and purification. Only after the ceremony could the first corn on the cob of the year be tasted, and only then could the celebratory meal begin. Everyone was careful not to blow on the freshly boiled cobs because they believed doing so would cause a windstorm that would beat down all the corn still standing in the fields. The feast was accompanied by prayers for happiness and prosperity for the coming year as well as for amnesty for criminals.

The Cherokee grew three varieties of corn, each with a different culinary use. "Six weeks corn" matured quickly and was eaten fresh or added to soups and stews. Once dried, it resembled popcorn. Flint or hominy corn, in hues of red, white, blue, or yellow, was soaked with ashes to remove the skin. It was then left whole or ground into what we would recognize as hominy grits. (Hominy is an Indian word from the Algonquian *tackhummin*, meaning "corn without skin.") The hominy might be added to stews or made into mush. A third kind, flour corn, had soft white kernels that could be ground into flour. The flour was mixed with water and then baked to make pone (another Indian word, meaning cornmeal cake) or boiled to make a kind of dumpling. These dumplings were often enriched by the addition of sweet potatoes, chestnuts, or beans.

Snaking up the corn stalks were vines bearing beans, which not only added protein to the diet but also gave back to the soil the nitrogen the corn had depleted. String beans were eaten fresh but they were also dried, as were the numerous kinds of multicolored beans. Boston baked beans may derive from an Indian dish of long-cooked beans sweetened with maple sugar. Succotash, traditionally a corn and bean stew, is certainly of native origin. In one Cherokee recipe that has come down to us, succotash is made by combining brown beans with hominy and black walnuts and

Europeans were amazed at the size of the native American sunflower. This woodcut appeared in an herbal, an illustrated guide to the vegetable kingdom, in London in 1597.

then thickened with pumpkin to make a hearty winter vegetable stew. During the summer, fresh beans and green corn were stewed together the same way.

Pumpkins and squashes matured in the fields once the corn and beans had been harvested. Harriot encountered them in "severall formes [though] of one taste and very good." He also noted that the inhabitants had both summer and winter squash.

Aside from corn, beans, and squash, the only other food crop cultivated by the Cherokees seems to have been sunflowers. These giant flowers with edible seeds amazed the Europeans. "There is also another great hearbe in forme of a Marigolde, about sixe foote in height; the head with the floure is a spanne in breadth," Harriot wrote, adding a culinary note, "...of the seedes heereof they make both a kinde of bread and broth."

Other vegetables and fruits were gathered in the wild. A wide variety of greens were boiled and enriched with oil extracted from acorns. Jerusalem artichokes (the root of a kind of sunflower), sweet potatoes, and other roots were roasted or boiled. Hickory nuts were the base of a soup. Wild onions or ramps (wild leeks) were used as a seasoning and vegetable. Strawberries (much larger than the European variety), blackberries, raspberries, blueberries, huckleberries, and wild grapes provided sweetness. A soup was made by boiling the grapes and thickening the liquid with cornmeal. When cool, it was eaten with wooden or buffalo-horn spoons.

Game and fish were also abundant. Men brought home buffalo (then still roaming the East), bear, venison, rabbit, opossum, squirrel, wild turkey, pigeon, quail, and numerous other small game. Fish were speared or trapped in weirs (fences or enclosures in the water), and numerous shellfish were there for the picking— lobsters, oysters, mussels, and clams. Native Americans were especially fond of the turtles that then lived along the coast.

Bear was an important source of meat and, even more so, of cooking fat. Food was fried directly in earthenware vessels, and the fat was also used as we use butter, to flavor vegetables and corn bread. Harriot was so impressed by the quantity of grease a bear yielded that he listed bears along with black walnuts and pecans as a potential source of marketable oil!

While the game animals were similar to those of the Old World, all of the vegetables eaten by the natives were totally unknown to the white settlers. It has been estimated that Native Americans were using about two thousand food plants before Columbus arrived. The varied civilizations and climates of the Western Hemisphere gave the world foods that revolutionized the cuisines of whole nations. Imagine Ireland without potatoes, Indian curries devoid of the fire of chiles, Italian food without tomatoes, or Parisians deprived of chocolate. Aside from the corn, beans, squashes, Jerusalem artichokes, and other foods originally from North America, from the South American tropics came pineapples, cassava (a staple starch throughout Africa), and vanilla; from Central America came chiles, chocolate, and tomatoes; from the Andean highlands came potatoes. Many foods from South or Central America were later introduced to North America after becoming common in Europe.

Besides introducing the Europeans to new foods, the natives also taught them new cooking methods, some of which are still used today. The New England clambake, where a pit is dug in the ground, heated with coals, and layered with clams, lobsters, corn, potatoes, and seaweed (to provide steam) is a glorious native celebration of the indigenous bounty. Even the classic American barbecue, with freshly boiled corn and meat cooking over open coals, hearkens back to the first American cooks.

In turn, the Native Americans, especially the versatile Cherokee, quickly adopted many of the Europeans' foods along with iron pots and firearms. Cattle and pigs were welcome additions to a culture whose only domesticated animal was a small hairless dog. Apples, peaches, and apricots were also quickly adopted. Peaches, first introduced in Florida in the sixteenth century, were so beloved that by the the time William Penn arrived in the Susquehanna region (or what would be Pennsylvania) a little over a hundred years later, he found that there was hardly an Indian group that was not growing the fruit.

Unfortunately, we have no Indian recipes from the years before the European conquest. Even the early descriptions given by the settlers are imprecise. It wasn't until the twentieth century, when the Native American cultures had been reduced to shadows of their past glory, that attempts were made to record their culinary heritage. For example, *The Indian Cook Book* by the Indian Women's Club of Tulsa was compiled in the 1930s in Oklahoma; the Cherokee had been forcibly removed there from their home in the Appalachians one hundred years earlier. The most comprehensive study of old-time Cherokee cooking was done in the 1940s by Mary Ulmer and Samuel E. Beck for the Museum of the Cherokee Indian in Cherokee, North Carolina. While European cooking technology and domestic animals play a role in the recipes in this collection, it is remarkable how little the foodways of the most traditional Cherokee had changed in over a century of hardship and oppression. The traditional dishes made by the cooks who contributed to the

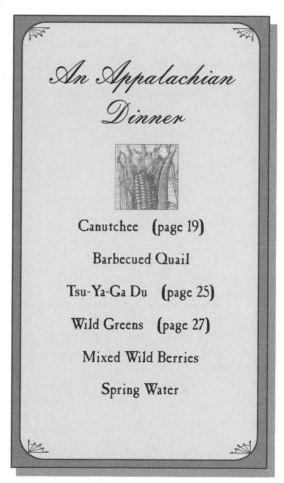

An Appalachian Dinner

Canutchee   (page 19)

Barbecued Quail

Tsu-Ya-Ga Du   (page 25)

Wild Greens   (page 27)

Mixed Wild Berries

Spring Water

collection use indigenous foods and age-old Native American methods of preparation. Similar recipes would have been familiar to the natives who held feasts for the first European settlers.

Thomas Harriot, for one, realized that there was more than one lesson to learn from the native people. "[T]hey are moderate in their eatinge wher by they avoide sicknes. I would to god wee would followe their exemple. For wee should bee free from many kynes of disseasyes which wee fall into by sumptwous and unseasonable banketts, continuallye devisinge new sawces, and provocation of gluttonnye to satisfie our unsatiable appetite."

But Europeans found the new continent's bounty too tempting to take much notice of his advice.

Chewing Gum

Native Americans gave us not only the blessing of corn but the mixed blessing of chewing gum. In New England, Indians were known to chew the resin of the black spruce—presumably as a way to stave off hunger—and taught the Puritan immigrants to do the same. The first commercial manufacture of chewing gum began in Maine around 1850. Following Indian practice, the confection was based on spruce resin flavored in a variety of ways. Some years later, American industry discovered that chicle, a substance the United States had been importing as a rubber substitute, had been used as a chewing gum by Central Americans for centuries. The rest, as they say, is history. Today, the United States leads the world in per capita gum chewing.

Canutchee

HOMINY AND HICKORY NUT SOUP

In order to preserve them, hickory nuts were ground, combined with water, and formed into balls. The nuts were later used as a base for a nourishing soup or stew. Like the peanut, pecan, and black walnut, the hickory nut (from the Indian *pawcohiccora*) is native to the New World. The European settlers occasionally also called it the butter nut. If you cannot find hickory nuts, pecans are a close relative. Whole hominy or posole is available canned in any supermarket that caters to a Hispanic population. You will find that the soup is very rich because of the nuts, so a small serving is probably sufficient.

Combine the ground nuts, hominy, chicken broth, and potatoes. Bring to a boil, then simmer until the potatoes are tender, about 20 minutes. Season with salt.

The Indian Cook Book by the Indian Women's Club of Tulsa, Oklahoma

1 cup finely ground hickory nuts, or substitute pecans

2 cups whole hominy (posole)

3 cups chicken broth or water

1 pound sweet potatoes, peeled and cut into 1-inch dice

Salt

SERVES 6

Kee-qus-no-swa Po-son-gee
Smoke-Preserved Trout

Natives throughout North America cooked fish over or in front of a slow fire. Thomas Harriot described the way the coastal Indians barbecued fish in his account of the first English settlement on the eastern seaboard:

> They sticke upp in the grownde 4. stakes in a square roome, and lay 4 poles uppon them, and others over thwart the same like unto an hurdle, of sufficient heigthe and layinge their fishe uppon this hurdle, they make a fyre underneathe to broile the same. They take good heede that they be not burntt. When the first are broyeld they lay others on, that weare newlye broughte, continuinge the dressinge of their meate in this sorte, untill they thincke they have sufficient.

Harriot points out that other Indians use a similar method to dry the fish for later storage. The Piankeshaw dried fish this way also, and the recipe below is based on their technique. The fish was slowly cooked and smoked over the fire, dried in the sun to prevent spoilage, then stored in buckskin bags.

Thomas Harriot's depiction of Native Americans grilling fish.

The Cherokee used these dried fish as a base for soup. Incidentally, the fish is also delightful prepared just through the end of step 2 and served as you would serve smoked trout. The dried fish makes a hauntingly smokey fish chowder.

1. Soak 2 cups of hardwood chips (such as hickory or apple) in water for 1 hour. Drain. Prepare a barbecue, preferably using real hardwood charcoal rather than briquettes. The coals should be covered with a pale gray ash and glowing red underneath.

2. Prepare the cleaned trout by splitting them in half lengthwise. Do not remove the bones at this point. Rub each half all over generously with salt and oil. Arrange the charcoal so that it is underneath only half of the grill rack. Sprinkle the charcoal with the wood chips. Set the trout, skin side down, in one layer on the side of the grill rack away from the charcoal. Cover the barbecue and cook about 15 minutes, until the fish is completely cooked through. Let cool. Carefully remove all the bones and skin.

3. Preheat oven to 225°F.

4. Set the fish on racks in the oven and bake for 8 to 12 hours, until the fish is dry. Store in an airtight container in the refrigerator.

The Indian Cook Book by the Indian Women's Club of Tulsa, Oklahoma

2 cups hardwood chips

4 trout, about 8 ounces each

Salt

Vegetable oil

MAKES 8 TROUT FILETS

Brunswick Stew

CHICKEN AND VEGETABLE STEW

The credit for Brunswick stew is claimed by just about everyone who has made a sizable contribution to the cuisine of the American South, including both African Americans and the descendants of English settlers. But how could a squirrel stew enriched by corn, potatoes, and beans be anything but an Indian dish? This particular recipe comes from a nineteenth-century source, *Housekeeping in Old Virginia*. There are two schools of thought about the correct consistency of Brunswick stew. To some, including the author of this recipe, it should be a hearty soup, whereas others swear by a thicker, stewlike consistency.

¼ pound lean bacon or ham, coarsely chopped

2 large squirrels or a 3½-pound chicken, cut into 8 pieces

1 large onion, chopped

Salt

4 cups peeled tomatoes, fresh or canned

2 cups sweet corn kernels, frozen or fresh (about 3 ears)

3 medium red potatoes, peeled and cut into ½-inch slices

2 cups butter beans (small lima beans)

Cayenne pepper

Ground black pepper

½ cup bread crumbs

SERVES 6

1. Combine the bacon or ham, squirrel or chicken, and the onion in a large stew pot. Add 7 cups water and 1 teaspoon salt. Bring to a boil and simmer until the squirrel or chicken is just tender, about 45 minutes.

2. Add the tomatoes, corn, potatoes, beans, and cayenne to taste. Continue cooking 45 minutes, until the vegetables are very tender. Remove the squirrel or chicken from the pot and bone it. Return the meat to the stew and season with black pepper. Stir in the bread crumbs. Serve in deep soup bowls.

Housekeeping in Old Virginia edited by Marion Cabell Tyree

A-Su-Nv Ta-Na-Yv

SMOKE-DRIED JERKY

The Cherokee's most common way of preserving meat in the summer was to dry thin strips over a low flame. It was then stored, threaded on a thong made of bark or a plant called bear grass and hung in front of or above the fireplace. The resulting jerky could be easily carried by hunters in buckskin bags. It could be pounded and cooked into a tasty stew that was thickened with hominy and flavored with greens, wild onions, and garlic. Today, you might simmer it with vegetables to make a thick soup or stew.

2 cups hardwood chips

2 pounds lean beef (like top round) or venison

Salt

Vegetable oil

MAKES ABOUT ³/₄ POUND

1. Soak 2 cups of hardwood chips (such as hickory or apple) in water for 1 hour. Drain. Prepare a barbecue, preferably using real hardwood charcoal rather than briquettes. The coals should be covered with a pale gray ash and glowing red underneath.

2. Cut the meat into strips about ¼ by 2 by 4 inches. Rub with salt and oil. Thread each strip on a wooden or metal skewer.

3. Arrange the charcoal so that it is underneath only half of the grill rack. Add the soaked wood chips. Set the meat in one layer over the other side of the grill. Cover the barbecue and cook about 15 mintues, turning the skewers every few minutes. Remove the cover and continue to cook until the meat stops giving off beads of liquid and looks dry, about 45 minutes. Let cool completely.

4. Store in an airtight container in the refrigerator.

Cherokee Cooklore edited by Mary Ulmer and Samuel E. Beck

Roast Squirrel

Dress squirrel and wash clean, place on fork or stick in front of open fire turning often until thoroughly brown.

The Indian Cook Book by the Indian Women's Club of Tulsa, Oklahoma

Sweet Potato Bread
Indian Sweet Potato Corn Bread

In Cherokee cooking, sweet potatoes and cornmeal were often combined to make bread or dumplings. The baking powder is a modern addition, though it is possible that a leavening may once have been made from wood ashes; ash can combine with the natural acids of corn to form carbon dioxide. Before European ovens came along, the bread was probably baked by setting it on a stone that had been heated with hot coals. An earthenware pan was then set over the bread and more coals heaped on top of it.

This "bread" is very moist and somewhat like a dense spoon bread. It will be a little richer if you use milk, though water is more authentic.

2 pounds sweet potatoes

1 tablespoon butter

1 cup cornmeal

½ teaspoon salt

2 teaspoons baking powder

1 cup water, or substitute milk

Serves 6

1. Preheat oven to 375°F.

2. Set the sweet potatoes in a small baking pan and bake until very tender, about 1 to 1½ hours, depending on size. Cool briefly, then scoop out and mash the pulp. Measure 2 cups pulp.

3. Butter a 10-inch cake pan or similar baking dish.

4. Stir together the cornmeal, salt, and baking powder. Add the water or milk. Stir in the mashed potatoes. Spoon into the prepared dish and bake 30 to 40 minutes, until firm.

The Indian Cook Book by the Indian Women's Club of Tulsa, Oklahoma

Tsu-Ya-Ga Du

CORN AND BEAN DUMPLINGS

This bread, similar to a dumpling, was cooked much the same way by Cherokee women whether in North Carolina or Oklahoma. It would have been served as an accompaniment to stews or alone, with a little fat for flavor.

In one variation, slightly undercooked chunks of sweet potato are added to the cornmeal dough instead of the beans. In another variation, called broadswords, dried stalks of corn (or hickory or oak leaves) are wrapped around the dumplings before boiling. A similar affect can be achieved by using the dried corn husks available at Mexican markets. Soak the corn husks in warm water until pliable, wrap the dumplings in the husks, and secure by tying with a thin strip of the husk. Wrapping helps the bread hold its shape better, and slightly enhances the flavor, depending on what you wrap it in.

1. Cover the dried beans with cold water and soak overnight. The next day, drain them, cover with 2 cups water, bring to a boil, and simmer until tender, about 1 hour. Drain the beans, reserving the cooking liquid.

2. In a medium bowl, combine ¾ cup of the bean cooking liquid and the masa flour. Knead until smooth. Add the beans, and mix until they are fully incorporated.

3. Bring a large pot of water to a boil, then lower the heat to a bare simmer. Do not add any salt. Form the corn mixture into balls about 1½ inches in diameter. Drop the balls into the simmering water and cook, uncovered, until cooked through, about 45 minutes. Remove from the water with a slotted spoon.

Cherokee Cooklore edited by Mary Ulmer and Samuel E. Beck

½ cup dried pinto beans

1½ cups masa flour (available in Hispanic markets)

MAKES 20 TO 30 DUMPLINGS, SERVING 4 TO 6

On Making Hominy

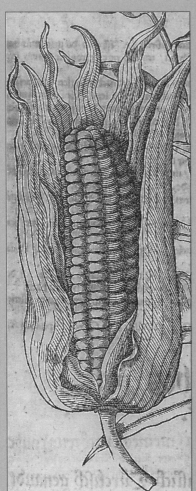

This woodcut of corn appeared in an herbal published in Prague in 1563

The Cherokee people made bread before the white man came along with his mills for grinding corn into meal or his soda for making the bread rise. This corn is skinned with wood ashes. Sieve the ashes, put these ashes into an iron pot or well-made pottery over the fire. When the water begins to boil put in the corn, stir once in a while to make sure the corn does not stick. Let this boil until it is thick enough to bubble. Take the corn off the fire. Go to the branch, or whatever source of water that is nearby, wash the corn in the running water by placing it in a sieve and letting the water run through it until it is clean. The sieve is a basket that is made so that there will be little holes in the bottom to let the water get through. After washing the corn let it drip until all extra water is dropped off it. While the corn is still damp pound it into meal by using the old homemade corn beater. This beater is made by hollowing out a log or stump and beating with a pole with the piece the size of the tree left at the top to give it weight.

Cherokee Cooklore edited by Mary Ulmer and Samuel E. Beck

Wild Greens

Native Americans depended on the forests and fields for greens. Rich in vitamins, the greens might be simply boiled and eaten plain, but the Cherokee preferred to dress them with meat drippings, the favorite being bear grease. The greens used depended on the season and region; the author recommends wild mustard, wild lettuce, polk, thistle, and lamb's quarters. (A variety of domesticated greens should serve equally well.) It is unlikely the flavorful (and nutritious) cooking water would have been discarded; it may well have been used as a base for a soup such as Canutchee (page 19).

1. Bring a large pot of water to a boil. Add the salt and the greens and bring to a boil. Simmer until tender, about 20 to 30 minutes. Drain well and chop coarsely.

2. Heat the bacon drippings in a large skillet. Add the greens and sauté, stirring to coat, until heated through.

The Indian Cook Book by the Indian Women's Club of Tulsa, Oklahoma

1½ pounds mixed greens, such as collard greens, mustard greens, kale, dandelion greens, Swiss chard, and so on, tough or thick stems removed

1 teaspoon salt

2 tablespoons bacon drippings

SERVES 4

Pilgrim's Progress
Puritans Adapt English Recipes to America's Bounty

Nineteenth-century Americans developed and embellished the Thanksgiving tradition, giving us the holiday we know today.

Massachusetts, 1650

The first Puritans who disembarked from the *Mayflower* in late December were greeted by a bleak landscape in the grip of a harsh New England winter. They were exhausted by their sixty-five-day crossing and desperately short of stores. Half did not make it through the first winter. The others survived by supplementing the remnants of the ship's food supply with fish and lobsters. Luckily, they also happened on a cache of Indian provisions. It is no wonder they were eager to give thanks once their first harvest came in the following year.

Seldom had a group of people been so ill-prepared to plant roots on an unknown shore. They were middle-class town dwellers who knew little about farming and even less about hunting or firearms, which in England were a prerogative of the aristocracy. Though game was incredibly abundant in the New World, they often could not bring it down. John Smith, an earlier visitor to New England, had found himself in much the same predicament as the Puritans: "Though there be fish in the sea, fowls in the air, and beasts in the woods," he wrote, "their bounds are so large, they so wild, and we so weak and ignorant, we cannot much trouble them."

The settlers would never have managed their first crop if not for the help of the Native Americans. They were lucky to find any natives at all. Contrary to Governor William Bradford's description of the New World as a "hideous and desolate wilderness, full of wild beasts and wild men," New England was practically empty of its first people. The region had recently been severely depopulated by an epidemic brought by European explorers. One historian has suggested that as many as 90 percent of the coastal Massachusetts Indians may have died or fled their villages. Salem itself was established on the site of a previous Native American settlement, surrounded by fields, conveniently, already cleared for the Englishmen. Fortunately for the settlers, at least a few natives were nearby to show them how to plant and prepare corn, squashes, and beans. Among them was Squanto, who had learned English during years of captivity in Europe. When the Puritans' first crop came in, they invited ninety Wampanoag men to celebrate a three-day feast of Thanksgiving.

We do not know exactly what they served, but we can make a good guess. The most complete account of the event comes from a letter by Edward Winslow, written on December 11, 1621:

> Our harvest being gotten in, our Governour [William Bradford] sent foure men on fowling, that so we might after a more speciall manner rejoyoce together, after we had gathered the fruit of our labours; they foure in one day killed as much fowle, as with a little helpe beside, served the Company almost a week, at which time amongst other Recreations, we exercised our Armes, many of the Indians coming amongst us, and amongst the rest their greatest King Massasoyt, with some nintie men, whom for three dayes we entertained and feasted, and they went out and killed five Deere, which they brought to the Plantation and bestowed on our Governour and upon the Captaine [Miles Standish], and others. And although it be not alwayes so plentifull, as it was at this time with us, yet by the goodnesse of God, we are farre from want, that we often with you partakes of our plentie.

So the main feature of the feast was game birds, most likely wild turkeys, ducks, geese, and pigeons. The Indians contributed deer, which the unskilled settlers could not bring down themselves. The guests also probably brought squashes, corn, and beans. The Puritans had enjoyed a harvest of corn, barley, and possibly wheat, so there was likely to be some sort of bread. Cod and sea bass were

Turkey by John James Audubon

probably also served, but it is unlikely that the Englishmen would have resorted to serving the shellfish that had often been their only source of sustenance in the previous winter. There is a chance that domestic geese, chickens, and ducks were also on the menu, but there were not yet any domestic turkeys. Some sort of cranberry sauce sweetened with maple sugar may have accompanied the roast meats since these tart berries native to America are similar to the English barberry, often made into a conserve there. There were no potatoes, either sweet or white, no coffee, and no tea. They probably drank beer. The first Thanksgiving took place sometime between September 21 and November 9 of 1621.

The next harvest was bad, but by 1623 the little colony was on its way to prosperity. That year, Governor William Bradford noted of the inhabitants of the "Plimoth Plantation" that "any general want or famine hath not been amongst them to this day."

In the following decades the colonists not only became self-sufficient but soon started exporting salt cod, cattle, and eventually rum. In the Mediterranean, the best-quality salt cod was exchanged for wine, oranges, and lemons. In the Caribbean, cattle and the lesser grades of salt cod were traded for molasses, sugar, and spices. "It is a wonder," one New Englander wrote in 1660, "to consider how many thousand neat beasts and hogs are yearly killed and have been for many years past for provision in the country and set abroad to supply Newfoundland, Barbados, and Jamaica." Once in New England, the molasses was transformed into rum, which, in turn, was often traded for slaves in Africa. Slaves were exchanged in the West Indies for more molasses for Massachusetts distilleries.

By mid-century, even before this commerce was to erect one splendid house after another in the port of Boston, the colony was booming. English visitors, used to a country where the gentry dined in ostentatious opulence but the peasants barely existed on a diet of barley bread, beer, and cheese, were impressed by the New World's abundance.

> "[T]here are not many Towns in the Country," wrote Edward Johnson in the 1650s, "but the poorest person in them hath a house and land of his own, and bread of his own growing, if not some cattle; beside, flesh is now no rare food, beef, pork, mutton being frequent in many houses, so that this poor wilderness hath not onely equalized England in food, but goes beyond it in some places for the great plenty of wine and sugar, which is ordinarily spent, apples, pears, and quince tarts instead of their former Pumpkin Pies, Poultry they have plenty, and great rarity, and in their feasts have not forgotten the English fashion of stirring up their appetites with variety of cooking their food."

The unusually literate Puritans consulted the latest English cookbooks to keep up with the trends. Even as the immigrants were learning how to grow pumpkins and cook corn, in England the culinary arts were going through a revolutionary transformation. When Charles I ascended the throne in 1625, English cooking was much the same as it had been in the Middle Ages. Both sweet and savory foods were heavily spiced, and sugar was included in dishes that contained meat and fish as well as in dishes we might think of as dessert. Sauces were thickened with ground almonds or bread crumbs, and great festive displays of food (blackbirds flying out of pies and such) were as important as flavor. By the mid-seventeenth century, though, spices were much cheaper, since they were now being brought on Spanish, Portuguese, and Dutch ships, instead of over the long, slow land route of Marco Polo. At the same time, the price of sugar was dropping year by year as the sugarcane plantations of the West Indies and Brazil increased their exports. It may have been the very commonness of spices and sugar that led the aristocracy to give them up in favor of a simpler cuisine. This new and relatively lighter way of cooking originated in France, where it emphasized herbs and citrus fruits instead of cloves, nutmeg, and ginger. When Charles II returned from exile in France in 1660, he brought with him a preference for this new way of cooking. Dish by dish, first the aristocracy and then the middle classes abandoned their medieval tastes in favor of a cuisine we would be likely to recognize today.

In Salem, the more affluent households would have looked to imported English cookbooks for ideas on entertaining, and as tastes changed in England, they followed suit in the colonies. They adapted the English recipes to suit the local foods, such as corn and beans.

They also followed English custom when it came to drinking. Beer, not water, was the early Puritan's beverage of choice, and adults downed as much as a gallon a day. (It was probably not a shortage of beer alone that lead to the Pilgrims' landing at Plymouth instead of heading on, but it was certainly noted as a contributing factor. "We could not now take time for further search or consideration," wrote one of the passengers, "our victuals being much spent, especially our beere.") Children as well as adults started the day with bread and beer, though at about 3 percent alcohol the murky beverage probably provided a lot more nutrition than hilarity. Later in the century, cider, fresh in season but fermented at other times of year, replaced beer as the colony's favorite drink. For those who drank for reasons beyond slaking thirst, rum was readily available as soon as molasses became a regular import. The well-to-do favored sack (sherry), malmsey (a sweet white wine), and claret (red wine from Bordeaux). The wine was often heavily spiced, probably to disguise flavors acquired on long ocean voyages. Puritans were certainly not against drink, though they did publicly disapprove of drunkenness.

However, their dour religion did prohibit almost all forms of entertainment and revelry. Easter and Christmas celebrations were forbidden, but they were not against an occasional feast to celebrate a good harvest. As a consequence, harvest festivals became a popular tradition in New England.

When in 1798 George Washington declared the first national holiday of Thanksgiving, he was thinking not of the Puritan settlers but of the newly minted Constitution. Thanksgiving, as we know it now, was a nineteenth-century invention; even the term "Pilgrim" was not used until then. The holiday came about largely because of the single-handed activism of Sarah Josepha Hale. From her soapbox as editor of *Godey's Lady's Book*, the most widely read publication in antebellum America, she wrote editorial after editorial until she finally convinced President Lincoln to declare a

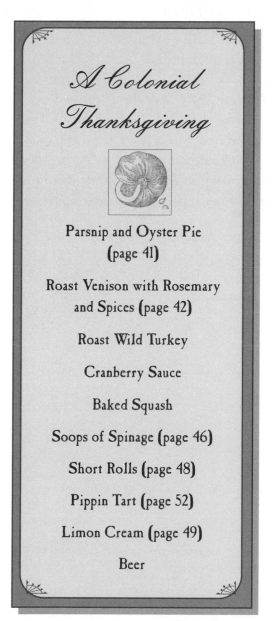

A Colonial Thanksgiving

Parsnip and Oyster Pie
(page 41)

Roast Venison with Rosemary
and Spices (page 42)

Roast Wild Turkey

Cranberry Sauce

Baked Squash

Soops of Spinage (page 46)

Short Rolls (page 48)

Pippin Tart (page 52)

Limon Cream (page 49)

Beer

national day of Thanksgiving in 1863. In part, Lincoln was motivated to create this national nonsectarian holiday to help heal the wounds of the Civil War.

Sarah Hale's enthusiasm for such a holiday had begun when she was growing up in New England, the only part of America where a Thanksgiving harvest dinner had a long tradition. In her 1827 novel *Northwood*, she described one of those feasts at which a roast turkey trailed a "rich odor of savory stuffing" and was presented in the company of meats, chicken pies, ducklings, vegetable platters, gravy pickles, preserves, cakes, and a "variety of sweetmeats." Sadly, the Indians were no longer there to share the feast, but perhaps some of their spirit remained.

A Small Gathering

John Murrell's popular *A New Book of Cookerie*, published in England in 1631, contains several sample menus for both grand occasions and simple meals. Though each menu contains numerous dishes, it is unlikely that there would have been enough of any single food for everyone. The diners would have had to choose among their favorites or, at a large table, lunge for whatever was closest. It is likely that Puritan meals of the mid-seventeenth century would have been served much the same way.

This is the menu for what Murrell calls a "small gathering"—the large feast has double the dishes.

The first Course for a small common Service of Meate, to direct them which are unperfect, to bring them to further knowledge of greater Service.

1 A Boyld Capon or Chicken.
2 A Legge of Lambe farc'd of the French fashion, or neats-tongue [beef tongue].
3 A boyld Mallard [duck] or Rabbet.
4 A dish of boild Olives [small pieces] of Veale, or Collops and Egges.
5 A piece of roast Beefe.
6 A dish of Chewets of Veale, or Mutton pyes, if it be Winter, but if it be summer an Olive-pye.
7 A legge of Mutton roasted whole, or a Loyne of Veale or both.
8 A pigge.
9 A Swan, Goose, or Turkey.
10 A pasty of Venison, or forequarter of Mutton, or a fat rumpe of Beefe.
11 A Capon, phesant, or Hearne [hen].
12 A Custard.

A second Course to the same dyet [meal].

1 A Quarter of Lambe.
2 A couple of Rabbets.
3 A Mallard, Teale, or Wigin [all water birds].
4 A brace of partriges or Woodcocks.
5 A Chicken or pigeon-pie.

6 A dish of plovers or Snites [game birds].

7 A couple of Chickens.

8 A Warden [a kind of pear] or Quince-pie

9 A sowst [jellied] pig or Capon.

10 A Cherrie or a Gooseberrie Tart, or a Quarter-Tart
of pippins [apples].

11 A dish of some kinde of sowst fish.

12 Lobstars or pickled Oysters.

To stew muscles

STEAMED MUSSELS WITH HERB AND ORANGE SAUCE

Robert May, the author of *The Accomplisht Cook or the Art & Mystery of Cookery*, published in 1685, was himself a professional cook who had worked for several aristocratic households both in England and in France. His cookbook was aimed at the few wealthy households that could afford a male chef, but that was no impediment to the book's popularity. Though he makes much of the French influence, his cooking is fundamentally English. This mussel recipe is a fine example of the sophisticated English cuisine of the time. In New England, of course, mussels were abundant.

1. Combine the mussels and beer in a large saucepan, cover, bring to a boil, and steam the mussels until they just open. Drain, reserving the cooking liquid. Discard any unopened mussels and remove the mussels from the shells.

2. Heat the butter in a large skillet over high heat. Add the mussels and fry 2 minutes. Add the basil, marjoram, thyme, parsley, wine, nutmeg and ¼ cup of the mussel cooking liquid. Bring to a rapid boil and cook 2 more minutes. Remove the mussels with a slotted spoon and divide them among 4 warm scallop shells or small dishes.

3. In a bowl stir together the vinegar and egg yolks. Stir in 2 tablespoons of the cooking liquid. Remove the skillet from the heat and immediately stir in the yolk mixture. If necessary, set the skillet back over low heat and stir the sauce until thickened. Add the diced orange. Pour the sauce over the mussels. Serve immediately.

The Accomplisht Cook or the Art & Mystery of Cookery by Robert May

2 pounds mussels, cleaned and with beards removed

1 cup beer

2 tablespoons butter

¼ teaspoon dried basil

¼ teaspoon dried marjoram

¼ teaspoon dried thyme

1 tablespoon chopped fresh parsley

¼ cup dry white wine

Large pinch grated nutmeg

1 small orange, peeled and diced

1 tablespoon wine vinegar

2 egg yolks

Salt

SERVES 4 AS AN APPETIZER

To fry lobsters

PAN-FRIED LOBSTER WITH RED WINE AND ORANGE

Lobsters were amazingly plentiful when the white settlers first came to North America. During one storm in Plymouth, lobsters washed up on the beach, gathering in piles two feet high. When a new group of colonists arrived at the Plantation in 1622, Governor Bradford was humiliated because the colony was so short of food that the only "dish they could presente their friends with was a lobster…without bread or anything els but a cupp of fair water." The ill-fated residents of an earlier settlement in Maine rose up in mutiny to protest being fed lobsters for breakfast, lunch, and dinner. No doubt the settlers devised numerous ingenious ways to cook *Homarus americanus.*

Salt

4 1½-pound live lobsters

3 eggs, beaten

3 tablespoons light cream

Flour

1 garlic clove, lightly bruised

6 tablespoons cold butter

3 tablespoons vegetable oil

¼ cup orange juice

¼ cup red Bordeaux

Large pinch grated nutmeg

Orange and lemon slices, for garnish

SERVES 4

1. Bring a very large pot of salted water to a boil. Add the lobsters and boil 12 minutes. Drain and cool. Remove the meat from the bodies, tails, and claws. Slice the tail meat crosswise into ½-inch thick slices.

2. Stir together the eggs, cream, and 3 tablespoons of the flour to make a batter.

3. Rub a deep serving dish with the garlic.

4. Heat 2 tablespoons of the butter and the vegetable oil in a large skillet over moderately high heat.

5. Dredge the lobster slices in flour, dip them in the batter, and fry them on both sides, in batches, in the hot fat until golden. Drain on paper towels.

6. Meanwhile, bring the orange juice, wine, and nutmeg to a boil in a wide saucepan over high heat. Boil until reduced to about 2 tablespoons. Reduce the heat to very low and gradually stir in the remaining 4 tablespoons cold butter, piece by piece, until the butter is just lique-fied. Immediately remove the pan from the heat. The sauce should be creamy. Season with salt.

7. To serve, place the fried lobster pieces in the garlic-rubbed dish, pour the sauce over them, and garnish with orange and lemon slices.

The Accomplisht Cook or the Art & Mystery of Cookery by Robert May

To make a pie with parsnips and oysters very good
PARSNIP AND OYSTER PIE

Medieval England was greatly enamored of large pies, or "coffins" as they were called. Everything from stews to large cuts of meat or fish to sweet or savory puddings was cooked within a shell of flour and water. At one time, the pastry crust was merely a watertight container for the food, but by the seventeenth century it had become delicate enough to eat. The recipe includes egg yolks for extra richness, but you can omit them.

1. To make the pastry, combine the flour and butter in a medium bowl. Using your hands or a pastry cutter, break up the butter into the flour until the mixture is about as fine as rolled oats.

2. Stir the egg yolk into ⅓ cup ice water. Sprinkle over the dough. Toss to form a rather dry dough, adding a little more water if necessary. Do not overmix. Gather the dough and wrap in plastic film. Refrigerate at least 2 hours.

3. To make the filling, simmer the parsnips in a saucepan of lightly salted boiling water until just tender, about 10 minutes. Drain. Cool and cut into ¼-inch slices.

4. Preheat oven to 400°F.

5. On a lightly floured surface, roll out half of the pastry to form the bottom crust for a 9-inch pie. Fit into 9-inch pan. Arrange one third of the parsnips on the pastry, add half the oysters, then sprinkle with half of the mace, flour, pepper, and salt to taste. Scatter half the egg yolks over the top and dot with half the butter. Add another layer of parsnips, oysters, spices, flour, egg yolks, and butter, then finish with the remaining parsnips. Brush the edge of the dough with water. Roll the remaining dough into a round on a lightly floured surface and place it over the filling. Trim the edges and crimp. Cut vent holes in the top crust.

6. Set the pie on the bottom shelf of the oven and bake for 20 minutes. Reduce the heat to 350°F and continue baking 40 minutes longer. Serve hot.

The Queen-Like Closet by Hannah Woolley

PASTRY

2¼ cups flour

¾ cup cold butter, cut into small pieces

1 egg yolk

FILLING

1½ pounds parsnips, peeled

1½ cups shucked oysters, well drained

½ teaspoon ground mace

1 tablespoon flour

½ teaspoon cracked pepper

Salt

4 hard-boiled egg yolks, crumbled [optional]

4 tablespoons cold butter, cut into small pieces

SERVES 6 TO 8 AS AN APPETIZER, 4 AS A MAIN COURSE

To roast a haunch or shoulder of venison or a chine of mutton
ROAST VENISON WITH ROSEMARY AND SPICES

In England, the middle class cooked mutton much like the wealthy cooked venison. In the New World, venison was available to just about anyone, whereas mutton was rare. An early visitor to the New York colony described "a roasted haunch of venison…which weighed thirty pounds. The meat was exceedingly tender and good and also quite fat. It had a slight spice flavor." Today, venison is hard to come by and mutton is almost unheard of. To replicate the recipe, you will need a large cut of venison, whether it comes from the shoulder, loin, or haunch (the thigh or leg of the animal). You can also make the recipe with a leg or shoulder of lamb.

In the original recipe the meat is studded with narrow strips of lard. Much the same effect can be achieved by "barding" it, that is, laying strips of

Eating with Pilgrims

When the Puritans sat down to a grand feast, their table manners were as different from ours as their spiced roasts and sweetened meat pies were unlike our Butterball turkeys and sweet potatoes with marshmallows. Diners ate off shallow wooden bowls called "trenchers," which were often shared. Pewter cups might also be shared. Bowls and spoons were used to eat thick stews and potages. Everyone received a large linen napkin and a pointed knife with which to cut off hunks of meat from a roast; the knife's pointed end was also used instead of a fork. The napkin was essential.

In England, the invention of the fork later in the seventeenth century led to the evolution of a knife with a rounded end, but the fashion for forks (considered by some a "diabolical luxury") arrived here much later. In the meantime, Americans became accustomed to using the spoon to hold down food as it was cut and then putting down the knife, shifting the spoon to the right hand, and spooning up the food. When the fork finally arrived in the eighteenth century, the habit remained. Europeans still remark on this peculiarly American way of eating, pointing out how much more practical it is to lift the food with the fork remaining in the left hand.

pork fatback or even salt pork over the venison as it roasts. You need not do this with lamb; if using lamb, follow the same cooking times as for venison.

1. Preheat oven to 450°F.

2. Divide the rosemary into little sprigs of 3 or 4 leaves each. (You will need about 30 of these sprigs.) Make little incisions all over the meat, always cutting with the grain, and slip a rosemary sprig into each slit. Season with salt and pepper.

3. Set the meat on the rack in a roasting pan. Cover the surface of the venison with the fatback. Place the pan in the oven and roast about 12 minutes per pound for rare meat, about 15 minutes for medium. The meat will register 130°F to 140°F on an instant-reading heat thermometer. After 45 minutes, remove the fatback and baste the venison every 15 minutes with a little butter. When done, set the roast upside down on a serving platter, cover loosely with foil, and let rest 20 minutes in a warm place.

4. Pour off all the fat from the roasting pan, add the broth and wine to the pan, and bring to a rapid boil. Add the cinnamon, ginger, cloves, bread crumbs, sugar, and vinegar. Boil rapidly until the sauce is reduced to 1 cup and thickened. Remove from heat and whisk in 2 tablespoons cold butter. Season with salt and pepper to taste.

5. Turn the venison right side up and carve. Serve the sauce on the side.

The Queen-Like Closet by Hannah Woolley

1 large sprig of fresh rosemary

A 6- to 7-pound shoulder or haunch of venison

Salt

Pepper

¼ pound sliced fatback

Butter

½ cup beef broth

1 cup red Bordeaux

½ teaspoon ground cinnamon

1 teaspoon ground ginger

3 whole cloves

2 tablespoons fine bread crumbs

2 tablespoons sugar

2 tablespoon red wine vinegar

SERVES 8-10

To fry pompion
SAUTÉED PUMPKIN WITH SHERRY

Long before the Puritans set off for the New World, pumpkins had been brought to England, possibly from Spain or its possessions. And they were still something of a novelty there. Not so in the New World, where immigrants had had more than enough of them after the first few years. No doubt their pumpkin recipes became quite creative after a while.

1 pound cooking pumpkin or squash (see note, page 236)

1 cup cream sherry

4 tablespoons butter

2 eggs, lightly beaten

Coarse sea salt

SERVES 4

1. Using a paring knife or vegetable peeler, peel the pumpkin or squash. Cut into ¼-inch thick slices. Set in a bowl and cover with the sherry. Allow to marinate at least 2 hours, or overnight. Drain well, reserving the sherry. Blot the pumpkin slices dry on paper towels.

2. Heat the butter in a large skillet over moderate heat until hot and foamy. Dip the pumpkin slices lightly into the eggs. Add the slices in a single layer to the skillet and fry on both sides until tender, about 6 to 8 minutes in all. Remove with a slotted spoon to a warm serving platter.

3. Pour ¼ cup of the reserved sherry into the skillet and bring to a rapid boil. Boil until reduced to a thick glaze. Pour over the pumpkin and sprinkle with the sea salt. Serve at once.

The Queen-Like Closet by Hannah Woolley

To make a sallad with fresh salmon
FRESH SALMON AND APPLE SALAD

Today it is hard to imagine, but salmon were once so plentiful in New England that during spawning time, even the inexperienced Salem colonists could scoop them by the dozen out of the rivers and streams.

1. In a saucepan wide enough to accommodate the salmon steaks side by side, combine the white wine, ⅓ cup vinegar, anchovy, bay leaves, cloves, and mace with 2 cups water. Bring to a boil and simmer 10 minutes. Add the salmon and return to a boil. Turn off the heat and let the salmon cool in the poaching liquid. Refrigerate overnight in the liquid.

2. Drain the salmon, remove the bones and skin, and break into 1-inch pieces. In a bowl toss with the apple, onion, olive oil, remaining vinegar, and salt and pepper to taste. Transfer to a serving bowl and decorate with the capers and lemon slices.

The Queen-Like Closet by Hannah Woolley

1 cup dry white wine

⅓ cup plus 2 tablespoons white wine vinegar

1 anchovy fillet

2 bay leaves

4 whole cloves

2 blades mace or ½ teaspoon ground

2 pounds salmon steaks, cut 1 inch thick

1 large tart apple, such as a Granny Smith, peeled, cored, and cut into ½-inch dice

2 tablespoons finely chopped red onion

2 tablespoons olive oil

Salt

Pepper

1 tablespoon capers

Lemon slices, for garnish

SERVES 4 AS A MAIN COURSE, 6 TO 8 AS AN APPETIZER

Soops or Butter'd Meats of Spinage
Sautéed Spinach with White Wine and Currants

Hannah Woolley in her 1684 cookbook notes that a variety of root vegetables can be cooked the same way: carrots, sweet potatoes, skirrets [a root vegetable], parsnips, turnips, Jerusalem artichokes, onions, or beets. The vegetables would have been cooked, mashed, then served on "sippets," large croutons that would absorb the juices. The colonists had no shortage of vegetables, as William Bradford wrote: "All sorts of roots and herbs in gardens grow, Parsnips, carrots, turnips, or what you'll sow, Onions, melons, cucumbers, radishes, Skirrets, beets, coleworts [member of the cabbage family], and fair cabbages."

1½ pounds spinach, cleaned and tough stems removed

3 tablespoons butter

2 slices hearty white bread, cut in half

3 tablespoons dry white wine

1 tablespoon dried currants

2 pitted dried dates, sliced thin

Large pinch ground cinnamon

Pinch sugar

Salt

2 hard-boiled eggs, quartered (optional)

Serves 4 as an appetizer or side dish

1. Place the spinach in a large saucepan, cover tightly, and set over moderate heat. Do not add water. Steam the spinach until just wilted. Drain in a colander, pressing down on it to remove excess liquid. Let cool, then chop the spinach fine.

2. Heat 2 tablespoons of the butter in a large skillet. Add the bread and fry on both sides until golden. Set aside.

3. Combine the wine and currants in a medium saucepan and simmer 5 minutes. Add the remaining 1 tablespoon butter, the spinach, dates, cinnamon, sugar, and salt. Cook, stirring, until just heated through.

4. To serve, arrange the croutons on a platter, and spoon the spinach mixture over them. Garnish with the hard-boiled eggs, if you wish.

The Queen-Like Closet by Hannah Woolley

Other Grand Sallets

MIXED GREEN SALAD WITH BEETS, OLIVES, AND CURRANTS

Many people are surprised to learn that raw vegetables and mixed salads are not modern inventions. The Pilgrims cooked most vegetables, but the baby greens of spring were simply tossed with oil and vinegar, as they have been prepared since at least Roman days. Robert May suggests "[a]ll sorts of good herbs" as ingredients for this salad, including sage, sorrel, parsley, spinach, burnet, lettuce, endive, and chervil. He emphasizes that only the "youngest and smallest leaves" should be used. These days the mixture of baby greens often sold as *mesclun* in fancy markets as well as supermarkets would make an adequate substitute. (If you can, add a little sage, parsley, and chervil to the blend.) May notes that the salad should be "swung in a strainer or clean napkin," the seventeenth-century version of a salad spinner, and "well drained of water."

Lemons, capers, currants, and olives would have been expensive but routinely available, as they were acquired from the Mediterranean region in exchange for dried codfish.

1. Arrange the greens in the center of a large platter. Sprinkle with the capers, currants, and olives. Arrange the pieces of lemon and beet around the edge of the greens.

2. Serve the salad, allowing each person to dress his or her own with oil, vinegar, salt, and pepper

The Accomplisht Cook or the Art & Mystery of Cookery by Robert May

6 cups mixed baby greens, cleaned and spun dry

2 tablespoons capers

2 tablespoons dried currants

¼ cup small green olives

1 lemon, cut into wedges

1 medium beet, cooked, peeled, and cut into slices

Extra-virgin olive oil

Wine vinegar

Salt

Pepper

SERVES 4

To make short rolls
SPICED SHERRY DINNER ROLLS

The American tradition of serving warm dinner rolls with meals goes back to British cooking. Hannah Woolley's somewhat extravagant recipe below would not have been everyday fare. At the governor's house, though, the "fine flower" and "Sack" the recipe calls for would have certainly been there for the cook's asking. Woolley writes that the rolls "eat finely if you butter some of them while they are hot."

1 cup milk

1 tablespoon sugar

1 teaspoon active dry yeast

About 4½ cups unbleached all-purpose flour

½ teaspoon salt

2 teaspoons ground coriander seed

Pinch grated nutmeg

Pinch ground cloves

¾ cup cold unsalted butter, cut into small pieces

½ cup cream sherry

MAKES 25 TO 30 ROLLS

1. In a saucepan heat the milk to lukewarm. Remove the pan from the heat and stir in the sugar and yeast until dissolved.

2. In a large bowl, stir together 4 cups of the flour, the salt, coriander, nutmeg, and cloves. Stir in the butter, then the milk mixture and finally the sherry. Knead on a well-floured board until smooth and elastic, about 10 minutes. Add more flour as needed to prevent the dough from sticking. Set the dough in a lightly oiled bowl, cover with plastic wrap, and let rise in a warm place until doubled in bulk, 2 to 3 hours.

3. Punch the dough down and form into 25 to 30 round rolls. Place these, just barely touching, on a baking sheet. Cover loosely with plastic wrap and let rise in a warm place until doubled in bulk, 1 to 2 hours.

4. Preheat oven to 375°F.

5. Bake the rolls 15 to 20 minutes, until the tops are golden. Serve warm.

The Queen-Like Closet by Hannah Woolley

To make limon cream
LEMON CUSTARD

In the seventeenth century, custard was made by stirring the milk and yolk mixture in a saucepan over glowing coals. While you can also make it by cooking it in a heavy saucepan set over low heat, it is much easier to bake custard in a hot water bath in the oven. The result is much the same. You can cook the custard below either in six individual custard cups or one large dish; the large dish will take about an hour to cook.

Orange flower water is an extract of orange flowers; it can be found in specialty food stores and Middle Eastern markets.

1. Preheat oven to 350°F.

2. Bring the cream and milk to a boil in a medium saucepan.

3. Whisk together the egg yolks, whole eggs, and sugar until light and creamy. Stir in the lemon juice and orange flower water and then the hot cream mixture.

4. Pour the custard mixture into six 6-ounce custard cups or into one large ceramic or glass baking dish. Set in a large baking pan on the lowest rack of the oven and pour boiling water into the pan to come halfway up the sides of the cups or dish.

5. Bake until a toothpick inserted in the custard comes out clean, about 40 to 50 minutes. Remove the cups from the water bath, let the custards cool, and then refrigerate them at least 2 hours. Serve cold.

The Queen-Like Closet by Hannah Woolley

2 cups heavy cream

1 cup milk

5 egg yolks

2 eggs

1 cup sugar

6 tablespoons lemon juice

4 teaspoons orange flower water

SERVES 6

Baked Quaking Pudding
ALMOND BREAD PUDDING WITH DATES

The British settlers brought with them a strong affection for puddings of endless variety. A visitor to England in the 1690s was quite baffled by trying to define them: "The pudding is a dish very difficult to be described, because of the several sorts there are of it; flour, milk, eggs, butter, sugar, suet, marrow, raisins, etc., etc., are the most common ingredients of a pudding. They bake them in an oven, they boil them with meat, they make them fifty several ways." Quaking pudding, an ancestor of bread pudding, was usually boiled, though it was sometimes baked, as it is here. It is particularly good served hot with a little whipped cream or vanilla ice cream—neither of which is authentic.

2½ cups light cream

2 cups bread crumbs, made from day-old bread

⅓ cup dried currants

6 ounces blanched almonds (about 1¼ cups)

¾ cup sugar

1 tablespoon rosewater

¼ teaspoon nutmeg

Large pinch salt

2 egg yolks

2 whole eggs

¼ pound pitted sliced dates

2 tablespoons chopped marrow, or substitute melted butter

SERVES 8 TO 10

1. Preheat oven to 350°F. Butter a shallow 8-cup baking dish.

2. In a saucepan bring the cream to a boil. In a large bowl combine it with the bread crumbs and currants.

3. Grind the almonds as fine as possible in a food processor. Add the sugar and continue to process, scraping down the sides of the bowl occasionally, until very finely ground. Add to the cream mixture along with the rosewater, nutmeg, salt, and egg yolks. Mix until smooth. Stir in the dates and marrow or butter.

4. Spoon into the buttered dish and bake until firm, about 45 minutes. Serve warm.

The Accomplisht Cook or the Art & Mystery of Cookery by Robert May

To Make Pompion Pie

Having your paste ready in your pan, put in your pompion [pumpkin] pared and cut in thin slices, then fill up your pie with sharp apples and a little pepper and a little salt then close it and bake it then butter it and serve it hot to the table.

The Queen-Like Closet by Hannah Woolley

To make a pippin tart
APPLE PIE WITH CANDIED ORANGE

It is essential that you use a firm cooking apple for this pie. The truly old varieties of apples (pippins, for example) are virtually impossible to find today, but several newer varieties, developed in the nineteenth century, will work well. Northern Spy and Baldwin are superior cooking apples, but Granny Smiths or even Delicious apples will do in a pinch. McIntosh and their like will not—they fall apart. Though claret (Bordeaux wine) would have been available to the more affluent settlers, it is likely the average Puritan would have used cider. The taste is quite different but equally delicious.

Every Puritan home was centered on the hearth which was not only used for cooking but was usually the only source of heat and hot water in the house.

1. To make the pastry, combine the flour and butter in a medium bowl. Using your hands or a pastry cutter, break up the butter into the flour until the mixture is about as fine as rolled oats.

2. Stir the egg yolk into ⅓ cup ice water. Sprinkle over the dough. Toss to form a rather dry dough, adding a little more water if necessary. Do not overmix. Gather the dough together and wrap in plastic film. Refrigerate at least 2 hours.

3. To make the filling, combine the apples, wine, cinnamon, and ginger in a medium saucepan. Cover, bring to a boil, and simmer until cooked through but not falling apart, about 10 to 15 minutes. Let cool in the liquid, then drain well.

4. Preheat oven to 400°F.

5. On a lightly floured surface, roll out half of the pastry to form the bottom crust for a 9-inch pie. Fit into 9-inch pan. Arrange the apples on the dough, pressing down to eliminate air pockets. Sprinkle with the citron, orange rind, and sugar. Brush the edge of the dough with water. Roll the remaining dough into a round on a lightly floured surface and place it over the filling. Trim the edges and crimp. Cut vent holes in the top crust.

6. Set the pie on the bottom shelf of the oven and bake for 20 minutes. Reduce the heat to 350°F and continue baking 30 to 40 minutes until golden. Cool on a rack to room temperature.

7. To make the icing, cream the butter and the confectioners' sugar together until fluffy. Add the rosewater and beat until smooth and light. With a metal spatula, spread the icing over the top crust of the pie.

The Accomplisht Cook or the Art & Mystery of Cookery by Robert May

PASTRY

2¼ cups flour

¾ cup cold butter, cut into pieces

1 egg yolk

FILLING

3 pounds apples, peeled, quartered, and cored

2½ cups red Bordeaux

Two 3-inch cinnamon sticks

2 small slices crystallized ginger

2 tablespoons diced citron

2 tablespoons diced candied orange rind

¾ cup sugar

ICING

4 tablespoons butter, softened

1 cup confectioners' sugar

1 tablespoon rosewater

SERVES 8

Founding Mothers

Dining with Plantation Society in the Old South

George Washington, before and after his presidency, was an important Virginia plantation owner. His home was exemplary of Virginia hospitality of his time.

Virginia, 1800

In the summer of 1800, a group of slaves in Richmond, Virginia, was arrested for trying to organize an uprising to gain their freedom. At their trial, most exposed their plans to burn down the capitol, the penitentiary, and armory and to kill any white man who opposed them. One of the leaders, "General" Gabriel, was quoted as saying he would spare one white person only and that was Mrs. David Meade Randolph, because he wanted to make her his queen since she knew so much about cooking. He wasn't the only one to acknowledge her talents. Mary Randolph was renowned as the best cook in Richmond at a time when the Southern gentry set the standard for all American cookery.

At the same time that Virginia was cradling many of the Founding Fathers, it was here, among the wealthy households that could afford lavish hospitality, that the nation's mothers gave birth to an authentically American cuisine. Mary Randolph is the best-known of these cooks today because of a gem of a cookbook she wrote in Washington some years later. This book, *The Virginia Housewife,* might never have been written had several misfortunes not befallen the Randolphs. The first was the election of Thomas Jefferson in 1800, which lost David Randolph his job as Marshal of Virginia. His rabid anti-Jefferson stance ruled out any other federal appointments, and with debts accumulating, the couple was forced to sell their house. To keep bread on the table (no doubt some of the best bread in town), Mrs. Randolph ran a series of boarding houses. A visitor to Richmond who had met her at a tea found her "a middle-aged lady, and very accomplished; of charming manners and possessing a masculine mind" distinguished by "acute penetration" and "informed judgement." She later moved to Washington, where *The Virginia Housewife* was probably composed. The first edition was published in 1824, another in 1825, and a third revised edition in 1828, the year of her death.

Mrs. Randolph's book reflects a sophisticated familiarity with an unexpectedly wide range of food and dishes. There are lots of recipes for that American favorite, ice cream. Vegetables, from pattypan squash to asparagus, sorrel and even green salads, have a prominent place. Interestingly enough, there are recipes for foreign dishes that we normally think of as recent additions to the American table, such as gazpacho. Broccoli and mushrooms, considered exotic for many years after the turn of the twentieth century, were readily available. Indeed this must have been a golden era of American cooking for those who could afford it. As early as 1607, a visitor wrote that Virginia was "nature's nurse to all vegetables." Later visitors from New England and abroad invariably gave high marks to the hospitality they received at the plantations of the new republic. At the grand estates, an ornate dinner was served between two and three o'clock in the afternoon. The food came in two courses. The first course would have consisted of one or more large roasts, perhaps a Virginia ham alongside a leg of venison, veal or lamb, or a turkey, goose, or shoat (a young pig—often a whole quarter would be roasted). With the main roast or roasts, there might be a soup, a dish of fried chicken, meat pies, fish, and shellfish as well as cooked vegetables and salads. In the summer, the roasts were often presented cold, and seafood salads dressed with olive oil and vinegar would have been included. The whole first course was served more or less simultaneously and the guests would help themselves. The second course consisted of desserts, which might include pies and custards as well as various English-style baked and steamed puddings. By the early 1800s ice cream was rapidly becoming popular. Wine, possibly claret (Bordeaux) but more likely Madeira, would have also been poured.

While putting together a meal like this is formidable in our modern age of supermarkets and kitchens with food processors, ranges, dishwashers, and microwaves, imagine what it was like when everything except for a few exotic ingredients like wine, oranges, and spices was produced and processed in the home. Chickens had to be butchered and plucked, butter churned, hams smoked, lard rendered, preserves put up, bread made (with homemade yeast), coffee roasted and ground, sugar (which came in loaves) pulverized. Everything had to be beaten, chopped, ground, and mixed by hand and then cooked in a hearth over an open fire, even in the middle of a scalding Virginia summer. Cooks did not even have the convenience of running water. Cooking was an exhausting, full-time job which, in the larger houses, took a large staff. Even though the plantation mistress was unlikely to do any actual cooking, she still needed the skills of a drill sergeant to keep the whole operation running. After all, the good name of Southern hospitality was on the line.

Though much of the food described in *The Virginia Housewife* is already recognizably Southern and American, its English heritage is apparent. This is not, however, the British cooking with which we are familiar and which was to plague the United Kingdom after the Industrial Revolution. Eighteenth-century English cooking, at least as it was prepared by the middle classes, showed remarkable élan, particularly in its use of herbs, spices, and wine. The fashion was to serve most roasted meats rare. Writing in the mid-1700s, Hannah Glasse, the most popular cookbook author not only in her native England but also in the American colonies, gave advice on cooking vegetables that should still be well-heeded today, "Most people spoil garden things by over-boiling them," she wrote. "All things that are green should have a little crispness, for if they are over-boiled they neither have any sweetness or beauty."

In Virginia, the upper-class women who ran households were

naturally very conscious of the latest English styles, but they were by no means slavish imitators, especially after the Revolution. There were several influences that made Southern cooking distinct. The mild climate and long growing season allowed the area to grow almost everything that ended up on the table. The native foods, at first adopted from the Indians out of necessity, had become so integral to the Virginian diet that when Thomas Jefferson, one of the great gourmets of the Revolutionary era, was residing in Paris, he had corn planted in his garden so that he would not be deprived of fresh corn on the cob.

Besides the culinary traditions of England, the greatest influence on Southern food came from Africa, often by way of the West Indies. It was seldom that the lady of the house did the back-breaking labor that went into making the lavish meals that won Virginia renown. Slaves of African descent did the actual cooking, even though the mistress might stand in the kitchen reading for and instructing the cooks. In 1840, a man named Isaac, who had been a

The American Plan

Up until the Industrial Revolution, generations of Americans ate their meals along the same pattern. The day began with an early copious breakfast that might include anything from cornmeal mush to eggs to braised partridges. Dinner, the main meal of the day, was served at midday. Unlike in Europe, it would almost always include at least one meat, along with some kind of bread and vegetable. Supper, an informal repast served in the early evening, was often the smallest meal of the day, with cold meats sometimes supplemented by eggs. In overwhelmingly rural America, meal times would be adjusted to the season. As the country became increasingly urban and industrial and husbands could no longer come home at midday, the evening meal slowly took over as the main focus of home cooking.

slave at Monticello, recalled that during his childhood Mrs. Jefferson would come into the kitchen with a cookery book in her hand and read to Isaac's mother how to make cakes, tarts, and so on. However, the talent, African foodways, and imagination of the black cooks could not help but shine through. Without that heritage, *The Virginia Housewife* would never have included recipes for African ingredients like okra and eggplant or the chiles and tomatoes that blacks had encountered in the West Indies. Certain techniques, especially deep frying, became popular here because they were so common in Africa.

Even French cooking entered the Southern repertoire through the medium of African-American cooks. When he was in the White House, Jefferson brought from home two slaves, Edy and Fanny, to learn French cooking from his French chefs at the presidential residence. When he returned to Monticello, the two African-Americans became his cooks there and improvised on what they had learned. Some years earlier, while he was still secretary of state, Jefferson had agreed to free his cook (and slave), but only under the condition that he first return to Monticello to train a new cook: "Having been at great expence [*sic*] in having James Hastings taught the art of cookery," the document of agreement reads, "desiring to befriend him, and to require from him as little in return as possible, I do hereby promise & declare, that if the said James shall go with me to Monticello in the course of the ensuing winter…and shall there continue until he shall have taught such person as I shall place under him for that purpose to be a good cook…he shall be thereupon made free."

Even Jefferson, as fond as he was of his French wines, his tender corn, and his garden-fresh asparagus and peas, would probably not have given food a central place in the events that led up to the Revolution. Nevertheless it was taxes on molasses, sugar, Madeira, and finally tea that stirred up the colonies against England. Down in Virginia, the mothers of the American Revolution were serving up fried chicken, corn bread, and ice cream, declaring independence on their own.

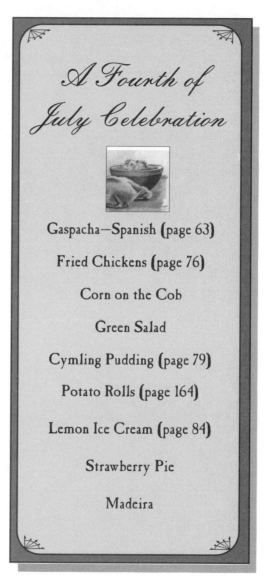

A Fourth of July Celebration

Gaspacha—Spanish (page 63)

Fried Chickens (page 76)

Corn on the Cob

Green Salad

Cymling Pudding (page 79)

Potato Rolls (page 164)

Lemon Ice Cream (page 84)

Strawberry Pie

Madeira

Early Cooking Fats

Before vegetable oils came into common use around the turn of the twentieth century, Americans could choose among three possible cooking fats, all of animal origin. Butter was the favorite, but it was expensive and spoiled so easily that it was usually only reserved for special occasions. In early America, lard was used universally for everything from frying to making pie crusts. Beef suet had more special applications. Because chopped suet melts relatively slowly, it was often added to steamed puddings and stuffings to add richness and moistness. In later American cooking, suet came to be used only in dishes closely associated with their British origins, such as mincemeat pie and Christmas pudding. For information on buying suet today, see the ingredients notes in the preface.

Gaspacha — Spanish
CHILLED TOMATO AND CUCUMBER SOUP

Mary Randolph's recipe for *gazpacho* may have come to her from her relative who had lived for some time in Spain or it may have arrived indirectly from Spanish America. Randolph's instructions do not give the proportion of bread to liquid but it is likely that the "soup" bore a closer resemblance to the Italian bread salad, *panzanella,* than modern Spanish *gazpacho.*

1. To peel the tomatoes, core them and make an X in the bottom of each. Plunge into boiling water for about 15 seconds. Cool under cold running water and peel off the skin. Set about one quarter of them aside.

2. Coarsely chop the remaining tomatoes, place in a saucepan, and simmer, covered, for 20 minutes. Pass through a food mill or press through a coarse sieve. (You should have about 3½ cups juice.) Chill.

3. Slice the reserved tomatoes. Peel the cucumbers, cut into fourths lengthwise, and slice thin. Put a layer of bread in the bottom of a shallow bowl, cover with a layer of tomatoes, then cucumbers, and sprinkle with a little onion, salt, and pepper. Add another layer of bread, tomatoes, and cucumbers and so on until the bread and vegetables are all used up.

4. Stir the olive oil and mustard into the reserved tomato juice. Season with salt and pepper. Pour over the bread and vegetable mixture. Allow to stand 2 hours before serving. Serve at room temperature.

The Virginia Housewife by Mary Randolph

4 pounds ripe tomatoes

2 medium cucumbers

6 slices hearty white bread, toasted and broken into several pieces each

Salt

Ground black pepper

1 small red onion, finely chopped

⅓ cup olive oil

1 tablespoon prepared mustard

SERVES 6

Asparagus Soup
CREAMY CHICKEN AND ASPARAGUS SOUP

The Virginia Housewife's technique for making a silky cream soup may be different from the process commonly in use today but the result is remarkably similar (and delicious).

1½ pounds asparagus
¼ pound slab bacon, in 1 piece
1 medium onion, coarsely chopped
Salt
Pepper
½ chicken (with bones), about 1½ pounds, cut into about 12 pieces
2 tablespoons flour
2 tablespoons butter, softened
1 cup milk

SERVES 4

1. Cut off 1 inch of the asparagus tips and set aside. Coarsely chop the remaining asparagus and combine with the bacon, onion, and 5 cups water in a medium saucepan. Season with salt and pepper. Bring to a boil and simmer until the asparagus is beginning to fall apart, about 45 minutes. Remove the bacon and press the soup, asparagus, and onion through a sieve into a bowl or pass through a food mill.

2. Pour the soup back into the saucepan. Add the chicken pieces and simmer until tender, about 30 minutes, skimming off the scum that forms on the surface. Add the reserved asparagus tips and cook until just barely tender, about 5 minutes.

3. Combine the butter and flour to make a paste and whisk it into the soup. Stir in the milk and bring the soup to a simmer; cook 5 minutes. Season with salt and pepper to taste if necessary.

The Virginia Housewife by Mary Randolph

Green Peas Soup

FRESH GREEN PEA SOUP WITH MINT

Garden peas were a great favorite among early Americans. Here, a soup is made by cooking some of the legumes until they are falling apart, while the rest are added towards the end of cooking. Adding mint to the soup may show a French influence, though the British were also using an abundance of herbs at the time. The recipe comes from Eliza Leslie, one of the first women to have a successful career as a cookbook writer. Here she recommends adding a little spinach juice (put a half cup of tightly packed spinach through a juicer or purée and strain) fifteen minutes before the soup is done to brighten its color. She also notes that you can substitute lima beans for the peas.

1. Combine the broth, bacon, and 2 sprigs of the mint in a large soup pot with 4 cups water. Bring to a boil and simmer 1 hour, skimming off the scum as it forms on the surface. Strain and return the liquid to the pot.

2. Add 2 cups of the peas, bring to a boil, and simmer 1 hour. Purée in a blender and return the purée to the pot.

3. Meanwhile, in another saucepan, combine the remaining mint with the sugar and 2 cups water. Bring to a boil, add the remaining 4 cups peas, bring to a boil, and simmer 15 minutes. Remove the mint, drain the peas, and add the peas to the soup. Cook 10 minutes longer. Season with salt and pepper to taste.

Miss Leslie's Complete Cookery by Eliza Leslie

4 cups veal broth or chicken broth

6 ounces slab bacon, cut into 4 pieces

4 large sprigs mint

6 cups green peas, fresh or frozen

1 tablespoon sugar

Salt

Pepper

SERVES 4 TO 6

Oyster Sausage
Oyster and Veal Sausage Patties

The oyster appears in myriad forms throughout nineteenth-century cookbooks. Oysters were broiled, scalloped, devilled, stewed, added to stuffings, and, of course, served on the half shell. As might be expected, Boston, New York, Philadelphia, and Baltimore had oyster houses galore but even in the American interior, oysters were common. Years before the railroads started shipping oysters to Chicago and points beyond, express oyster wagons rushed across the Alleghenies, shifting frequently to fresh horses, so that wealthy people could give oyster parties where bushels of the crustacean would be devoured.

2 cups shucked oysters, drained and coarsely chopped

$\frac{1}{4}$ pound ground veal

$\frac{1}{4}$ pound suet, ground

1 cup bread crumbs

1 egg, beaten

Salt

Ground black pepper

1 tablespoon vegetable oil

Makes 12 to 16 patties

1. Combine the oysters, veal, and suet in a food processor. Pulse until coarsely ground. Add the bread crumbs and egg and pulse until combined. Season with salt and pepper.

2. Using lightly oiled hands, form the mixture into 2½-inch patties. (You should have about 14 patties.) Refrigerate, covered, until ready to fry.

3. To cook, heat the oil in a large skillet over moderately high heat. Add the patties in batches and fry until browned and cooked through, about 3 minutes per side. Drain on paper towels.

Housekeeping in Old Virginia edited by Marion Cabell Tyree

Brisket of Beef Baked
BACON AND OYSTER-STUFFED BRISKET WITH RED WINE

In the early days of the republic, oysters were not only eaten by themselves but were often included in other dishes. Oyster stuffings were especially popular, not only for turkey but also for other meats. Here, a forcemeat (as stuffings were called in those days) of bacon, oysters, and spices is inserted into incisions made in a large cut of beef. The meat would then have been slowly cooked in a Dutch oven until the oysters and bacon almost melted into the beef.

1. Preheat oven to 350°F.

2. Stir together the bacon, parsley, oysters, cloves, nutmeg, black pepper, and salt to taste.

3. Using a small sharp knife, make about ten to twelve 2-inch incisions all over the brisket, cutting along the grain of the meat rather than across it. Stuff these with the oyster mixture.

4. Sprinkle the brisket with the flour, then set the meat in a Dutch oven. Add the wine, lemon juice, and rind. Cover and bake until tender, about 3 hours.

5. Remove the brisket to a serving platter. Skim the fat from the gravy and season with salt and pepper to taste. Carve the brisket and serve the gravy on the side. Garnish the platter with green pickles.

The Virginia Housewife by Mary Randolph

---

4 slices bacon, finely chopped

½ cup chopped fresh parsley

6 large oysters, shucked, drained, and finely chopped

Large pinch ground cloves

¼ teaspoon grated nutmeg

½ teaspoon ground black pepper

Salt

A 4-pound brisket

2 tablespoons flour

1½ cups dry red wine

1 tablespoon lemon juice

1 teaspoon grated lemon rind

Green pickles (cucumbers or green tomatoes) for garnish

SERVES 6

To roast goose
ROAST GOOSE WITH SAGE

Geese, ducks, and other poultry were usually roasted on a spit before "a good clear fire." When cooked properly the resulting roast would have been tender, juicy, and usually rather pink. In general, Mrs. Randolph recommends very quick cooking times for all her roasts. She suggests cooking a large goose 1½ hours. Of course, we have no way of knowing what "large" meant in those days, but even if we assume that it was the size

Fire in the Kitchen

As late as 1800, the technology used for making dinner had not changed much since the Middle Ages. There had been a few minor innovations like the movable crane, which allowed the cook to remove a pot from the fire, or adjust its proximity without having to reach over the burning flames. Spits could now be turned with mechanical gadgets driven by weights, and a few new pots and pans were available. But cooking was fundamentally the same: over an open fire or embers in a large hearth. Soups and stews were suspended from the crane in large cast-iron pots. Frying was done in skillets called spiders because they sat on three legs so that the pan would not touch the embers. Gridirons, used for grilling, were grills on legs. Roasting was done on a spit in front of (never over) the fire, with a pan set underneath to catch the drippings. One of the most useful pans was the Dutch oven, which came in various sizes to accommodate everything from a small batch of corn bread to a whole turkey. The iron "oven" was set in the fireplace and glowing embers were piled over it. Of course, the heat could not be set to low, medium, or high.

In the winter, fireplaces also provided heat and hot water, but in the summer cooking often took place outdoors or in a separate building. In the days before matches, a fire was never intentionally allowed to go out. Embers were carefully banked so that they could be fanned into flame at five in the morning when preparations for breakfast began. The fires were a constant source of danger to the house and to the cooks with their voluminous floor-length skirts. In fact, one historian has calculated that only childbirth killed more women than hearth fires!

of a medium-sized goose today, about 10 pounds, it still requires a rather hot fire. To simulate the action of roasting when you are baking in an oven, cook the meat at a very high temperature on a roasting rack so that the hot air can circulate all around. Make sure to allow all roasted meat to "rest" at least 20 minutes after cooking so the juices can redistribute throughout the meat. Roast goose, like roast pork, was invariably served with apple sauce (see page 101).

1. Preheat oven to 450°F.

2. Stir together the sage, onions, butter, black pepper, and salt. Rub the inside of the goose with the mixture. Prick the skin of the goose all over with a fork. Truss and set on a roasting rack in a roasting pan. Dust with flour.

3. Set the pan in the oven and roast, basting regularly with the drippings after the first half hour. (If the fat spatters too much, add a little water to the pan.) Cook about 10 minutes per pound. The breast should still be a little pink when done.

4. Transfer the goose, breast side down, to a serving platter. Cover with foil, and let rest in a warm place 20 minutes before serving. To serve, set breast side up and carve.

The Virginia Housewife by Mary Randolph

20 large sage leaves, finely chopped

2 small onions, finely chopped

2 tablespoons butter, softened

1 teaspoon ground black pepper

2 teaspoons salt

1 young goose, 8 to 10 pounds

Flour

SERVES 6

To roast veal
HERB-STUFFED ROAST VEAL

One of the most popular cookbooks in the years after the Revolution was Susannah Carter's *The Frugal Housewife*. Though the book was English, numerous editions were published in the United States, including an 1803 edition that had an appendix that featured recipes using American ingredients, such as "Indian meal," which of course was cornmeal. For the roast veal, the author recommends using a veal filet, essentially the same cut as a top round of beef. It should be boneless and cut in such a way that you can open it like a book, to accommodate the stuffing.

Nutmeg and Mace

Both nutmeg and mace come from the fruit of the nutmeg tree. Each oval nutmeg has a thin, red covering that becomes mace when dried. Nutmeg has a stronger, muskier flavor, while mace is more delicate. Today nutmeg is used much more often, but in the eighteenth and nineteenth centuries, they were equally popular and flavored both sweet and savory foods. Mace used to be added in whole "blades" (irregular filigreed pieces), but today is almost always sold already ground. If you can, grind or grate whole nutmeg and mace as you need them to better retain their flavor.

1. Preheat oven to 450°F.

2. Toss the bread crumbs together with the suet, parsley, thyme, savory, nutmeg, lemon rind, and eggs. Season with salt and pepper.

3. Spread the stuffing over the veal and enclose it with the meat. Tie the roast with kitchen twine to secure, and rub it with butter. Set on a rack in a roasting pan, put in the oven, and roast for 20 minutes. Reduce the heat to 350°F and continue roasting about 2½ hours, basting with the butter and pan juices at least every 15 minutes, until the veal is is no longer pink and registers at least 155°F on a meat thermometer. About 30 minutes before the meat is done, dust with flour. Continue basting until done.

4. Remove the roast from the pan, set on a serving platter, and cover loosely with aluminum foil. Set aside in a warm place for 20 minutes.

5. Pour off all the fat from the roasting pan. Add the broth and bring to a simmer, scraping the bottom of the pan. Stir together the remaining 1 tablespoon butter and 1 tablespoon flour. Stir into the pan juices. Cook at a bare simmer 10 minutes.

6. To serve, remove the kitchen twine and carve the veal into slices. Serve the gravy on the side.

The Frugal Housewife: or, Complete Woman Cook by Susannah Carter

3 cups fresh bread crumbs

½ pound ground suet, or substitute butter

½ cup chopped fresh parsley

1 teaspoon dried thyme

1 teaspoon dried savory

1 teaspoon grated lemon rind

½ teaspoon grated nutmeg

2 eggs, beaten

Salt

Pepper

A 4-pound boneless veal roast (see introduction to recipe)

4 tablespoons butter, melted, plus 1 tablespoon butter

Flour for dusting, plus 1 tablespoon flour

1 cup beef broth

SERVES 6 TO 8

A Fowl or Turkey Roasted with Chestnuts

ROAST TURKEY BREAST STUFFED WITH CHESTNUTS AND HERBS

The domestic turkeys available two hundred years ago would have been the size of wild turkeys rather than the huge birds we see today. The original recipe calls for a whole turkey of eight to ten pounds, but a whole boned turkey breast also works very well and is easier to find. The garnish of watercress and oranges suggested by Susannah Carter is very authentic to the period.

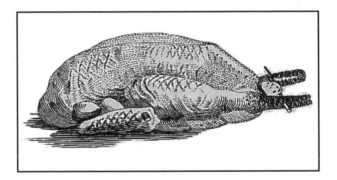

1. Preheat oven to 400°F.

2. Using a serrated knife, slit the skin of each chestnut. Set the chestnuts in one layer on a baking sheet, sprinkle with water, place in the oven, and roast 20 to 30 minutes. Take out of the oven and with a small paring knife remove both the exterior shell and the interior skin. (The hotter the chestnuts are, the easier they are to peel.) Set 8 of them aside and chop them coarsely.

3. Increase the oven temperature to 450°F.

4. In a food processor, combine the remaining chestnuts with the ham, chicken livers, marjoram, thyme, basil, parsley, mace, and nutmeg. Process until the mixture is finely chopped. Season with salt to taste.

5. Lay the turkey breast skin side down on a cutting board. Starting from the center where the breast bone was removed, make a long incision in each of the two breast pieces parallel to the cutting board so that you can open up the whole breast to accomodate the stuffing. Arrange the chestnut stuffing in the center, and fold the meat over to cover. Tie with kitchen twine to secure.

6. Set the turkey breast skin side up on a rack in a roasting pan. Roast until the turkey is just cooked through and registers 165°F on a meat thermometer, about 1 hour 40 minutes, basting every 15 minutes with a little melted butter.

7. Remove the turkey from the pan and set on a serving platter. Cover loosely with aluminum foil and set aside in a warm place for 20 minutes.

8. In the meantime pour off all the fat from the roasting pan. Add the beef broth and wine and bring to a simmer, scraping the bottom of the pan. Stir together the butter and flour. Stir into the gravy until thickened. Add the reserved chopped chestnuts and cook at a bare simmer 10 minutes.

9. To serve, garnish the roast with oranges and watercress. Carve the roast and serve the gravy in a sauceboat on the side.

The Frugal Housewife: or, Complete Woman Cook by Susannah Carter

25 large chestnuts

¼ pound ham, coarsely chopped

2 chicken livers

½ teaspoon dried marjoram

½ teaspoon dried thyme

½ teaspoon dried basil

1 tablespoon chopped fresh parsley

Large pinch mace

Large pinch grated nutmeg

Salt

1 boneless turkey breast, about 5 pounds

Butter

1 cup beef broth

¾ cup dry white wine

2 tablespoons butter, softened

2 tablespoons flour

Sliced oranges, for garnish

Watercress, for garnish

SERVES 8 TO 10

To roast quails

Roast Quail with Orange Shallot Sauce

Quail were even more common here than they were in England, and the same recipes were used on both continents. In order to make sure they remained succulent, quail were stuffed with suet; if you rub the inside cavity with butter, much the same result will be achieved. The simply roasted birds were often served with a barely thickened sauce made of "gravy" (which meant a hearty meat broth) and enlivened by the addition of an anchovy and wine or, as here, orange juice. The bread crumbs are a holdover from the earlier era when the crumbs were used to thicken the sauce. Here they just absorb it.

½ cup bread crumbs	1. Preheat oven to 500°F.
2 tablespoons butter plus melted butter for basting	2. Fry the bread crumbs in the 2 tablespoons butter until golden. Set aside.
¼ pound beef suet, ground, or substitute softened butter	3. Combine the suet with the marjoram, thyme, basil, mace, nutmeg, and pepper to taste. Rub a little of this mixture on the inside of each quail.
½ teaspoon dried marjoram	
½ teaspoon dried thyme	4. Truss the birds and set them breast side up on a rack in a roasting pan. Set in the oven and roast 10 minutes, basting once or twice with a mixture of 2 tablespoons water combined with 1 teaspoon salt. Remove the quail from the oven and sprinkle with flour. Return to the oven and continue to cook 10 to 12 minutes longer. The thigh meat should still be a little pink. Baste two or three times with melted butter. Remove the birds from the oven, set breast side down on a platter, and cover lightly with aluminum foil. Allow to rest while you make the sauce.
½ teaspoon dried basil	
Large pinch ground mace	
Large pinch grated nutmeg	
Pepper	
Salt	
8 quail	
Flour	
1 cup beef broth	
2 anchovy fillets	
4 shallots, sliced	5. Pour off all the fat from the roasting pan. Add the beef broth, anchovies, shallots, and orange and lemon juices. Bring to a rapid boil and cook until reduced to ¾ cup.
½ cup orange juice	
1 tablespoon lemon juice	
Lemon wedges, for garnish	6. To serve, set each quail breast side up and spoon a little sauce over it. Sprinkle some of the reserved bread crumbs on top and garnish with lemon wedges.
Serves 4	

The Frugal Housewife: or, Complete Woman Cook by Susannah Carter

To make polenta

CORNMEAL MUSH BAKED WITH CHEESE

How Mary Randolph came to call this dish of cornmeal mush cooked with cheese by the Italian name is a mystery, though the name clearly shows that an American food had become part of Italian cooking, and then came back to its land of origin. When made with white cornmeal, which is more common in the South, the dish bears a close resemblance to grits.

1. Bring 3 cups water to a boil in a medium-sized heavy saucepan. Add the butter and salt to taste. Mix the cornmeal into 1 cup cold water. Add the cornmeal mixture to the boiling water and stir energetically. Bring to a boil, stirring continuously. Reduce the heat to low and cook 15 minutes, stirring frequently to prevent sticking and breaking up any lumps. The mixture will be very thick. Scrape into a bowl and allow to cool completely. Unmold.

2. Preheat oven to 375°F. Butter a 6-cup casserole.

3. Slice the cornmeal mush into ½-inch slices. Layer the mush with the cheese in the casserole, finishing with a layer of cheese. Bake until golden, 30 to 40 minutes.

The Virginia Housewife by Mary Randolph

2 tablespoons butter

Salt

1 cup cornmeal

6 ounces sharp cheddar cheese, cut into thin slices

SERVES 6

Fried Chickens

FRIED CHICKEN WITH CREAM GRAVY

This is the first known recipe for that most Southern dish, fried chicken with cream gravy. It appeared in a 1828 edition of Mary Randolph's *The Virginia Housewife.* Lard, plentiful and tasty, would have been used for frying, but peanut oil will do the job. After you have fried the chicken and parsley, use the same fat for frying the fritters in the recipe that follows.

A 3½-pound chicken, cut into 8 pieces

Flour

Lard, or substitute peanut oil

¾ cup milk

¼ cup heavy cream

Ground black pepper

1 tablespoon chopped fresh parsley

20 small parsley sprigs

Indian Fritters (recipe follows)

SERVES 3 TO 4

1. Season the chicken with salt. Dredge the chicken pieces in the flour. Set aside on paper towels while the fat heats.

2. Add enough lard or peanut oil to a large heavy pan so that it is about 1½ inches deep. Heat the oil to moderately hot (about 350°F). Add the chicken pieces, starting with the largest ones first. Fry for about 20 minutes, until the chicken is cooked through. Drain on paper towels, then arrange on a serving platter and keep warm.

3. To make the cream gravy, combine the milk and cream in a small saucepan. Bring to a simmer. Stir together 1 tablespoon butter and 1 tablespoon flour. Whisk this mixture into the milk. Bring to a boil and simmer 10 minutes, stirring occasionally. Add the chopped parsley and season with salt and pepper. Keep warm.

4. When the chicken is cooked, fry the parsley sprigs in the same fat until crisp. Drain on paper towels.

5. To serve, pour the cream gravy over the chicken and garnish with the fried parsley sprigs and the fritters.

The Virginia Housewife by Mary Randolph

Indian Fritters
CORNMEAL FRITTERS

Mary Randolph suggested serving cornmeal fritters with fried chicken, but failed to include a recipe. She probably had in mind fritters like these, which are remarkably similar to hush puppies. This recipe appeared in a pamphlet written by Eliza Leslie in 1846 to introduce English cooks to this most American of grains (as an alternative to potatoes, which were being wiped out by a blight).

2 eggs

⅓ cup milk

1 cup cornmeal

Pinch salt

Lard, or substitute peanut oil

MAKES 12 TO 16 FRITTERS

1. In a medium bowl, beat the eggs with an electric mixer until light and fluffy, about 5 minutes. Stir in the milk, cornmeal, and salt, and continue beating until ingredients are incorporated.

2. Fill a heavy saucepan or deep skillet with lard or oil to a depth of 1½ inches. Heat until hot but not smoking, to about 375°F. Drop the batter by tablespoonfuls into the oil and cook until puffed and golden, 3 to 5 minutes. Drain on paper towels and serve immediately.

The Indian Meal Book by Eliza Leslie

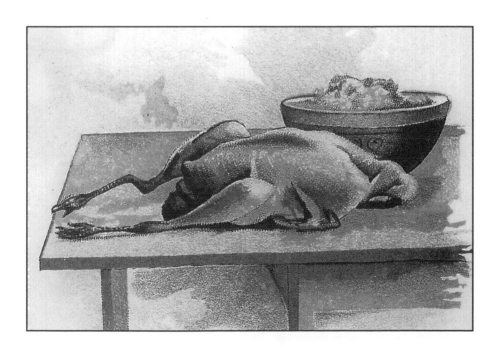

Spinach with Sorrel

SAUTÉED SPINACH WITH SORREL

Sorrel, a leafy green with a pleasantly acidic flavor, was quite common in Jefferson's day. Though it is still widely used in France, in the United States it may be a little tricky to find. It is stocked by some specialty grocers and an occasional farmers' market. The sorrel gives the spinach a delightfully lemony edge. Cook the two greens separately, because sorrel cooks much more quickly. Mrs. Randolph mentions that you can garnish the vegetables with poached eggs if you so desire.

1 pound fresh spinach leaves, cleaned

1 pound sorrel leaves, cleaned

2 tablespoons butter

Salt

Ground black pepper

SERVES 4 TO 6

1. Steam the spinach and sorrel separately until just wilted. Drain in a colander and press out as much liquid as possible. Chop coarsely.

2. Melt the butter in a medium skillet over moderate heat. Add the greens and sauté about 2 minutes, until they are heated through and quite dry.

The Virginia Housewife by Mary Randolph

To dress salad

To have this delicate dish in perfection, the lettuce, pepper grass, chervil, cress &c. should be gathered early in the morning, nicely picked, washed, and laid in cold water, which will be improved by adding ice; just before dinner is ready to be served, drain the water from your salad, cut it into a bowl, giving the proper proportions of each plant; prepare the following mixture to pour over it: boil two fresh eggs ten minutes, put them in water to cool, then take the yelks [sic] in a soup plate, pour on them a table spoonful of cold water, rub them with a wooden spoon until they are perfectly dissolved, then add two table spoonsful of oil; when well mixed, put in a teaspoonful of salt, one of powdered sugar, and one of made mustard; when all these are united and quite smooth, stir in two table spoonsful of common, and two of tarragon vinegar; put it over the salad, and garnish the top with the whites of the eggs cut into rings, and lay around the edge of the bowl young scallions, they being the most delicate of the onion tribe.

The Virginia Housewife by Mary Randolph

Cymling Pudding
SUMMER SQUASH SOUFFLÉ

Delicate pattypan squash, called cymling at the time, was a favorite in antebellum Virginia. It was often boiled and then mashed with butter and cream, much like turnips. Here the squash are turned into a savory pudding that is almost a soufflé. The inclusion of soda crackers in the recipe is likely to be a later addition. If pattypan squash is unavailable, any summer squash will do.

1. Steam the squash until tender, about 10 minutes. Purée in a food processor. In a bowl combine the purée, 1 tablespoon of the butter, the milk, and eggs. Add salt and pepper to taste.

2. Preheat oven to 350°F.

3. Spread butter on both sides of the bread, using a total of 2 tablespoons of the butter. Line a 2-quart baking dish with the bread, then pour in the squash mixture. Sprinkle with the cracker crumbs and dot with the remaining 1 tablespoon butter. Bake until puffed and golden, about 1 hour. Serve immediately.

Housekeeping in Old Virginia edited by Marion Cabell Tyree

1½ pounds pattypan squash, cut into ½-inch slices

4 tablespoons butter, softened

1 cup milk

3 eggs

Salt

Ground black pepper

6 slices day-old hearty white bread

¼ cup crushed soda crackers

SERVES 4 TO 6

Tomata Catsup

TOMATO KETCHUP

This is the earliest recipe we have for tomato ketchup, and it's a little unusual for its time. In the eighteenth and early nineteenth centuries, catsup usually referred to an aged vinegary condiment most commonly made with mushrooms or walnuts. It was added as a flavor enhancer to dishes much as we might add Worcestershire sauce today. As the 1800s progressed, tomato ketchup became much more popular, with sugar becoming an important addition by the century's end. Mrs. Randolph knew well that there was only a single month when tomatoes are ripe enough to preserve. Her instructions are to the point: "Make it in August."

6 pounds ripe tomatoes, cored and quartered

Salt

1 onion, finely chopped

2 teaspoons mace blades, coarsely ground, or substitute 1 teaspoon ground mace

1 tablespoon whole black peppercorns

MAKES 4 CUPS

1. Put the tomatoes in a large nonreactive saucepan over moderate heat. Sprinkle with 1 teaspoon salt. Cover tightly and bring to a boil, stirring occasionally. When the mixture begins to look soupy (after about 15 minutes), remove the lid and cook at a steady simmer for 45 minutes more. Pass through a food mill, or purée briefly in a food processor, then pass through a coarse sieve.

2. Return the tomatoes to the pan, add the onion, mace, and peppercorns. Cook at a steady simmer, stirring regularly, until the catsup cooks down to 4 cups, about 45 minutes. Add more salt if necessary. Strain, being careful not to press the peppercorns and mace through the sieve.

Note: The ketchup can be stored for up to two weeks in the refrigerator. To store longer, ladle into sterilized canning jars and process according to the jar manufacturer's directions.

The Virginia Housewife by Mary Randolph

Excellent Recipe for Pastry
PIE DOUGH

When making pie pastry Mrs. Margaret Cabell Tyree, one of the numerous contributors to *Housekeeping in Old Virginia*, was obviously aware of the advantages of mixing butter and lard. Not only was lard more economical than butter, but it also yielded a flakier pastry; the butter made the dough much tastier than the traditional American recipe, which called for lard alone. The butter should be very slightly softened. Using half butter and half vegetable shortening yields much the same result.

1. Stir the flour and salt together in a medium bowl. Add the butter and lard and, using a large flat knife, cut the fats into the flour until the flakes are no larger than oatmeal.

2. Sprinkle the mixture with about ⅓ cup ice water, a few tablespoons at a time, stirring with the knife after each addition. Add only enough water so that the dough just barely sticks together. The dough should be very dry. Gather the dough into a ball, divide in half, and wrap each half in plastic wrap. Refrigerate at least 1 hour before using.

Housekeeping in Old Virginia edited by Marion Cabell Tyree

2 cups bleached all-purpose flour

½ teaspoon salt

6 tablespoons unsalted butter, cut into small pieces

6 tablespoons chilled lard

MAKES ENOUGH DOUGH FOR ONE 9-INCH DOUBLE-CRUST PIE OR TWO 9-INCH SINGLE-CRUST PIES

Burnt Cream
ORANGE CUSTARD WITH CARAMELIZED CRUST

Once the "cream" is made and chilled, the "burnt" part needs to be added: sugar is sprinkled over the top, then lightly caramelized. In a modern kitchen, this is tricky. In Jefferson's time (this recipe was apparently used by the Jefferson family at Monticello) the cook had at her disposal something called a salamander, essentially a thin slab of iron attached to a long metal handle. The salamander would be set on the coals until it was glowing red and then held just above the sugar for a moment or two. Modern chefs often use a small blowtorch to caramelize the tops of their crème brûlée (literally *"burnt cream"*). At home, the trick is to get the top of the custard as close to the broiler as possible without actually burning it or heating up the custard too much. A few dark specks are okay.

The pamphlet in which this recipe originally appeared was published anonymously, presumably from an old family collection.

1 orange
4 cups milk
½ cup sugar, plus 4 tablespoons sugar
3 egg yolks
1 whole egg
¾ cup all-purpose flour
2 tablespoons butter

SERVES 6

1. Using a vegetable peeler, remove two 4-inch strips of orange rind. Heat the milk with the rind in a medium saucepan. Bring to a boil and simmer 10 minutes. Remove the rind.

2. In a medium bowl, beat together the ½ cup sugar, the egg yolks, and egg. Stir in the flour, then gradually beat in the hot milk.

3. Pour the mixture into a heavy saucepan. Cook over low heat, stirring, until thickened—it should just barely come to a simmer. Pour into an shallow flameproof dish. Let cool, then refrigerate. To prevent a skin from forming, lay a piece of wax paper or plastic wrap directly on the surface of the custard.

4. Preheat the broiler.

5. Sprinkle the top of the chilled custard evenly with the remaining 4 tablespoons sugar. Set the custard about 1 inch from the heat source and, watching it carefully, move it around so that the sugar melts. Try to minimize any burning. Refrigerate briefly. Serve as soon as the sugar hardens.

Eighteen Colonial Recipes

Watermelon Ice

Mrs. J. Johnson of Abingdon, Virginia, calls this dessert "beautiful and delicious." The watermelon must be very ripe. Adding a few reserved seeds is a decorative touch.

1. Scoop out the watermelon flesh and remove the seeds. Reserve about 1 tablespoon of the seeds.

2. Purée the pulp in a food processor, and measure 4 cups. Stir in the sugar and the seeds. Refrigerate until very cold.

3. Pour into an ice-cream freezer and freeze according to the manufacturer's directions. Serve slightly soft.

Housekeeping in Old Virginia edited by Marion Cabell Tyree

1 small ripe watermelon, about 4 pounds

¾ cup extra-fine granulated sugar

SERVES 6

Lemon Cream

LEMON ICE CREAM

In Mrs. Randolph's day there were already several popular flavors of ice cream. Her book lists both vanilla and peach (chocolate was still far in the future). Lemon was much in favor then and deserves to be again. Until 1848, when the hand-cranked ice-cream maker was introduced, the confection was made by immersing a pewter tub filled with the cream mixture into another tub containing salt and ice. A spoon was used to keep the cream moving until frozen throughout.

4 lemons

3 cups heavy cream

1 cup sugar

1 cup milk

MAKES ABOUT 2½ PINTS

1. Using a vegetable peeler, peel the yellow lemon rind from each lemon. Combine with the cream in a medium nonreactive saucepan. Bring to a boil and cook at a bare simmer for 20 minutes. Cool and strain into a bowl.

2. Squeeze and measure 3 tablespoons lemon juice. Pour the sugar over the juice until the sugar is completely saturated. Stir the sugar into the cream until dissolved. Stir in the milk. Chill until very cold.

3. Pour the mixture into an ice-cream freezer and freeze according to the manufacturer's directions.

The Virginia Housewife by Mary Randolph

The Ice-Cream Revolution

George Washington spent $200 on ice cream in New York City in the single summer of 1790—an astronomical sum in those days. While in the city, he bought it from a commercial ice-cream seller but back home at Mount Vernon he already had a "cream machine for making ice," which he had bought six years before. He also had an ice house that kept ice from melting well into the summer. Thomas Jefferson also apparently owned an ice-cream machine. Mrs. Alexander Hamilton was known to serve the confection, as was Dolley Madison. A guest of Mrs. Madison at the White House was duly impressed when presented with "a large, shining dome of pink Ice Cream."

The Italians had introduced ice cream to the English and French, but it is not clear which of the three countries introduced us to our favorite dessert. The continental recipe always begins with an egg-custard base, whereas some American ice creams use just plain cream with flavoring. The 1754 edition of the English cookbook *The Art of Cookery Made Plain and Easy* by Hannah Glasse includes a custardless ice cream, and this influential cookbook may have played a role. *The Virginia Housewife* includes recipes using both techniques.

Nowhere else was it as popular. By 1837, the English Captain Frederick Marryat noted with surprise about the "one great luxury in America...the quantity of clear pure ice...even in the hottest seasons, ice creams are universal and even cheap." He was also taken aback to see "common laborers" take a midday break to eat a dish of ice cream. By that time, ice was already big business, with whole ponds being "harvested" in the winter and carefully stored in insulated warehouses until the summer.

A Victorian Christmas

Americans Celebrate Their Favorite Holiday

Waiting for the Christmas pudding. An engraving by Thomas Nast, who gave us our visual image of Santa Claus.

Philadelphia, 1860

A s the Christmas season approaches," Christine Terhune Herrick wrote, sitting at her desk in Philadelphia at the offices of *The Ladies' Home Journal* in 1886, "the thoughts of the housekeeper turn towards the preparation of those dainties which seem to belong par excellence to the holiday time. It is the period for social reunion, for unbending from the cares and dignities which cumber the rest of the year and yielding mind and body to the genial relaxations that restore even to the most blasé something of the freshness of youth." Christmas, with its cheer and goodwill, its decorative exuberance and edible abundance, as well as its sentimentality and commercialism, was America's favorite holiday in the nineteenth century. Mrs. Herrick's reflections, appearing in the nation's most widely read publication, acted as both mirror and beacon to the era's Victorian sentiment.

The Victorians invented Christmas as we know it today, with its turkey dinner, Santa Claus, greeting cards, and Christmas tree. Because of Philadelphia's large German population, it had been one of the first communities to adopt the Christmas tree in the early 1800s. By mid-century, the whole country had adopted the custom. In the old days, the tree had been small enough to fit on a table, but it grew until its shining star grazed the ceiling and the branches sparkled with tinsel, glass ornaments, and candles. Santa Claus, descended from an Old World bishop named St. Nicholas, was transformed into an icon of generosity and good cheer by Clement C. Moore's *A Visit from Saint Nicholas* in 1823 and thereafter given a starring role on numerous advertisements and greeting cards. Philadelphia had also played a role in making Christmas cards popular when a local printer came up with an inexpensive color printing process. This allowed just about everyone to send a vibrant season's greeting.

It was also in the middle of the nineteenth century that the stuffed and roasted turkey became the centerpiece of the American Christmas feast, accompanied by oyster dressing, sweet potatoes, cranberry sauce, mincemeat pie, oranges, and nuts. The coming of the railroads helped to make the feast standard all over the country. After the Civil War, the railroads brought New England oysters to Chicago, Southern sweet potatoes to Boston, Midwestern wild turkeys to Baltimore, and Florida oranges to Philadelphia.

The first European settlers had celebrated a very different holiday. Certainly the Puritans disapproved of revelry to commemorate Christ's birth. As late as 1846, Philadelphia Methodists bade parishioners a happy Christmas, "but not a merry foolish one devoted to mirth and trifling and mingled with sin." As the century neared the Gilded Age, the good residents of Philadelphia did not take this advice too closely to heart; in 1848, *The Pennsylvanian,* a Philadelphia daily, was reporting that the city's markets were "almost impassable" as a result of the Christmas tree trade. Whether living in exclusive Society Hill or just scraping by in the working-class tenements off Front Street, Philadelphians did everything they could to ensure a merry Christmas.

The holiday season was a dizzying round of public and private events with concerts, exhibitions, masquerade balls, shooting matches, turkey hunts, and billiard tournaments mingled with skating parties, sleigh rides, games of cards for the adults, and more active amusements like blindman's buff for the children. It was the time of year for "candy parties" at which women and children pulled sheets of candied sugar and molasses into brittle or turned the candy syrup into toffee or chocolate caramels. No self-respecting hostess would let an occasion go by without a welcoming spread of sandwiches, turnovers, gingerbread, doughnuts, crullers, and the universally adored ice cream. Chestnuts were indeed roasted on an open fire but so were popcorn and even oysters. Ella Myers, in her *Home Cookbook*, published in Philadelphia in 1884, has detailed instructions on how to welcome home a ravenous party returning from a day of sledding:

> A delicious supper may be provided…by having an oyster roast. The preparations for this are simple. An open fireplace and a bed of glowing coals, or a stove with the oven well-heated, are essentials. The shell oysters, carefully washed are brought in by the basket full and laid among the coals or on the oven floor. When the heat opens the shell, the oysters are done. The shell is wrenched in two by a stout knife, the oyster treated with a little pepper, salt and a dash of lemon juice and is ready for eating. A good plan is for each man to open the oysters for himself and his partner at the supper table. They must be eaten very hot, as soon as possible after they are drawn from the fire and should be accompanied by crackers, or bread and butter, and coffee. Cake and fruit may finish the repast, if desired, but they are not absolutely necessary. Oysters must be provided in generous measure, for the exercise in the frosty air develope [sic] astonishing appetites and the tempting bivalves disappear with marvelous rapidity.

Oysters were cheap in those days. In fact, especially when compared to Europe, most food was plentiful and relatively inexpensive. When it came to Christmas dinner, even the most modest household could usually afford a festive dinner with a turkey, stuffing, vegetables, and a pie or two.

Wealthier families sat down to multi-course feasts at tables radiant with their best crystal and silverware. Aside from the turkey stuffed with a chestnut, oyster, or corn bread dressing, dinner might include ham, goose, pheasant, duck, broiled salmon, and chicken or game pie. Porcelain tureens held turnips, mashed potatoes, creamed onions, creamed chestnuts, and baked stuffed potatoes as well as beets, fried celery, candied sweet potatoes, and cranberry jelly. Creamed oysters, shrimp salad, and cheese croquettes might further augment the meal. Then, of course, came dessert: sponge cake, banana cake, fruit cake, lemon pudding, cranberry pie, mince pie, and ice cream, as well as the indispensable steamed pudding with hard sauce. "Christmas without plum pudding would seem like...*Hamlet* with Hamlet left out," declared a writer in the *Woman's Home Companion.*

It's hardly surprising that Christmas dinner invariably called for some trepidation and much planning. Mrs. Herrick was ever ready with sound advice: "the hostess should diligently guard against over-tasking her strength or her pocket. The simplest form of entertainment is preferable to an elaborate one which must be paid for later by worn nerves or an exhausted purse....Make the house gay with Christmas greens, have a cordial welcome ready for

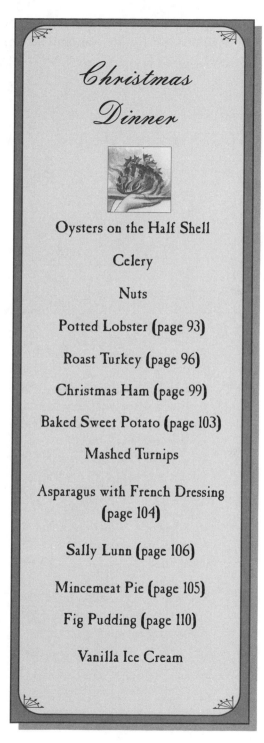

Christmas Dinner

Oysters on the Half Shell

Celery

Nuts

Potted Lobster (page 93)

Roast Turkey (page 96)

Christmas Ham (page 99)

Baked Sweet Potato (page 103)

Mashed Turnips

Asparagus with French Dressing
(page 104)

Sally Lunn (page 106)

Mincemeat Pie (page 105)

Fig Pudding (page 110)

Vanilla Ice Cream

guests, give them of the best of yourself and of your belongings, and it will be a difficult visitor who will not thoroughly enjoy the party be it what style it may."

Preparing for Christmas

Here are a few decorating ideas from Mary Virginia Terhune's *House and Home*, published in Philadelphia in 1889.

If there are no small children in the house you will probably dispense with a tree but a few flowers and a few yards of evergreen tastefully arranged will give your parlor quite a holiday appearance. A few potted plants in blossom may be grouped in the centre of the dinner-table, the pots concealed by evergreen or holly. Take [a] wooden bowl and place it on a small table or stand, fill with evergreen—ground pine is preferable—add holly berries here and there, or pressed autumn leaves and ferns, and let the evergreen creep over the edges of the bowl to cover it entirely.

Wood brackets entirely covered with evergreen and holding a small plant blossom or a slender vase with a few choice flowers, serve to brighten the corners of a plainly furnished room. Should you have a large dish of yellow glass, fill it with green and pink or scarlet blossoms and set it in the centre of the dinner table upon a square of pale blue or peacock blue satin.

Potted Lobster

Lobster Pâté

The most popular cookbook writer of antebellum America was Eliza Leslie. This receipt is adapted from the *fifty-ninth* edition of her masterwork, *Miss Leslie's Complete Cookery*. Miss Leslie was a proponent of simple, straightforward (but never plain!) cooking.

In the days before canning, all kinds of seafood were "potted." Shrimp, crab, or lobster (still cheap in the nineteenth century) were partially cooked, sealed with clarified butter, and then put in the ice box for meals later that week. The result is similar to seafood pâté. The author notes that "potted lobster is used to lay between thin slices of bread for sandwiches." Just the thing with a cup of tea, or as an appetizer with a glass of sherry.

1. Bring a large pot full of water to a boil. Add the lobsters and cook 10 minutes. Drain and cool. Remove the meat from the bodies, tails, and claws. If the lobsters are female, remove the bright pink coral and reserve separately.

2. Preheat oven to 300°F.

3. Combine the lobster meat with the nutmeg, mace, cayenne, and salt to taste in a food processor. Process until the meat is finely chopped.

4. Spoon the chopped meat into a 2½-cup ovenproof dish (or 2 smaller dishes). Press down hard to eliminate any air pockets. If there is coral, rub it to a paste and arrange it between layers of the lobster meat. Melt the butter and pour over the lobster. Set the dish in the oven and bake 30 minutes. Remove.

5. When cool enough to handle, pour off the butter into a small saucepan, bring it to a boil, and simmer until almost no water remains. Be careful it does not burn. Skim off the solids and strain. Pack down the lobster again. Pour the clarified butter over the lobster. Cover. Refrigerate at least 24 hours before serving. Serve at room temperature with lightly toasted bread.

Miss Leslie's Complete Cookery by Eliza Leslie

Two 1½-pound live lobsters

Large pinch ground nutmeg

Large pinch ground mace

Large pinch cayenne pepper

Salt

¾ cup butter

Makes about 2½ cups, serving 6 to 8 as an appetizer

Salmon Steaks

SALMON BAKED IN PARCHMENT

To protect delicate fish from direct heat in a coal-fueled stove, it was wrapped in paper before being set on a gridiron on the coals. The fish steams inside the paper envelope, and also absorbs some of the smoky flavor of the fire. You can achieve much the same effect on a barbecue. Make sure the coals have burnt down and that there are no flames to set the parchment on fire. Eliza Leslie suggests serving the dish with fried parsley, a popular garnish at the time (page 76).

Butter

4 salmon steaks, about 6 ounces each

Salt

Pepper

Lobster Sauce (recipe follows)

SERVES 4

1. Preheat oven to 450°F.

2. Cut 4 pieces of cooking parchment large enough to wrap each piece of salmon. Rub each lightly with butter. Season the fish with salt and pepper, place a salmon steak in the center of each piece of paper, and wrap. Fold the ends under and set on a baking sheet.

3. Bake for 12 to 15 minutes, until the salmon flakes at the edges but is still bright pink at the center. Serve with Lobster Sauce on the side.

Lobster Sauce

Lobster Butter Sauce

The nineteenth-century American kitchen was as fond of sauces as the French kitchen was. Meat and fish were considered incomplete without a gravy or sauce. This lobster sauce could also be made with shrimp or crab and though it is particularly good with salmon, most other full-flavored fish would be a good foil for its buttery richness.

1. Simmer the mace and peppercorns with ¾ cup water in a small saucepan for 20 minutes. Strain out the spices and pour the water back into the saucepan. You should have about ½ cup. If necessary, add a little fresh water.

2. Remove the lobster meat from the shell. Finely dice the meat from the tail. Take the remaining meat from the claws and body (include the coral if there is any) and purée in a food processor.

3. Stir together the butter and flour.

4. Set the pan with the spice-infused water over moderate heat. Add the butter mixture and stir vigorously with a whisk. Keep stirring until the butter just barely begins to simmer but does not boil. Add the lobster purée and whisk until smooth. Stir in the diced lobster. Season with salt. Remove the pan from the heat.

8 blades mace, or substitute ½ teaspoon ground mace

4 black peppercorns

A 1-pound cooked lobster

¾ cup butter, softened

1 tablespoon flour

Salt

Makes 1½ cups sauce, serving 4 to 6

Miss Leslie's Complete Cookery
by Eliza Leslie

To roast a turkey

ROAST TURKEY WITH MARJORAM LEMON STUFFING

"The turkey is the true son of the soil. He has never been asked for his naturalization papers!" proclaimed the editors of the Philadelphia Women's Centennial Committee *National Cookery Book* as they gloried in the one hundredth anniversary of independence. This most American bird, "universally admitted to be the finest fowl brought to table" was much closer to its wild cousin in those days—a little leaner and a little tougher but much more flavorful. For Christmas, it was often served with oyster stuffing though there were numerous imaginative variations.

The bird would have been spit-roasted in front of a fire, with a pan set below to catch the drippings. It would have also been roasted rather quickly compared to today, but then in those days, a 20-pound turkey would have been a freak of nature. To simulate the nineteenth-century approach, cook a 10- to 12-pound turkey on a rack in a hot oven. To assure a juicy turkey, the Victorians dusted it with flour and then basted it diligently with butter. The flour absorbs a little of the butter each time and releases it slowly as the roast cooks. Use day-old stale bread to make the bread crumbs. Tear it into small pieces and then pulse in a food processor.

The recipe's author notes that "A turkey should be accompanied by ham or tongue. Have stewed cranberries on the table to eat with it." She also suggests serving it with mushroom sauce, made by adding sautéed mushrooms to the gravy.

At the holidays, turkey was the true national bird.

1. Preheat oven to 400°F.

2. To make the stuffing, stir together the bread crumbs, suet, lemon peel, marjoram, nutmeg, ham, and eggs. Season with salt and pepper. Stuff the craw with about 1½ cups of the stuffing, use another 1½ cups for the cavity. Reserve the remaining stuffing. Truss the turkey and dust with about 1 tablespoon flour. Set breast side up on a rack in a roasting pan. Roast, basting every 15 minutes with melted butter, for 2 hours.

3. Combine the neck and giblets with 4 cups water in a medium saucepan. Simmer for 2 hours. Strain. You should have about 1½ cups broth; add water if necessary to make the needed amount.

4. Brown 4 tablespoons flour by cooking it in a small skillet over moderate heat, stirring, until it is the color of peanut butter. You can also do this by sprinkling the flour on a baking sheet, and baking it until it reaches the same color. Stir into the giblet broth. Bring the gravy to a simmer and cook 10 minutes.

5. While the turkey is roasting, form the reserved stuffing into about a dozen 1-inch balls, by squeezing it in your hands.

6. Dust the turkey once more with flour and continue roasting and basting until done: the juices from the thigh should run clear, not pink. The total roasting time will be about 12 to 15 minutes per pound. Remove the turkey from the pan, set breast side down on a serving platter, and cover loosely with foil. Let rest in a warm place 20 minutes before serving.

7. Pour off and discard all the fat from the roasting pan. Add the gravy to the roasting pan and simmer 5 minutes, scraping the bottom of the pan. Season with salt and pepper to taste.

8. Fill a skillet with ½ inch vegetable oil and heat it over moderately high heat until hot. Add the balls of stuffing and fry until golden, 3 to 5 minutes. Drain on paper towels.

9. To serve, set the turkey breast side up on the platter, and surround it with the stuffing balls. Serve the gravy on the side.

Miss Leslie's Complete Cookery by Eliza Leslie

6 cups fresh bread crumbs

½ cup ground suet

2 teaspoons grated lemon peel

1 teaspoon dried marjoram

½ teaspoon grated nutmeg

¾ cup chopped ham

3 eggs

Salt

Pepper

A 10-pound turkey, neck and giblets reserved

Flour

Melted better, for basting

Vegetable oil, for deep frying

SERVES 6

Devilled Turkey

SPICED TURKEY DRUMSTICKS

Highly seasoned devilled turkey was considered a man's dish by nineteenth-century Americans. The female constitution was considered too delicate to be subjected to such strong flavors. Though leftover turkey legs could certainly be devilled the day after, it was the custom to present the whole roasted turkey at the table and then send the legs back to the kitchen to be devilled while the bird was carved. The seasoned limbs would then be served with the main course.

2 cooked turkey legs	1. Preheat oven to 450°F.
Salt	2. Slash the turkey legs with a sharp knife to the bone in several places. Season generously with salt, pepper, and cayenne. Stir together the flour and mustard and smear all over the turkey legs.
Black pepper	
Cayenne pepper	
4 tablespoons flour	
2 tablespoons brown mustard	
	3. Bake until brown and crusty, about 20 minutes.
SERVES 2	*National Cookery Book* by the Women's Centennial Committees, Philadelphia Centennial Exhibition 1876

Virginia Ham

Virginia ham has been considered one of the great delicacies of American cuisine since colonial days. Sir William Gooch, one of the colony's royal governors, used to send his home-cured hams to his brother, the bishop of Norwich, as well as to the bishops of Salisbury, London, and Bangor. In the nineteenth century, Queen Victoria was so fond of the hams that each week a standing order went out from Buckingham Palace for six Virginia hams.

The meat gets its special flavor from the peanuts that are fed to the hogs as well as from the distinctive curing process. The hams are first allowed to absorb salt, then are smoked over hickory or oak and finally rubbed with pepper. Covered with cotton, they are hung to cure for at least six months.

Today, Smithfield hams, the most famous Virginia hams, are readily available through mail order.

Christmas Ham

VIRGINIA HAM BAKED WITH SHERRY

Preparing a Virginia-style ham will give you a good sense of what cooking was really like in the nineteenth century. The ham must first be well scrubbed to rid it of the pepper and any surface mold that may have formed. It is then soaked in water to lessen its salty flavor. You can soak it overnight, but most people recommend at least forty-eight hours. William Byrd, an eighteenth-century Virginia plantation owner, recommended soaking it in a mixture of half water and half milk for thirty-six hours. It should then be cooked at a bare simmer; boiling it can make it stringy. You can cook it well ahead of time and then, when you are ready to serve it, roast it with the topping until just heated through. Serve in very thin slices.

1. Scrub the ham under cold running water with a stiff brush to remove the spices and any mold that might be present. Soak the ham overnight or as long as 48 hours in cold water to cover.

2. Drain. Place the ham in a large pot, cover with cold water, and bring it to a simmer. Poach at a bare simmer until tender, about 20 minutes per pound. The internal temperature should read 160°F on a meat thermometer. Drain, and remove the skin while still warm. Let the ham cool.

3. Preheat oven to 375°F.

4. Stir together the egg, brown sugar, and cracker crumbs and spread all over the ham. Place the ham in a roasting pan and pour the sherry all around it. Bake, basting frequently with the sherry, until all of it is absorbed and the top is well browned, about 45 minutes. Carve into thin slices.

1 dry-cured Virginia-style ham

1 egg, beaten

3 tablespoons brown sugar

¾ cup cracker crumbs

2 cups cream sherry

SERVES 10 TO 12

Famous Old Receipts by Jacqueline Harrison Smith

To roast a loin of pork

ROAST PORK STUFFED WITH MARJORAM AND SAGE

Before the great western cattle ranches began to produce an abundance of beef, pork was by far the most popular meat in America. The first settlers had found that if they let their pigs run wild in the forests, they would have a ready supply of very flavorful meat for winter. In Victorian times, roast pork was inevitably seasoned with sage and marjoram and always served with apple sauce. Miss Leslie also recommends mashed potatoes and turnips as an accompaniment.

3 slices stale white bread

2 egg yolks

2 teaspoons dried marjoram

3 teaspoons dried sage

Salt

Pepper

A 4-pound pork loin (have the butcher cut through the connecting bones so that the loin can be carved into chops)

1 tablespoon flour

1 cup chicken broth

SERVES 4 TO 6

1. Preheat oven to 450°F.

2. Using a food processor, break up the bread into crumbs, and measure 1 cup. Combine the crumbs with the egg yolks, marjoram, and 1 teaspoon of the sage. Season the stuffing generously with salt and pepper.

3. Make a 3-inch incision between every rib. Fill each with the stuffing. Lightly score any fat on the top of the meat with a crisscross pattern. Rub the loin all over with the remaining sage, salt, and pepper.

4. Place the loin on a rack in a roasting pan. Roast 20 minutes. Reduce the heat to 350° and continue roasting, basting occasionally with the pan juices, until the pork loses all traces of pink at the center, about another 1 hour and 40 minutes. Remove to a platter and let rest in a warm place for 20 minutes before carving.

5. Meanwhile, pour off all the fat from the roasting pan. Stir the flour into the broth. Add to the pan and bring to a boil, scraping the bottom of the pan to loosen the browned bits. Boil until reduced to ⅔ cup. Season with salt and pepper. To serve, carve the loin into chops. Serve the gravy on the side.

Miss Leslie's Complete Cookery by Eliza Leslie

Apple Sauce

In the nineteenth century sweetened apple sauce was always served with roast pork and goose. The sweetness and acidity of the apples are a natural foil for the rich, fatty flavor of both meats.

Combine the apples and lemon rind with ¼ cup water in a small saucepan over moderate heat. Cover tightly and cook until the apples fall apart, about 20 minutes. Stir in the sugar, butter, and nutmeg. Serve warm.

Miss Leslie's Complete Cookery by Eliza Leslie

2 pounds McIntosh apples, peeled, cored, and quartered

2 teaspoons grated lemon rind

¼ cup brown sugar

1 tablespoon butter

Large pinch grated nutmeg

MAKES ABOUT 3 CUPS

Macaroni

MACARONI BAKED WITH SWEETBREADS

Macaroni and cheese has been a favorite with Americans at least since the time of Jefferson. It is likely that it was introduced indirectly from Italy through France. By mid-century, there were all kinds of elegant variations on the basic pasta and cheese dish. Sweetbreads (the thymus gland of a calf or lamb), today associated in the United States with French cooking, were not exotic in the nineteenth century. They show up regularly in American cookbooks and on restaurant menus.

³⁄₄ pound veal sweetbreads

1 small whole onion, peeled

2 blades mace, or ¹⁄₂ teaspoon ground mace

Salt

¹⁄₂ pound macaroni

2 tablespoons butter, melted

2 cups drained canned plum tomatoes, coarsely chopped

³⁄₄ cup milk

1 teaspoon dry mustard

¹⁄₂ teaspoon ground black pepper

1 egg, lightly beaten

2 cups grated sharp cheddar cheese

SERVES 4 TO 6

1. Cover the sweetbreads with cold water and soak for 3 hours, changing the water every hour. Place in a saucepan, cover with water, bring to a boil, and simmer 3 minutes. Drain and cool under cold running water. Pull off the rubbery sinews. Wrap the sweetbreads in a clean kitchen towel or cheesecloth, set on a plate, place a board on top, and weigh it down with a pan full of water. Place in the refrigerator. Keep pressed for at least 4 hours or overnight. Remove weight and unwrap the sweetbreads and separate them into small pieces.

2. Preheat oven to 375°F. Butter a large shallow casserole.

3. Bring 2 quarts of water to a boil, add the onion, mace, and 1 teaspoon salt, and simmer 15 minutes. Add the sweetbreads and bring to a boil. Add the macaroni and simmer until the pasta is just tender, about 12 minutes. Drain, remove the onion, and in a large bowl toss with the butter and tomatoes.

4. Stir together the milk, mustard, pepper, egg, and 1¹⁄₂ cups of the cheese. Add to the macaroni and sweetbread mixture and stir to combine thoroughly. Spoon into the prepared casserole, and top with the remaining cheese.

5. Bake until bubbling and brown, about 40 to 50 minutes.

Housekeeping in Old Virginia edited by Marion Cabell Tyree

Baked Sweet Potato

SWEET POTATOES BAKED WITH SPICES

This native American vegetable has long been part of our Christmas feasts.

1. Preheat oven to 350°F. Butter a shallow 2-quart casserole.

2. Stir together all the ingredients, spoon into the casserole, cover, and bake 2 hours. Uncover and continue baking until golden and cooked through, about 30 minutes longer.

Famous Old Receipts by Jacqueline Harrison Smith

2½ pounds sweet potatoes, peeled and grated

1 tablespoon ground cinnamon

1 teaspoon ground black pepper

½ teaspoon salt

1 teaspoon ground allspice

½ cup light brown sugar

6 tablespoons butter, melted

2 eggs, lightly beaten

1 cup milk

SERVES 6

French Dressing

Malt Vinegar Vinaigrette

By the middle of the Victorian era, Christmas menus often included canned asparagus with French dressing. To Victorians, the salad dressing called "French" was a classic vinaigrette. The French normally use wine vinegar, but this dressing has the distinctive flavor of malt vinegar, showing an English influence. You can find malt vinegar in fancy food stores and upscale supermarkets.

⅓ cup English malt vinegar
2 teaspoons prepared mustard
⅔ cup olive oil
Salt
Freshly ground black pepper
Makes 1 cup

Whisk together the vinegar and mustard. Slowly whisk in the oil. Season with salt and pepper.

Famous Old Receipts by Jacqueline Harrison Smith

Aunty's Mince Meat

MINCEMEAT PIE FILLING

Famous Old Receipts, a collection of nineteenth-century heirloom recipes published in 1908, contains fourteen mincemeat recipes, some of which actually include meat (beef tongue). All include suet. The major difference among most of the receipts is the liquor they call for, some preferring Madeira or port, others brandy, applejack, or rum. This particular mincemeat is from Mrs. Prescott Adamson of Germantown, Pennsylvania. Redolent of spice, dried fruit, and most especially brandy, it bears only passing resemblance to the bland bottled mincemeat available commercially today.

The original recipe made enough filling for a dozen pies. This recipe will make enough for two. Preheat an oven to 400°F, line a pie pan with pastry (see page 81), fill it with the mincemeat, and top with a solid or lattice pastry crust. Bake the pie on the bottom shelf for 15 minutes, then reduce the heat to 350°F and continue baking until the mincemeat is bubbly and the pastry golden, another 45 minutes.

1. In a food processor, coarsely grind the almonds and add the sugar, raisins, and currants. Pulse until chopped but not puréed. In a bowl combine with all the remaining ingredients, reserving ⅓ cup of the brandy. Spoon into a crock, pressing down to make sure there are no air pockets. Top with the remaining reserved brandy.

2. Cover tightly and refrigerate at least 1 month before using.

Famous Old Receipts by Jacqueline Harrison Smith

---

3 ounces almonds

⅓ cup sugar

1 pound seedless raisins

½ pound dried currants

½ pound beef suet, ground (see page xiii)

1 pound apples, peeled, cored, and grated

2 tablespoons lemon juice

1 teaspoon grated lemon rind

1 teaspoon grated nutmeg

¼ teaspoon ground cloves

3 ounces citron, chopped

⅓ cup hard cider, imported French or English

¼ cup peach jam

About ¾ cup brandy

MAKES ABOUT 6 CUPS, ENOUGH FOR TWO 9-INCH PIES

Sally Lunn
BUTTERY YEAST BREAD

This version of the buttery loaf called Sally Lunn was contributed by Mrs. James T. Halsey of Philadelphia to *Famous Old Receipts*. The bread, which has the texture and richness of cake, was so popular that this single collection includes six recipes for it! They all use yeast except for one that has the audacity to use the newfangled baking powder.

Like biscuits, Sally Lunn is best served hot with butter. Its name was derived from the French *soleil et lune* (sun and moon), since at one time the dough was shaped into rolls and the golden top crust and the white bottom supposedly evoked an image of the two heavenly bodies. Sally Lunn is traditionally baked in a "turk's head," a pan somewhat like a large bundt cake pan. An angel-food cake pan is a good substitute.

Pine Apple Pudding

Grate 1 large pineapple, beat together half a pound of butter and half a pound of sugar, six eggs, the white and yolks beaten separately, one glass of brandy, one tablespoon of rosewater and a little nutmeg, grated. Mix the ingredients together with the juice and pulp of the pineapple, adding a little grated bread, and bake it for about 10 minutes in a crust.

Philadelphia Centennial Exhibition 1876, Women's Centennial Committees, *National Cookery Book*

1. Stir the yeast into ¼ cup lukewarm water.

2. Generously butter a 10-inch bundt cake pan (or tube pan).

3. Heat the milk together with the butter until the butter is melted. Stir in the salt. Let cool until lukewarm.

4. Stir the milk mixture together with the eggs and yeast mixture in a large bowl. Add the flour, 1 cup at a time, beating with a wooden spoon after each addition until smooth.

5. Spoon the dough into the prepared pan, cover with plastic wrap, and let rise in a warm place until doubled in bulk, about 2 hours.

6. Preheat oven to 375°F.

7. Bake the Sally Lunn until golden and a toothpick inserted in the center comes out clean, about 45 minutes. Let cool briefly, unmold and serve.

Famous Old Receipts by Jacqueline Harrison Smith

1 teaspoon active dry yeast

1 cup milk

½ cup butter

½ teaspoon salt

4 cups all-purpose flour

2 eggs, beaten

MAKES ONE 10-INCH TUBE LOAF

Metropolitan Cake
LEMON AND SPICE LAYER CAKE

This fancy cake would have been the centerpiece of an elaborate spread of desserts that any self-respecting nineteenth-century woman of society would have insisted upon for the holiday meal. This recipe comes from *Dr. Price's Excellent Recipes for Delicious Desserts*, a booklet promoting flavor extracts. Ideally, the cake should be made in five cake pans; however you can use two springform pans to bake the two separate mixtures (the baking time will be closer to 45 minutes). Chill the baked cakes thoroughly, then cut them into layers.

3½ cups bleached all-purpose flour

4 teaspoons baking powder

1 cup butter, softened

2 cups sugar

1 teaspoon lemon extract

1 cup milk

1 teaspoon ground cinnamon

½ teaspoon ground cloves

½ teaspoon ground allspice

1 cup raisins

⅔ cup diced citron

8 egg whites

Almond Icing (recipe follows)

SERVES 12

1. Preheat oven to 375°F. Butter and flour five 10-inch round cake pans. Sift together the flour and baking powder.

2. With an electric mixer, cream the butter with the sugar in a large bowl until creamy and light. Beat in the lemon extract. Gradually add the flour mixture and milk, alternating and beating well after each addition.

3. Transfer about ⅓ of the batter to another bowl. To the smaller amount of batter, add the cinnamon, cloves, allspice, raisins, and citron.

4. Beat the egg whites until firm and shiny. Fold about ⅗ of them into the plain batter and the remainder into the spiced batter. Divide the plain batter among 3 of the prepared cake pans and the remainder between the other 2 pans.

5. Bake until a toothpick inserted in the center comes out clean, about 20 to 25 minutes. Cool on wire racks. Spread each layer with a thin layer of Almond Icing, alternating light and dark layers. Use any remaining icing for the top.

Almond Icing

This frosting is a close cousin to marzipan. The more finely you are able to grind the almonds, the better.

1. Place the almonds in a food processor and grind as fine as possible. Add ½ cup granulated sugar and continue grinding until very fine.

2. Using an electric mixer, in a large bowl beat the egg whites until firm. Gradually add the confectioners' sugar and beat until shiny. Gradually beat in the ground almonds and finally the rosewater. You may need to use a wooden spoon at the end.

Dr. Price's Excellent Recipes for Delicious Desserts

½ pound blanched almonds

½ cup granulated sugar

3 egg whites

2½ cups confectioners' sugar

1 tablespoon rosewater

MAKES ABOUT 4 CUPS

Fig Pudding

STEAMED CHRISTMAS PUDDING WITH DRIED FIGS

Boiled and steamed puddings were a great favorite in both America and England during the age of Victoria. This is a traditional steamed "figgy" pudding, given a New World turn by the addition of molasses. Like all dishes of this type, it is dense and filling, so keep the servings small. The pudding can be steamed several days ahead of time and then reheated by steaming for about 45 minutes just before serving. Serve it hot with a little Foamy Sauce (page 111).

1 cup dried figs, chopped (about ½ pound)

½ cup molasses

½ cup chopped suet (about ¼ pound; see page xiii)

1 teaspoon ground cinnamon

½ teaspoon grated nutmeg

¼ teaspoon salt

½ teaspoon baking soda

½ cup milk

1 egg, lightly beaten

1¾ cups all-purpose flour

Foamy Sauce (recipe follows)

SERVES 6

1. Butter a 6-cup pudding mold or ovenproof bowl.

2. Combine the molasses, suet, cinnamon, nutmeg, salt, and figs in a large bowl. Stir the soda into a tablespoon of hot water until it dissolves. Stir into the milk. Stir the milk, the egg and finally the flour into the fig mixture. Spoon into the prepared mold and cover tightly with foil.

3. Place the mold on a rack in a large pan. Add enough water so that it just comes to the bottom of the mold. Cover pan tightly, bring to a simmer, and steam 3 to 4 hours, adding more water as necessary. Serve hot with Foamy Sauce.

Foamy Sauce
SHERRY "HARD" SAUCE

1. Using an electric mixer, beat the egg and sugar until smooth and creamy, 5 to 10 minutes.

2. Whip the cream until it forms soft peaks. Fold the cream into the sugar mixture, then stir in the sherry. Serve with steamed puddings.

Famous Old Receipts by Jacqueline Harrison Smith

1 egg

⅔ cup sugar

⅓ cup heavy or whipping cream

3 tablespoons cream sherry

MAKES ABOUT 2½ CUPS

For a dramatic presentation, Christmas pudding was sprinkled with warm brandy and then set aflame.

Lemon Jumbles

LEMON BUTTER COOKIES

Recipes for the thin, buttery cookies called "jumbles" abound in cookbooks of the eighteenth and nineteenth centuries. Lemon was one of the favorite flavors.

½ cup butter, softened

½ cup sugar

1 egg

2 tablespoons lemon juice

1 teaspoon grated lemon rind

1½ cups flour

Coarse granulated decorating sugar

MAKES ABOUT 4 DOZEN COOKIES

1. With an electric mixer or food processor, cream together the butter and sugar until light and fluffy. Gradually beat in the egg, lemon juice, and rind. Stir in the flour and combine until a dough forms. Refrigerate the dough about 1 hour, or until it is firm enough to roll.

2. Preheat oven to 375°F.

3. Roll the dough ⅛-inch thick on a floured board. Cut into fancy shapes. Arrange the cookies on ungreased cookie sheets and sprinkle with coarse granulated sugar. Bake until a very pale gold, about 8 to 10 minutes.

Famous Old Receipts by Jacqueline Harrison Smith

Claret Ice

LEMON AND RED WINE ICE

Ices were as required at elegant festivities as ice cream was at every proper dinner or tea party. Combining red wine and citrus, this sorbet tastes remarkably like frozen sangría. It would have been served as one of several desserts. Claret was the term generally used to denote red wine from Bordeaux.

1. In a large nonreactive bowl, combine the sugar, lemon juice and rind, and wine with 2 cups water. Stir until the sugar is thoroughly dissolved. Chill.

2. Just before freezing, stir in the egg white. Pour into an ice-cream freezer and freeze according to the manufacturer's directions. Serve slightly soft.

Famous Old Receipts by Jacqueline Harrison Smith

1¼ cups sugar

½ cup lemon juice

1 teaspoon grated lemon rind

2 cups red Bordeaux wine

1 egg white, lightly beaten

SERVES 6 TO 8

Melting Pot on the Delta

The Refined Cuisine of Creole High Society

The bounty of the Caribbean unloading in nineteenth-century New Orleans.

New Orleans, 1880

Céléstine Eustis, born and bred in Louisiana, set up house in Paris in the 1870s, a glittering, ostentatious period. The city swarmed with parvenu aristocracy that threw lavish dinner parties, which inevitably featured dishes showered with truffles and swimming in cream sauce. When Miss Eustis entertained, however, she treated her fashionable guests to gumbo and jambalaya. These strange creations must have caused many a whispered conversation while the hostess was busy in the kitchen supervising the last-minute details, but they must have also provided an exotic relief from the ornate preparations of *la grande cuisine,* for *Mademoiselle* Eustis received numerous requests for her recipes.

If this Louisiana belle was disinclined to abandon her native dishes in the world capital of gourmandise, she was certainly not going to do so when she arrived in the capital of the freshly re-United States to take care of her recently orphaned niece and nephews. Miss Eustis shared joint custody of the children along with their grandfather, W. W. Corcoran. Because this extraordinarily wealthy man had no lady to act as hostess, she also moved into his mansion to undertake that essential role. Once again, gumbo was the pièce de résistance at the midday Sunday dinner. In the introduction to *Cooking in Old Creole Days*, the cookbook that Celestine Eustis wrote in later life, a friend gives us a little insight into her character:

It is not to be wondered at that one who had been brought up in New
Orleans, where the bons vivants have for many years held sway, and
who went daily down to the French market to select her Bayou
Fourche oysters, ducks and geese in season from the swamps on the
River, turkeys from a long line that hung all plucked but their wings
to be used for brushes and their tails into fans; pompano from the
Gulf of Mexico, sea trout, red fish and sheepshead that were
unexcelled, red snapper from off the banks of Yucatan, frog's legs,
lake and river shrimp and prawns, should have brought to
Washington and the North the desire for the best of everything.

Celestine Eustis's passion for the culinary arts could have been
born in no other American city but New Orleans. "Cuisine is a
serious matter," she writes in her introduction in French, "the
health of mankind depends on it; internal happiness shows interest
in it and even justice has a say in its workings."

Like the Creole food that she championed, Celestine Eustis
was a mixture. Her father was a Yankee lawyer who had settled in
New Orleans and married into a plantation family that boasted
both French and Spanish blood. Creole is a term that the French
and Spanish (criollo) used for people of European and African
descent born outside of their native continents. In the Mississippi
Delta, the Creole developed a cuisine that merged all their
traditions. If there ever was a melting pot in America, it hung in a
hearth somewhere in New Orleans, its American, French, and
Spanish ingredients stirred and enriched by African hands.

Creole cooking was sophisticated, urban, and subtly spiced, its
French names often disguising local innovation. Typical French
preparations like trout *amandine* and sweetbreads *à la financière*
coexisted with redfish "courtbouillon"—which sounds like a French
poaching liquid but is, in fact, a fish stew—or "ratatouille de veau,"
containing such non-French ingredients as okra and sweet potatoes.

Louisiana's complex culinary heritage began in 1718, when the
French founded the small settlement of La Nouvelle Orléans at a
strategic crescent on the Mississippi some distance from the Gulf of
Mexico. The first maps indicated that "savage man eaters"
inhabited the area, but it is unlikely that the settlers, mostly brought

over from French jails, brothels, and debtors' prisons, would have survived if the local Natchez Indians had not shown them how to grow corn, squashes, and beans. The natives also taught the settlers how to use ground sassafras leaves, now known as filé, to thicken stews.

The early settlers were a rambunctious lot. The Compagnie des Indes, which had jurisdiction over the colony, soon saw New Orleans dissolving into chaos. In order to make the settlement a little more settled, they requested the assistance of the Ursuline order. Many of the nuns who arrived had aristocratic backgrounds and brought with them knowledge of the latest culinary fashions. They established herb gardens along with some modicum of bourgeois decency.

The second set of foreigners to arrive, and probably the group that most influenced Louisiana cooking, was the slaves brought from Africa, either directly or through the West Indies, to work the recently established sugar plantations. With them they brought okra and probably eggplant, as well as expertise at growing rice. Their most important influence was as cooks, since any white family with culinary aspirations had a black cook. Gumbo and similar one-pot meals that combine an assortment of meats and vegetables clearly had an African heritage. So did deep-fried dishes like the rice fritters called calas. In Louisiana, no matter what the ingredients or the original cuisine, food invariably passed through the hands of black cooks.

In 1762, Louis XV, in an effort to keep the colony out of British hands, secretly gave Louisiana to his royal Spanish cousin. For the Creole kitchen, at least, this was fortuitous. The Spaniards brought with them the chiles and tomatoes they had discovered in Central and South America, foods quite foreign at the time in France. Jambalaya and the sausage called "chaurice" (a corruption of chorizo) are another legacy of the Spanish period.

The same war that led the French to give away Louisiana also lost them their Canadian possessions. The British, who took control of Acadia, as today's provinces of Nova Scotia and New Brunswick were then known, demanded that the French colonists swear allegiance to the English crown. The majority refused, and were expelled from the land their ancestors had settled in the seventeenth century. Some of these Acadians settled in the American colonies, others returned to France, but many made their way down to French-speaking Louisiana. There they founded settlements deep in the swamps and bayous, often virtually inaccessible to the metropolis on the delta. The difference between Creole and Cajun (shortened from "Acadian") food can be explained by this divergent history. Where Creole cooking was cosmopolitan, urbane and—at least up until the Civil War—aware of the latest Parisian trends, Cajun cooking depended largely on what could be hunted or caught in the back country and seasoned with the hot red pepper that grew in everyone's backyard. The use of mace and cloves in Cajun food today has an echo in the cuisine of Quebec; both hearken back to French foodways of the late seventeenth century. Creole cooking, by contrast, is not particularly spicy. Typical of Cajun cooking are robust dishes such as crawfish *étouffé*, a mouth-scorching stew made with the crayfish once so disdained by the upper classes.

At about the same time, the French Revolution brought a flood of refugees fleeing the Terror, while the war of independence in Haiti brought Creole planters (and many of their slaves) from that French colony. For a short while, the flag that flew over the harbor of New Orleans was French once again but by 1803, with Jefferson's Louisiana Purchase, it was in American hands. With the Americans came the pies, puddings, and other staples of the Anglo-American repertoire, adding once again to the crescent city's melting pot.

In the mid-nineteenth century, New Orleans was a multinational city—in peoples and foods—unparalleled elsewhere in the United States. Cowboys arrived with the cattle they had driven from Texas, riverboats discharged settlers and their produce from the Midwest. The port attracted ships bearing Cubans and their cigars, Jamaicans bearing bananas and pineapples, the French with wine. Lafcadio Hearn, a journalist and cookbook writer, described the cries of the city's food peddlers in 1881:

> There have never been so many fruit peddlers and viand peddlers of all sorts as at the present time…with the first glow of sunlight the street resounds with their cries…these musical announcements, sung by Italians, negroes, Frenchmen, and Spaniards. The vendor of fowls pokes in his head at every open window with cries of "Chick-EN, Madamma, chick-EN!" and the seller of "Lem-ONS—fine Lem-ONS!" follows in his footsteps. The peddlers of "Ap-PULLS!" of "Straw-BARE-eries!"…all own sonorous voices.…Then there is the canteloupe man, whose cry is being imitated by all the children: "Cantel-lope-ah! / Fresh and fine, /Jus from the vine,/ Only a dime."

Although after the Civil War the streets seemed as vibrant as before, there was a crisis in the kitchens of New Orleans, at least as the whites saw it. In a foreword to Celestine Eustis's collection of recipes, S. Weir Mitchell quotes a Southern friend, "[He] once said to me, that the surrender at Appomatox had brought about two serious calamities—an end to dueling and the disappearance of the colored cook. We may at least agree with him that the latter result is a matter deeply to be deplored by all who, like myself, remember the marvelous skill of the Southern cooks." Though some of the expert cooks of African descent remained in the wealthy white households, many looked for work elsewhere.

Until this time, recipes had been passed by word of mouth, but now that the continuity was broken this was impossible. This accounts for the many Creole cookbooks that were written and published late in the nineteenth century. The comprehensive culinary guide published by the *Picayune* newspaper gives as its aim: "to preserve to future generations the many excellent and matchless recipes of our New Orleans cuisine, to gather these up from the lips of the Old Creole negro cooks and the grand old housekeepers who still survive, ere they too pass away, and Creole cookery, with all its delightful combinations and possibilities, will have become a lost art."

Though much of New Orleans has been conquered by the more robust Cajun and Cajun-influenced cooking, there still exist remnants of the subtle and sophisticated Creole past. Traditions are maintained among the old French families and even the casual tourist can savor the past at ancient New Orleans restaurants like Antoine's and Galatoire's.

Celestine Eustis once wrote that taste is to cooking what emotion is to poetry and art; it is its animating genius. It is a genius that lives on in New Orleans today.

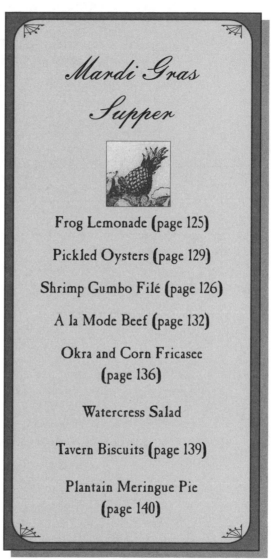

Mardi Gras Supper

Frog Lemonade (page 125)

Pickled Oysters (page 129)

Shrimp Gumbo Filé (page 126)

A la Mode Beef (page 132)

Okra and Corn Fricasee
(page 136)

Watercress Salad

Tavern Biscuits (page 139)

Plantain Meringue Pie
(page 140)

The menu on the following pages comes from *Cooking in Old Creole Days*, where it was presented in the original French along with an English translation.

A SMALL CREOLE DINNER

TO THE DELEGATES OF

THE NEW ORLEANS PRESS CLUB.
INTERNATIONAL LEAGUE OF THE PRESS CLUB.

In the Atheneum, corner of Clio and St. Charles Streets,

SATURDAY, 19TH FEBRUARY, 1898

In the City of New Orleans, Louisiana,
Any time near nine o'clock

❦ ❦ ❦

Tattered rags are better than to go naked.

Absinthe and Anisette.

In Louisiana they find good calas, (cake eaten with coffee).
Oysters, Chooupique and bamboula (national dance).

Oysters from Mosquito Bayou.

With a good gombo prepared by Silvie,
Without ever scolding I would pass my life.

Gombo filé   Bisque 'crébiches [crawfish]

Small vegetables with salt.

When I was a little boy
My mother would say
Courtbouillon Créole
is a mightly fine dish.

Courtbouillon Patassa from Bayou Patassa.

HAUT SAUTERNE 1878

A cockroach never holds its own before a hen.

Chicken Paté.

A crawfish is a darned beast!

Boiled crawfish.

Everyone knows what boils in his own pot.

Red beans with rice ("Hopping John")

SAINT JULIEN 1876

They boast of their terrapin,
But once you taste Caoene,
You taste something just as fine.

Fricassee Caoene (Pig-skin).

Don't tie your dog with sausages.

Jambalaya Tchourisses (Rice and blood-puddings)

A Creole dinner is not complete
Without a little suckling pig.

A runaway pig, stuffed and roasted.
Sweet salad with chicory.

A bird in the hand
Is better than all the birds flying in the woods.

Snipes with laurel leaves en baguette.
Watercresses from Bayou des Herbes.

CHAMPAGNE

Lagniappe is something very good (a corruption of a Spanish word which
means thrown in a market basket over and above).

Popcorn, Sugared Pecans,
Sweet Potato Bread, Thick Molasses.
(The last drawn from the pots in the sugar-house before it turns to sugar)

A fourth of the ice cream. A fourth of a piece of cake.

Ice cream biscuit. Mulatto stomach (gingerbread).
Tante Zizine's poundcake.

There are no Skipenon grapes and no persimmons,
But we'll give you what there is.

Bananas, Oranges, Sugar Cane, Mandarins.
Black Creole coffee ("Morning Joy").

A singed cat fears the fire.

Brulo.
Cigarettes perique (corn paper).
Creole cigarettes (yellow paper).

When you have no horse, you ride a donkey;
When you have no donkey, you ride a goat;
When you have no goat, you go on foot.

The chile pepper, or *capsicum*, gave
Louisiana cooking its signature bite.

Frog Lemonade

PINEAPPLE LEMONADE

This delightful drink is named for the mascot of the *Picayune* newspaper. The drink was first served at a big charity event held for the benefit of a home set up to house the boys who sold newspapers in New Orleans.

1. In a punch bowl, combine the lemon juice and sugar with 6 cups of water. Stir until the sugar is dissolved. Add the pineapple juice, seltzer, strawberries, pineapple pieces, and lemon slices. Add a large block of ice.

2. To serve, fill each glass ⅓ full of crushed ice. Pour in lemonade, making sure to include a strawberry, a piece of pineapple, and a lemon slice.

The Picayune's Creole Cook Book

3 cups fresh lemon juice

1 cup sugar

1½ cups pineapple juice

1 liter seltzer (1 bottle)

18 strawberries

1 small pineapple, peeled, cored, and cut into pieces

2 lemons, sliced paper thin

1 block ice

Crushed ice

MAKES ABOUT 1 GALLON

Shrimp Gumbo Filé
SHRIMP SOUP WITH FILÉ

When asked to define gumbo, Celestine Eustis explained: "It is an Indian dish which we usually serve as a special treat on wedding days and other festivities, before a war and at intimate rendezvous after a dance. You can make it with game, poultry, turkey, veal, leftovers, if worse comes to worst, even an owl."

Generally, gumbos fall under two categories, those thickened with okra—thus the name, which comes from an African word for okra—and those with ground sassafras leaves, known as filé. The gumbos of Miss Eustis's era were closer to soups than to the stews often served today. You can make the soup thicker by using more roux or adding more filé powder.

"First you make a roux..."

Many of today's recipes for both Cajun and Creole cooking begin with these instructions. The method of using roux—a cooked mixture of an equal proportion of fat and flour—to thicken sauces comes, as the name would indicate, from France, but in Louisiana it is taken much more seriously. "The basis of all Creole cooking is roux," wrote Celestine Eustis. "You have to make sure it is well made, otherwise your food will be insipid and greasy." There is a mystique attached to roux, and the most careful practitioners of the art cook it over very low heat for up to an hour to develop its nutty taste. Roux vary depending on the desired flavor. Light-colored roux, sometimes called "blond," is cooked for a short time and have a subtle flavor, whereas the darker varieties are cooked until they reach the color of milk chocolate and give a robust underpining to the dish. In the nineteenth century, lard was always used as the fat component; today, oil is usually used instead.

The ingredients call for oyster liquor, the juice left over from opening oysters, which would have been abundant in an era when many meals began with oysters. Bottled clam juice or fish broth make suitable substitutes. Serve the gumbo over rice.

1. Combine the celery ribs, allspice, peppercorns, mace, cloves, thyme, parsley sprig, 1 of the bay leaves, $^1/_2$ teaspoon cayenne pepper, and $^1/_2$ teaspoon salt with 8 cups water in a large saucepan. Bring to a boil and simmer 20 minutes. Add the shrimp or crawfish and bring to a boil. Drain immediately, reserving the liquid. Peel the shrimp or crawfish and devein, if necessary. Set aside.

2. Heat the lard or oil in a large saucepan over moderate heat. Add the flour and cook, stirring, until it is a rich brown. Add the onion and parsley and sauté, stirring, until tender, about 5 minutes. Crush the remaining bay leaf and add it to the pan. Add the oyster liquor and 3 cups of the shrimp cooking liquid. Bring to a boil and simmer 20 minutes.

3. Add the shrimp or crawfish and remove the pan from the heat. Stir in the filé powder. Add more salt, pepper, and cayenne to taste if necessary. Serve over rice.

The Picayune's Creole Cook Book

4 celery ribs, coarsely chopped

8 whole allspice

20 whole black peppercorns

$^1/_4$ teaspoon ground mace

4 whole cloves

$^1/_2$ teaspoon dried thyme

1 large sprig parsley

2 bay leaves

Cayenne pepper

Salt

50 medium shrimp or crawfish in the shell (about 2 pounds)

4 cups oyster liquor, or substitute bottled clam juice or fish broth

$^1/_4$ cup lard, or substitute peanut oil

$^1/_4$ cup flour

1 large onion, finely chopped

$^1/_3$ cup chopped fresh parsley

3 tablespoons filé powder (available in specialty stores)

Ground black pepper

SERVES 4 TO 6

Gumbo aux herbes
STEWED GREENS WITH HAM AND VEAL

This soup, more popularly called gumbo z'herbes, breaks all the rules of a proper gumbo as it uses neither okra nor filé powder as a thickener. It is probably descended from similar African soups that were brought to this country by slaves. Originally, it was considered Lenten fare but, by and by, ham and veal were added to give it a more complex flavor. Use at least five different kinds of greens for this recipe, but if you can use more, by all means do so. Tradition has it that you will make as many new friends as the number of greens you put into it. Serve over rice.

Salt

1 teaspoon baking soda

3 pounds equal parts cabbage leaves, beet greens, turnip leaves, mustard leaves, spinach, collard greens, and kale, trimmed and coarsely chopped

1 small bunch parsley, large stems removed

1 bunch scallions, coarsely chopped

2 tablespoons lard, or substitute peanut oil

1 pound breast of veal, cut into $\frac{1}{2}$-inch pieces

2 tablespoons flour

$\frac{1}{2}$ pound smoked ham, cut into $\frac{1}{2}$-inch dice

1 large onion, finely chopped

Cayenne pepper

Ground black pepper

SERVES 8

1. Bring a large pot of water to a boil, and add about 1 tablespoon salt and the baking soda. Add the greens, parsley, and scallions and simmer for 45 minutes. Drain and let cool. Chop fine.

2. Heat the lard or oil in a large saucepan over moderate heat. Add the veal and cook until browned, about 5 minutes. Sprinkle the flour into the pan and cook until lightly browned. Add the ham and onion and continue cooking until the onion is golden, about 5 minutes. Add the chopped greens and cook 1 more minute. Add 8 to 10 cups water, season with cayenne and salt and black pepper to taste, and bring the mixture to a boil. Simmer 1 hour, until the veal is tender. Adjust the seasonings. Serve over rice.

The Creole Cookery Book by the Christian Woman's Exchange

Pickled Oysters
MARINATED SPICED OYSTERS

The Picayune's Creole Cook Book notes that "This is a delicious Creole luncheon dish," though more substantial dishes were sure to follow. Serve the oysters accompanied by lightly toasted bread and butter. When making the dish, make sure the poached oysters are very cold before they are added to the vinegar mixture, or they will be slimy.

1. Drain the oysters of their liquor. Add enough water to the liquor to make 1 cup. Bring the liquor to a boil in a nonreactive saucepan. Add the oysters and simmer just until their edges begin to ruffle, about 5 minutes. Drain, let the oysters cool, and refrigerate until cold. Measure and reserve ¾ cup of the cooking liquid.

2. Combine the reserved oyster cooking liquid with the wine vinegar, mace, allspice, cloves, cayenne pepper, peppercorns, and lemon juice, and salt to taste. Bring to a boil. Add the oysters and remove from the heat. Let cool, then refrigerate until cold. Drain the oysters and serve.

The Picayune's Creole Cook Book

36 shucked oysters with their liquor

¾ cup white wine vinegar

6 blades mace, or ½ teaspoon ground

1½ teaspoons whole allspice

1 teaspoon whole cloves

¼ teaspoon cayenne pepper

4 black peppercorns

2 tablespoons lemon juice

Salt

SERVES 6 TO 8 AS AN APPETIZER

Courtbouillon à la Creole
REDFISH STEWED WITH TOMATOES, HERBS, AND WINE

This is one of the many Creole dishes with a name that means something entirely different in France. On the Continent a courtbouillon is merely the flavored liquid used to poach fish.

"Those kings of the New Orleans French Market, the Red Snapper or the Redfish, are used in making the pride and glory of the New Orleans cuisine, a good 'Courtbouillon'" write the authors of *The Picayune's Creole Cook Book*. "More generally and with finer results the Redfish or 'Poisson Rouge' is used. This fish may always be known by the single spot on its tail." They recommend serving the dish with French fries, mashed potatoes, or potato croquettes, though rice will also certainly work just fine.

Terrapin

The variety of turtle called terrapin was rivaled only by oysters as the nineteenth century's favorite dish, especially when made into soup. Today Louisiana is probably the only state in the Union where you may still encounter the specialty. It is not easy to prepare, as this recipe for terrapin on toast makes clear.

Like crabs and lobsters, terrapins are thrown alive into boiling water and let boil till the outer shell and toe-nails can be removed. Then wash and

boil them in salted water till the fleshy part of the leg is tender. Put them in a bowl or deep dish, take off the second shell, remove the sand bag and gall bladder, and cut off the spongy part. Cut up the meat, season it with salt, pepper, cayenne and mace, thicken with butter and flour, and cook. Just before serving, put in a gill of sherry wine for every terrapin, and pour all over hot toast.

Creole Cookbook by Lafcadio Hearn

1. Heat the lard or oil in a large nonreactive saucepan over moderate heat. To make a roux, add the flour and cook, stirring until it is the color of peanut butter, about 15 to 20 minutes. Add the allspice, thyme, marjoram, bay leaves, onion, parsley, and garlic. Sauté until the onion is soft, about 10 minutes. Add the tomatoes, wine, and 2¼ cups water, bring to a boil, and simmer 20 minutes. Season with salt and cayenne to taste and continue cooking 5 minutes longer.

2. Gently add the fish steaks, then the lemon juice and simmer until the fish is just cooked, about 15 to 20 minutes. Serve in bowls.

The Picayune's Creole Cook Book

¼ cup lard, or substitute peanut oil

¼ cup flour

10 whole allspice, crushed

½ teaspoon dried thyme

½ teaspoon dried marjoram

2 bay leaves

1 large onion, finely chopped

¼ cup chopped fresh parsley

1 large garlic clove, minced

6 medium tomatoes, peeled and chopped, or 2½ cups canned tomatoes, drained and chopped

¾ cup dry red wine, preferably Bordeaux

¼ cup lemon juice

Salt

Cayenne pepper

A 3-pound redfish or red snapper, cut into 6 steaks or slices

SERVES 4 TO 6

A la Mode Beef
BRAISED BEEF WITH MADEIRA AND SPICES

As presented in *The Creole Cookery Book* by the Christian Woman's Exchange, this recipe begins with an 18- to 20-pound beef round that you are instructed to bone and then lard with the herbs and bacon. No doubt it would have made an impressive centerpiece, whether served hot or cold. This example of thoroughly classical French cuisine works equally well with a smaller cut of meat, one that might actually fit into a late twentieth-century oven.

6 ounces slab bacon
¼ cup finely chopped fresh parsley
2 tablespoons fresh thyme leaves, or 2 teaspoons dried
6 scallions, finely chopped
1½ teaspoons dried marjoram
1½ teaspoons dried basil
½ teaspoon grated nutmeg
½ teaspoon ground mace
¼ teaspoon ground cloves
1 teaspoon ground black pepper
1½ teaspoons salt
1½ cups dry Madeira
A 6- to 8-pound boneless round roast
2 tablespoons flour
1 tablespoon butter, softened

SERVES 8 TO 12

1. Cut the bacon into 2 dozen strips, each about ½ by ½ by 2 inches. Stir together the parsley, thyme, scallions, marjoram, basil, nutmeg, mace, cloves, pepper, salt, and ¼ cup of the Madeira.

2. With a sharp knife make narrow incisions—parallel to the grain of the meat—all over the roast, about 2½ inches deep. After making each incision, open up the slit slightly and put in a little of the spice mixture and a strip of the bacon. Set the roast in a large nonreactive bowl, pour the remaining wine over it, cover, and refrigerate overnight.

3. The next day, preheat oven to 450°F. Set the roast in a large Dutch oven along with the marinade and ½ cup water. Cover. Bake 20 minutes. Reduce the oven temperature to 325°F and bake until very tender, approximately an additional 30 minutes per pound.

4. Remove the roast to a serving platter and cover. Skim off as much fat as possible from the pan juices. To thicken the gravy, stir together the flour and butter. Add it to the pan juices and simmer, stirring, 10 minutes.

5. To serve, cut the meat across the grain into slices. Serve the gravy on the side.

The Creole Cookery Book by the Christian Woman's Exchange

Ratatouille de Veau à la Créole
VEAL STEW WITH OKRA AND SWEET POTATOES

This is a perfect example of a classic French dish transformed into a delicious New World recipe. In Provence, *ratatouille* is a mélange of eggplant, zucchini, and tomatoes. This New Orleans *ratatouille* is a mixture of American sweet potatoes and African okra, with tomatoes and peppers adding the Creole touch.

1. Season the veal generously with salt, black pepper, and cayenne. Heat 1 tablespoon of the fat in a large heavy casserole or Dutch oven. Add the veal and cook, stirring, until browned all over. Remove from the pan to a bowl and reserve.

2. Heat the remaining 1 tablespoon fat in the pan over moderate heat. Add the ham, bell pepper, onion, garlic, parsley, and thyme and cook until the onion is softened. Add the reserved veal, tomatoes, and bay leaf and stir to combine. Cover and cook at a bare simmer until the veal is just tender, about 1½ hours. Add the sweet potato and continue cooking 15 minutes. Add the okra and cook until both the sweet potato and okra are very tender, about 30 minutes. Adjust the seasonings to taste.

The Picayune's Creole Cook Book

---

2 pounds stewing veal, cut into 2- by 2- by 3-inch pieces

Salt

Black pepper

Cayenne pepper

2 tablespoons butter or lard

¼ pound smoked ham, cut into ½-inch dice

¼ cup chopped red bell pepper

1 large onion, finely chopped

1 garlic clove, minced

2 tablespoons chopped fresh parsley

½ teaspoon dried thyme

1½ cups canned plum tomatoes, drained and chopped

1 small bay leaf

¾ pound sweet potato, peeled and cut into 1-inch pieces

1 pound okra, cut into ½-inch slices

SERVES 4

Jumballaya

CHICKEN STEWED WITH RICE

Jambalaya, as it is more commonly spelled, is the dish most obviously associated with the brief period of Spanish domination in New Orleans. Even Celestine Eustis, writing at the turn of the twentieth century, refers to it as a "Spanish Creole dish." Interestingly, this early recipe is much closer to *paella* and to the Caribbean *arroz con pollo*, which shares the same ancestry, than it is to today's recipes for jambalaya, which have become considerably more complex, often adding seafood and sausages to the ham and chicken.

1 tablespoon lard, or substitute peanut oil

A 3-pound chicken, cut into 8 pieces

Salt

Ground black pepper

¼ teaspoon cayenne pepper, or to taste

½ pound smoked ham, cut into 1-inch long pieces

1 large onion, finely chopped

3 medium tomatoes, peeled and coarsely chopped, or 1½ cups drained canned tomatoes

¼ cup chopped fresh parsley

1½ cups rice

SERVES 4 TO 6

1. Heat the lard or oil in a large heavy stewpot over moderately high heat. Season the chicken generously with salt and black pepper, and the cayenne. Fry it in the hot fat until well browned on all sides, about 10 minutes. Remove to a plate and reserve. Add the ham to the pot, brown it, then remove and set aside. Lower the heat to moderate, add the onion, and cook, stirring, until transparent, about 5 minutes. Stir in the tomatoes and parsley and simmer briefly.

2. Return the chicken and ham to the pot, add 3 cups water, and bring to a boil. Cover and simmer until the chicken is just cooked through, about 30 minutes. Add salt and pepper to taste.

3. Add the rice and continue simmering, covered, until it is tender and the most of the liquid has been absorbed, about 20 minutes. Remove the pot from heat and let stand 10 minutes before serving.

Cooking in Old Creole Days by Celestine Eustis

To stew ducks

DUCK BRAISED WITH PEAS AND PORT

This preparation would easily be recognized in France as *canetton aux petits pois*. The ducks available in New Orleans a hundred years ago were probably smaller and leaner than the Long Island ducklings commercially available today, which would have made them less fatty. Today, the trick is to prick the duck very diligently all over and then roast it at a very high heat so that most of the fat is rendered before the flesh begins to cook.

1. Preheat oven to 500°F.

2. Prick the duck all over with a fork at ¼-inch intervals. Set on a rack in a roasting pan and roast 30 minutes. Remove duck. Reserve 1 tablespoon of the rendered duck fat.

3. Set a large Dutch oven over moderate heat. Add the reserved duck fat and the onion and sauté until soft, about 5 minutes. Add the sage, mint, basil, marjoram, thyme, and beef broth. Add the duck. Cover and cook at a slow simmer for 45 minutes; the duck meat should still retain a trace of pink.

4. Remove the duck from the pan. Strain the cooking liquid into a bowl and carefully skim off as much of the fat as possible. Return the skimmed cooking liquid to the pan, add the peas and the duck, cover, and simmer 10 minutes.

5. Remove the duck to a serving dish and keep warm. Add the Port to the peas. Stir together the flour and butter to form a paste and stir it into the Port mixture. Bring to a boil and simmer 10 minutes. Add salt and pepper to taste. Spoon the peas and sauce around the duck.

The Creole Cookery Book by the Christian Woman's Exchange

1 Long Island duckling (about 6 pounds)

1 large onion, sliced

½ teaspoon dried sage

½ teaspoon dried mint

½ teaspoon dried basil

½ teaspoon dried marjoram

½ teaspoon dried thyme

1 cup beef broth

3 cups green peas

½ cup Port

2 tablespoons flour

2 tablespoon butter, softened

SERVES 2 TO 3

Okra and Corn Fricasee

SAUTÉED OKRA WITH CORN

To those who are fond of okra—and there are millions in the South, the Caribbean, and Africa—its yielding texture and unique flavor can't be beat. Unfortunately the vegetable is often mishandled. Okra can have a slippery texture when it is merely boiled. Southern cooks learned long ago that if you fry the vegetable before proceeding with a recipe, there will be no slime. Here, it is combined with corn, evoking the succotash of the Eastern seaboard.

¼ cup peanut oil

2 cups sliced okra, cut about ½ inch thick

3 cups corn kernels, fresh or frozen (about 4 large cobs)

2 teaspoons flour

¾ cup milk

Cayenne pepper

Salt

Ground black pepper

SERVES 4

1. Heat the oil in a large skillet over moderate heat. Add the okra and fry 5 minutes. Pour off all but 1 tablespoon of the oil. Add the corn and continue cooking about 5 more minutes, until the okra and corn are both tender.

2. Stir in the flour and cook 1 minute. Add the milk, bring to a boil, and simmer 5 minutes. Just before serving, season with the cayenne and salt and pepper to taste.

Creole Cookbook by Lafcadio Hearn

Green Tomato Soy, or Sauce
GREEN TOMATO AND MUSTARD RELISH

Throughout the nineteenth century all sorts of "ketchups" and "soys" were enormously popular. They provided a refreshing counterpoint to meats that had been heavily salted to preserve them. They did not resemble the sauces we know by those names today. This recipe, for example, yields a sharp, chunky relish in which the mustard and vinegar are just barely contained by the sweetness of the unripe tomatoes. It's terrific with ham, but even better—though thoroughly inauthentic—on hamburgers.

1. Layer the tomatoes in a bowl, sprinkling each layer generously with the salt. Cover and let stand at room temperature overnight.

2. The next day, drain and rinse the tomatoes in cold water. Put them in a large nonreactive saucepan with the onions, mustard seed, peppercorns, allspice, mustard powder, and cayenne. Add the vinegar, cover, and bring to a boil over moderate heat. Remove the cover and simmer until the mixture is as thick as jam, about 2 hours. Stir frequently towards the end so that the bottom does not scorch.

3. Serve cold, or preserve in canning jars according to the jar manufacturer's instructions.

Creole Cookbook by Lafcadio Hearn

4 pounds green tomatoes, sliced very thin

½ cup salt

3 medium onions, chopped

3 ounces mustard seed (about ½ cup)

2 teaspoons whole black peppercorns

2 teaspoons whole allspice

½ teaspoon mustard powder

1 teaspoon cayenne pepper

2 cups white wine vinegar

MAKES 5 CUPS

Potato Corn Bread

SWEET POTATO CORN BREAD

This "bread" is so rich and sweet that it is reminiscent of shortbread. Cut it in small squares and serve it hot.

1 medium sweet potato (½ pound), peeled and quartered

½ cup butter, softened

¾ cup brown sugar

4 eggs

1 cup milk

½ teaspoon salt

2 cups white cornmeal

SERVES 6 TO 8

1. Boil the sweet potato in lightly salted water until tender. Drain and mash.

2. Preheat oven to 400°F. Butter a shallow baking pan about 10 by 14 inches.

3. With an electric mixer, cream together in a large bowl the butter and sugar until light. Beat in the eggs, one at a time. Beat in the mashed sweet potato, milk, and salt. Lastly, stir in the cornmeal until the batter is combined.

4. Pour into the prepared pan and bake until firm, about 30 minutes. Serve hot.

The Creole Cookery Book by the Christian Woman's Exchange

Tavern Biscuits

SPICED BAKING POWDER BISCUITS

These biscuits are a little fancier than the average Southern variety, no doubt to keep the drinking clients amused.

1. Sift together in a bowl the flour, baking powder, baking soda, allspice, and salt. Using a pastry cutter or your hands, work the butter into the flour mixture until it is the texture of oatmeal. In a bowl stir together the cream, wine, and brown sugar. Add the cream mixture to the dry ingredients and stir just until a dough forms. Do not overmix. Wrap the dough in plastic wrap and refrigerate at least 20 minutes.

2. Preheat oven to 450°F.

3. Roll out the dough ¾ inch thick on a lightly floured surface. Cut the dough into rounds with a 2- to 3-inch biscuit cutter. Place the biscuits on a baking sheet and bake until golden brown, 12 to 15 minutes. Serve warm.

The Creole Cookery Book by the Christian Woman's Exchange

4¼ cups bleached all-purpose flour

2 tablespoons baking powder

¼ teaspoon baking soda

2 teaspoons ground allspice

½ teaspoon salt

⅔ cup butter

1 cup heavy cream

½ cup dry white wine

⅓ cup brown sugar

MAKES ABOUT 16 BISCUITS, DEPENDING ON SIZE

Plantain Meringue Pie

Even after New Orleans was added to the United States in 1803, it continued to have a much closer relationship to the Caribbean than to the rest of the Union. Because the fastest form of transportation was a ship, bananas and plantains from Santo Domingo arrived in New Orleans much faster than even the news from the Yankee north. Plantains were introduced into the Caribbean from Africa, and while even bananas were unheard of in New York and Boston until well after the Civil War, these tropical staples were a common sight in New Orleans markets. The plantain is a starchy relative of the banana that is always cooked, in either its green or ripe state. When ripe, plantains should be almost entirely black and soft to the touch.

2 ripe plantains, peeled and coarsely chopped

$\frac{1}{2}$ cup brown sugar

1 teaspoon ground cinnamon

$\frac{1}{2}$ teaspoon ground ginger

$\frac{1}{4}$ teaspoon grated nutmeg

$\frac{1}{4}$ teaspoon ground cloves

1 recipe pastry pie dough (page 81)

3 egg whites

6 tablespoons white sugar

1 tablespoon vanilla extract

SERVES 8

1. Combine the plantains, brown sugar, and 1½ cups water in a small saucepan. Cover and simmer 15 minutes, until the plantains are very soft. Purée the mixture in a blender or food processor. Stir in the cinnamon, ginger, nutmeg, and cloves.

2. Roll out the dough into a 12-inch circle on a well-floured board. Roll loosely around the rolling pin, then unroll over a 9-inch pie pan. Crimp the edges to make a raised lip about ¼ inch high around the edge of the pie. Refrigerate the shell.

3. Preheat oven to 400°F.

4. Line the dough with aluminum foil and fill with pie weights or dried beans. Set in the oven and bake 15 minutes. Remove the weights and foil.

5. Reduce the oven temperature to 350°F. Pour the plantain filling into the pre-baked crust and bake 20 minutes, until the crust is cooked through. Remove the pie from the oven and increase the temperature to 425°F.

6. To make the meringue, beat the egg whites with the white sugar until stiff and glossy. Beat in the vanilla. Spread the meringue over the pie.

7. Bake until the top is golden, about 6 to 8 minutes. Let cool on a wire rack. Serve at room temperature.

The Picayune's Creole Cook Book

Fiery Finale

Grand dinners in late nineteenth-century New Orleans would end with a spectacle: Once the gentlemen had retired to smoke their cigars they would be presented with a flaming bowl of brandy. The flamed coffee, the brûlot, that is served today at fancy New Orleans restaurants is a dim reminder of those displays. In his Creole Cookbook of 1885, Lafcadio Hearn gives specific instruction for a "Grand Brulé à la Boulanger":

The crowning of a grand dinner is a brûlé. It is the piece de résistance, the grandest pousse café of all. After the coffee has been served, the lights are turned down or extinguished, brûlé is brought in and placed in the centre of the table upon a pedestal surrounded by flowers. A match is lighted, and after allowing the sulphur to burn entirely off is applied to the brandy, and as it burns it sheds its weird light upon the faces of the company, making them appear like ghouls in striking contrast to the gay surroundings. The stillness that follows gives an opportunity for thoughts that break out in ripples of laughter which pave the way for the exhilaration that ensues.

Pour into a large silver bowl two wineglasses of best French brandy, one half wineglass of kirsh [sic], the same of maraschino, and a small quantity of cinnamon and allspice. Put in about ten cubes of white sugar; do not crush them, but let them become saturated with the liquor. Remove the lumps of sugar, place in a ladle and cover with brandy. Ignite it as before directed, then lift it with the contents from the bowl, but do not mix. After it has burned about fifteen minutes serve in wine glasses. The above is for five persons, and should the company be larger add in proportion. Green tea and champagne are sometimes added.

Creole Cookbook by Lafcadio Hearn

Big Breakfast at the Little House

The Morning Meal on the Open Prairie

With timber unavailable on the open prairie, pioneer families often had to build houses out of sod.

Kansas, 1880

When Mary and Laura Ingalls awoke to the crisp air of a spring prairie morning they were greeted with a familiar smell. "Mary and Laura looked at each other and laughed. They could smell the bacon and coffee and hear pancakes sizzling, and they scrambled out of bed." And soon the two young heroines of Laura Ingalls Wilder's *Little House on the Prairie* were sitting on the grass, eating pancakes with molasses and bacon from the tin plates on their laps. They had a long day ahead of them. A substantial breakfast was essential to anyone trying to make it on the frontier.

During the early spring of the mid-1870s, Mary, Laura, and their parents, Charles and Caroline, had driven their covered wagon across the frozen Mississippi in order to stake a claim on the prairie of Kansas. Years later, Laura recounted her childhood in a series of children's books—from *Little House on the Prairie* through *The First Four Years*—that chronicled the family's trials and adventures as they kept moving from Wisconsin to Kansas to Minnesota and finally to the Dakota territory. Since on the frontier getting enough food was a full-time job for everyone in the family, food is often at the center of her books.

In the 1860s and '70s, the families who ventured out of the sheltering woods of the eastern United States onto the seemingly limitless plains lived a life that wasn't all that different from that of the first European settlers on Chesapeake Bay. The pioneers had to be almost entirely self-sufficient. Even when there was a little town with a general store, the scruffy families seldom had any cash. In the early days, Laura Ingalls Wilder writes how her Pa, after trudging many miles to the store, returned with a tiny sack of white sugar that Ma immediately squirreled away for those special occasions when company called. On the other hand, as Pa told Ma after his first reconnaissance of their new Kansas home, "This country's cram-jammed with game. I saw fifty deer if I saw one, and antelope, squirrels, rabbits, birds of all kinds. The creek's full of fish....We can live like kings!" Nevertheless, the family was thrilled when they were able to get a taste of salt pork again.

In general, one pioneer meal was much like the next; the first meal of the day was as hearty as supper and often it was the same thing—reheated if you were lucky. In *These Happy Golden Years*, Laura is served salt pork for dinner and salt pork with potatoes for breakfast and thinks nothing of it. In Kansas, the Ingallses feast on a roast prairie chicken at night and have cornmeal mush with the leftover gravy in the morning of the next day. Similarly, the pancakes with molasses that the girls enjoyed for breakfast on the prairie might easily have been served late in the day.

In their Kansas log cabin, Ma produced meals with only a rough fireplace and a couple of pans. Her larder was more often empty than full. The family traded for flour and molasses when they had something to trade, but mostly they lived on what they could raise or hunt. Even the furniture was homemade. The family ate sitting on chairs that consisted of big logs at a table "Pa had quickly made...of two slabs of oak. One end of the slabs struck in a crack of the wall, and the other end [rested] on short, upright logs."

When they relocated to South Dakota just a few years later, the contrast could not have been greater. It was as if they'd stepped from the seventeenth century into the Industrial Age. No longer were they self-sufficient pioneers but rather farmers, raising a cash crop and dependent on the marketplace for their successes as well as their needs. Like farmers all across the Middle West, they were increasingly tied to the large food companies of the industrial heartland, and their income became a function of prices set in Chicago and New York. The railroads, which had spanned the continent in the 1860s, now assured urban America an abundance of inexpensive wheat and corn, while at the same time providing the factories with a growing market for their newfangled ploughs, patent stoves, canned vegetables, and soda crackers. Of course, this new bounty came at a price. Laura may not have understood the intricacies of commodity price fluctuations in an industrial society but she knew the results: "...a farmer never has any money. He can never make any because the people in towns tell him what they will pay for what he has to sell and then they charge him what they please for what he has to buy."

The fact was that farmers did occasionally have money, but it was quickly gone. Nevertheless, the standard of material existence was unquestionably better than it had been for the pioneers. For example, when Laura married (at the age of nineteen), she moved into a house built of milled planks with a large cast-iron, coal-burning stove and a pantry full of white flour, whole-wheat flour, cornmeal, and sugar, both brown and white. A large jar of lard was on hand. Only the stone cookie jar and the doughnut jar awaited Laura's attention. Although the young couple had little cash to spare, we see them sitting at the (store-bought) table entranced by a Montgomery Ward catalogue, pondering which set of glassware to order. "They needed it for the table," Wilder wrote, "and there was such a pretty set advertised, a sugar bowl, spoon-holder, butter dish, six sauce dishes, and a large oval-shaped bread plate." (Wilder still had the bread plate when she died, at ninety, in 1957.) With the improved cooking equipment and more varied food supplies, people started paying attention to fancier cooking. By the 1880s, *The Sun-Flower Cook Book,* with recipes collected by the ladies of the You and I Club of Lawrence, Kansas, shows a sophistication undreamed of by Laura's mother only ten years earlier.

The changes that Laura Ingalls experienced in her youth in the West reflected the enormous upheaval that the Industrial Revolution was bringing to the East and Midwest. At about the time the Ingallses first began cooking on a cast-iron stove, Alexander Graham Bell was demonstrating his telephone at the 1876 Great Centennial Exhibition in Philadelphia, and Gustave W. Swift had devised a way to ship meat butchered in Chicago to Boston and Baltimore in refrigerated railroad cars.

By the early years of the twentieth century, stoves had become sophisticated. This model sold for around thirty dollars in the 1914 Montgomery Ward catalog.

The next decade saw huge increases in the size and population of the cities. For example, Kansas City, Kansas, grew by 1,000 percent. Increasing numbers were making a living sitting behind a desk in occupations such as bank clerk or typewriter (the original term for typist). This new urban life began to affect the way people ate. And the first meal to be transformed was breakfast.

On the farm, breakfast was still a multi-dish affair and was considered by many the most important meal of the day. At a series of lectures she gave at the Cincinnati Pure Food Exposition (a glorified farm trade show) in 1894, Sarah Rorer, a nationally renowned cooking teacher, proposed several breakfast menus. A typical one consisted of grapes, oatmeal, fried black bass, "parisienne" potatoes, sliced cucumbers, rolls, and coffee. Other suggestions included fried cucumbers, stewed potatoes, beef hash, broiled chops, boiled sheep's kidneys, and fried eggplant as well as the eggs, bacon, omelets, and muffins that we associate with breakfast today.

It was only in the late 1800s that Americans began to think of some foods as specifically intended for the morning meal. By that time, oatmeal porridge or cornmeal mush with molasses and cream had become a popular side dish to eat with breakfast and, for the hard-up and some health food eccentrics, might even have been breakfast in its entirety.

While an everyday breakfast of chops, griddle cakes, eggs, sausages, fried potatoes, and vegetables was fine for farmers and longshoremen, telegraph clerks were eating the same way. It's little wonder that the press was full of lamentations on the state of the American digestive tract. There were some, most notably Dr. Harvey Kellogg of Battle Creek Sanitarium in Michigan, who thought that even oatmeal was a dangerously rich breakfast dish. In his search for a more "digestible" food, Dr. Kellogg and his brother Will invented wheat flakes and then corn flakes. Ready-to-eat breakfast cereals were eagerly received by harried urban women and—aided by advertising—became an overnight success. To many Americans, breakfast now meant a hurried bowl of Corn Flakes or Grape Nuts. Back at the farm, though, the morning meal changed much more slowly.

In 1894, Laura Ingalls was twenty-five, married to Almanzo Wilder, and a mother. The breakfast she would have cooked on her farm would have been just like her mother's, copious and varied when a good harvest brought in some cash, and filling and dull when the many scourges that beset a farmer's life left the larder bare. In trying times they might have recalled a day when Laura's father visited her future husband's family. Wilder recounts the event in *The Long Winter*:

> Then [Pa sat] down, as they urged him, and lifting the blanket cake on the untouched pile, he slipped from under it a section of the stack of hot, syrupy pancakes. [Alamanzo's brother] forked a

brown slice of ham from the frying pan onto Pa's plate and Almanzo filled his coffee cup.

"You boys certainly live in the lap of luxury," Pa remarked. The pancakes were no ordinary buckwheat cakes. Almanzo followed his mother's pancake rule and the cakes were light as foam, soaked through with melted brown sugar.

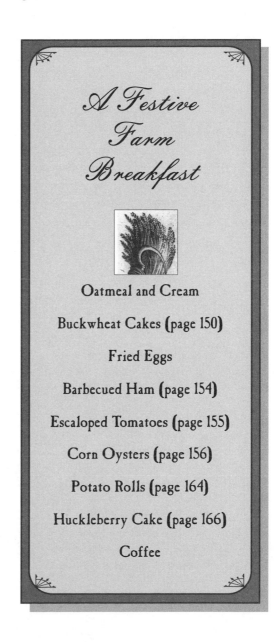

A Festive Farm Breakfast

Oatmeal and Cream

Buckwheat Cakes (page 150)

Fried Eggs

Barbecued Ham (page 154)

Escaloped Tomatoes (page 155)

Corn Oysters (page 156)

Potato Rolls (page 164)

Huckleberry Cake (page 166)

Coffee

Buckwheat Cakes
YEAST-RISEN BUCKWHEAT PANCAKES

These pancakes have a tangy, almost sourdough flavor because the batter rises overnight. The recipe can be made more quickly by using a whole envelope of yeast (2 teaspoons) and only 1½ teaspoons of salt, and leaving the batter to rise about 1 hour.

By the late nineteenth century, many farm women could buy cakes of yeast from the general store instead of making it at home. Fleischmann's, then as now, had a virtual monopoly on the product. Mr. Fleischmann was a Jewish Hungarian immigrant who originally sold the yeast cakes door to door. In 1876, he set up a special "Vienna Bakery" at the Philadelphia Centennial exhibition, where visitors could sip coffee while they watched bread being made. It was a huge success.

All yeast was sold in fresh cakes until the 1930s when Fleischmann's perfected a commercial dry yeast. These buckwheat cakes come from one of their promotional pamphlets, *The Bread Basket*.

Poor Man's Wheat

As late as the end of the eighteenth century, wheat was much more expensive than corn, rye, and buckwheat. Out of necessity, there were lots of recipes developed for these grains, which were never much in favor back in England. By a hundred years later, when the development of western farmland sent the price of wheat (along with most other foods) plummeting, the taste for corn bread and buckwheat pancakes had been firmly established.

Buckwheat in particular grows well under conditions that would barely produce a crop of wheat. New England, with its cold climate and rocky landscape, is especially well suited to this hearty grain. Because buckwheat is unsuitable for making bread, it was most often eaten in the form of pancakes, smothered with native maple syrup or imported molasses.

Buckwheat is available in most health food stores.

1. Dissolve the yeast with the molasses in the lukewarm water. Combine the milk and salt in a medium saucepan, bring to a boil, then cool to lukewarm. Add to the yeast mixture. Gradually stir in the buckwheat and white flours and mix until the dough is smooth. Cover with plastic wrap and set aside to rise in a cool place overnight.

2. Heat a griddle or large heavy skillet until hot. Brush with oil. Pour the batter by scant $1/4$-cupfuls onto the hot griddle, forming 4- to 5-inch pancakes. Turn when bubbles form and break on the top of each pancake and the bottoms are golden. Continue cooking until cooked through, about 5 minutes in all. Place on heated plates and keep warm while you make the next batch. Brush the griddle with more oil if necessary.

3. Serve with butter and syrup or molasses.

The Bread Basket by Standard Brands

$1/2$ teaspoon active dry yeast

3 tablespoons molasses

$2^1/4$ cups lukewarm water

1 cup milk

2 teaspoons salt

2 cups buckwheat flour

1 cup all-purpose white flour

Vegetable oil, for cooking

Butter and syrup or molasses, for serving

MAKES ABOUT 2 DOZEN PANCAKES

Cheese Omelet

This omelet, which resembles a crustless quiche, was surely intended to be a portion for one. Unless you are planning to go out and plough the fields afterwards, it will serve two handsomely.

1 teaspoon butter

1 cup grated cheddar cheese, about 3 ounces

3 eggs, well beaten

½ cup milk

Salt

Pepper

SERVES 2

1. Preheat oven to 400°F. Butter a 2-cup gratin or shallow baking dish.

2. Stir together the cheese, eggs, and milk and season with salt and pepper. Pour into the prepared gratin dish.

3. Bake in the middle of the oven until lightly puffed and golden, about 20 minutes. Serve immediately.

The Sun-Flower Cook Book by The You and I Club of Lawrence, Kansas

Chicken Croquettes

CHICKEN CROQUETTES WITH LEMON

One of the ways many leftover foods were turned into a second meal was to combine them with a little thick white sauce, dredge them with bread crumbs and fry them. Croquettes of chicken, salmon, veal, or turkey were a favorite morning dish. (Salmon cakes still find their way onto the Southern breakfast table.) No matter what the ingredient, they can all be made as the following recipe describes. If you do use salmon, substitute fish stock or clam juice for the chicken broth.

1. Combine the chicken, broth, milk, butter and flour in a medium saucepan. Bring to a simmer over moderate heat and cook, stirring, until the sauce thickens. Remove from the heat and stir in the egg yolks, lemon rind, and salt and cayenne pepper to taste. Refrigerate until firm, about 30 minutes to 1 hour.

2. Using well-floured hands, form the chicken mixture into about a dozen oblong croquettes, each about 3 by 2 inches. Refrigerate until ready to cook.

3. Fill a deep skillet with about 1 inch of the lard or oil and heat it over moderate heat.

4. Lightly beat the egg whites. Dip the croquettes into the beaten whites, then into the bread crumbs. Fry the croquettes in the hot oil until golden, about 5 minutes. Remove with a slotted spoon and drain on paper towels. Serve with lemon wedges.

The Sun-Flower Cook Book by The You and I Club of Lawrence, Kansas

2 cups finely minced leftover cooked chicken

$^3/_4$ cup chicken broth

$^1/_2$ cup milk

2 tablespoons butter

2 tablespoons flour

2 eggs, separated

1 teaspoon grated lemon rind

Salt

Cayenne pepper

About $^3/_4$ cup bread crumbs

Lard or peanut oil, for frying

Lemon wedges

SERVES 4

Barbecued Ham
PAN-FRIED HAM GLAZED WITH CIDER VINEGAR

To the Kansas lady who contributed this dish to *The Sun-Flower Cook Book*, barbecue does not refer to a method of cooking but rather to a sweet-sour sauce that goes on the meat. It may be that her family hailed from the Carolinas, where a related vinegar and sugar condiment is used on pork that has been slowly cooked over coals.

1 tablespoon butter or lard

Four ¼-inch-thick slices ham (about 1 pound in all)

¼ cup cider vinegar

2 teaspoons prepared brown mustard

½ teaspoon sugar

¼ teaspoon ground black pepper

SERVES 4

1. Heat the butter or lard in a large skillet over moderately high heat. Add the ham slices and cook until lightly browned on both sides, about 8 minutes. Remove from the pan and keep warm.

2. Add the vinegar to the pan and bring to a rapid boil. Stir in the mustard, sugar, and pepper. Pour over the ham, let stand 1 minute, then serve.

The Sun-Flower Cook Book by The You and I Club of Lawrence, Kansas

Escaloped Tomatoes

Cooked vegetables were as likely to be part of a hearty farmhouse breakfast as eggs and sausage. To save time the next morning, you can assemble the dish entirely the night before.

1. Preheat oven to 350°F. Butter a medium-sized shallow casserole with 1 tablespoon of the butter.

2. Heat 1 tablespoon of the remaining butter in a medium skillet over moderate heat. Add the onion and sauté until golden, about 10 minutes. Set aside.

3. Sprinkle about ¼ of the crumbs over the bottom of the prepared casserole. Dot with 2 teaspoons of the butter. Spread with ⅓ of the tomatoes, then ½ of the onions and season with salt and pepper. Make another layer with the crumbs, butter, tomatoes, onions, salt, and pepper. Finish with another layer of crumbs, butter, tomatoes and finally the remaining crumbs and butter.

4. Bake until bubbling and golden, about 45 minutes.

The Sun-Flower Cook Book by The You and I Club of Lawrence, Kansas

4 tablespoons butter

1 medium onion, sliced

1 cup crumbled soda crackers

2 pounds ripe tomatoes, peeled and cut into ½-inch slices

Salt

Ground black pepper

SERVES 4

Hashed Browned Potatoes

Chop two cold boiled potatoes fine, dust with salt and pepper. Put a tablespoonful of butter in a frying-pan, when hot put in the potatoes. Spread them out perfectly even and about half an inch in thickness. Stand the pan over a moderate fire and cook slowly without stirring for about fifteen minutes. Then begin at one side of the pan and roll over carefully as for an omelet. Pack or bank the potatoes against one side of the pan. Take a small meat dish, place it against the side of the pan, turn the pan over, turning out the potatoes on to the dish in a roll nicely browned over the outside. Considerable practice is required before one can manage the roll without breaking.

How to Cook Vegetables by Mrs. S. T. Rorer

Corn Oysters
FRESH CORN FRITTERS

These mock oysters made of freshly shucked corn were a great favorite in the America of the late 1800s and through the early years of this century. Some recipes call for deep frying the "oysters" and others—most likely for reasons of economy rather than health—instruct you to cook them more like griddle cakes. These are terrific with breakfast, but make an equally good appetizer, especially when served with tartar sauce.

4 to 5 cobs sweet corn, shucked, or substitute 2 cups frozen kernels, thawed

2 eggs, separated

⅓ cup flour

Pinch cayenne pepper

Salt

Ground black pepper

Butter, melted

MAKES ABOUT 2 DOZEN CORN "OYSTERS"

1. Cook the fresh corn in lightly salted boiling water until tender, about 10 minutes. Drain and cool. Using a sharp knife, cut the kernels off the cobs. Measure 2 cups corn into a bowl.

2. Stir the egg yolks and flour into the corn. Season with cayenne and salt and pepper to taste. Beat the egg whites until firm and shiny. Fold into the corn mixture.

3. Heat a griddle or heavy frying pan over moderate heat. Brush with melted butter. Drop the corn batter by spoonfuls the size of a fried oyster (about 2 inches in diameter) onto the griddle. Brown on both sides, about 2 to 3 minutes per side. Serve immediately.

Mary at the Farm and Book of Recipes by Edith M. Thomas

Parsnip Fritters

Parsnips, which are too rarely cooked today, were essential to a well-stocked root cellar on the prairie. Along with carrots, turnips, onions, and potatoes, they assured that a long hard winter would not be devoid of vegetables. Parsnips were often simply boiled, then mashed and flavored with butter. The dish was sweet and had a comforting texture. Here, in a recipe that appears in one form or another in almost every collection of the day, is a slightly fancier version of those simple mashed parsnips.

1. Boil or steam the parsnips until very soft (about 30 minutes). Drain, let cool, and mash. Stir in the egg yolk, flour, baking powder, and salt to taste. Beat the egg white until firm, then fold into the parsnip mixture. Using well-floured hands, mold the mixture into a dozen ¾-inch-thick cakes, each about 2 inches in diameter.

2. Heat the butter and oil together in a large skillet over moderately high heat. When the butter is sizzling, add the fritters and cook until golden on both sides, about 4 minutes per side.

Mary at the Farm and Book of Recipes by Edith M. Thomas

1½ pounds parsnips, peeled and cut into 1-inch pieces

1 egg, separated

2 tablespoons flour, plus additional flour for dredging

¼ teaspoon baking powder

Salt

1 tablespoon butter

1 tablespoon peanut oil

SERVES 3 TO 4 AS A SIDE DISH

Egg Plant
FRIED EGGPLANT

Eggplant, which we associate with Mediterranean cooking, was by no means exotic in nineteenth-century America. Almost every sizable cookbook has at least one recipe for the vegetable. Though eggplant was occasionally boiled, stuffed, and then baked, it was most often fried.

2 medium eggplants, about 1½ pounds, peeled

Salt

Pepper

2 eggs, lightly beaten

About 1 cup bread crumbs

About ¼ cup peanut oil

SERVES 4

1. Cut the eggplant into ½-inch-thick rounds. Sprinkle generously with salt, set in a colander, and let drain 1 hour. Rinse well in cold water, drain, then blot dry with paper towels. Season with pepper.

2. Dip the eggplant rounds into the eggs, then into the bread crumbs, coating both sides.

3. Heat ¼ cup of the oil in a large skillet over moderately high heat until hot. Add as many eggplant slices as will fit comfortably in one layer in the pan. Fry on both sides until golden and cooked through, about 6 to 8 minutes in all. Remove the eggplant slices with a slotted spatula and drain on paper towels. Fry the remaining eggplant in batches until all of it is cooked. Use more oil as necessary.

Mother Hubbard's Cupboard by The Young Ladies' Society

Spanish Beans

SLOW-COOKED BEANS WITH TOMATO AND CHILE

Baked beans in one form or another have long been a staple in this country from Boston to New Orleans. In the Yankee version, yellow eye or navy beans were cooked with salt pork and sweetened with molasses or maple sugar. Towards the Mexican border, chiles and tomatoes were used. The directions for making these "Spanish" beans come from the Garfield Woman's Club of Garfield, Utah. If their plain, no-nonsense recipes are any indication, Garfield was a place where the women-folk had better things to do than to stay all day in the kitchen.

Beans were as much a part of breakfast as they were of any meal; however, they were not specific to breakfast. Likewise, eggs were also eaten for supper.

1. Soak the beans overnight in cold water to cover. Drain.

2. Put the beans in a soup pot. Cover with water. Bring to a boil and simmer until the beans are just tender, about 1 hour.

3. Meanwhile, heat the butter, lard, or oil in a skillet, add the onion and sauté it until golden, about 10 minutes. Add the cooked onion to the beans along with the plum tomatoes, chiles, and ½ teaspoon salt. Cook at a bare simmer for 1½ hours. Season with salt and pepper.

The Garfield Woman's Club Cook Book

1½ cups dried red kidney beans (about ½ pound)

3 tablespoons butter, lard, or vegetable oil

1 large onion, chopped

2 cups canned plum tomatoes with juice, chopped

2 dried whole New Mexico or Anaheim chiles

Salt

Pepper

SERVES 6 TO 8 AS A SIDE DISH

Bread in America

In nineteenth-century America, no proper meal would have been served without home-baked bread. Women prided themselves on

their loaves, much as Southern cooks still boast today of their airy rolls.

The feeling that bread was almost a sacrament was raised to its highest level in the teachings of Sylvester Graham, a clergyman and self-styled physician. Graham decreed that not only did bread have to be made at home but the task was never to be delegated to a servant, as only the wife and mother could instill the staff of life with the necessary spiritual as well as healthful properties. Moreover, when he wasn't denouncing such hellish abominations as liquor, pork, salt, featherbeds (they induced unchastity), tight corsets, and hot mince pie, Graham railed against refined white flour. His advocacy took such hold that "Graham flour" became synonymous for whole-wheat flour for most of the century.

When the settlers first arrived from Europe they came from towns and villages where there was almost always a professional baker, or at least a large communal oven. This evolved because people lived close together, and also because fuel to fire individual ovens was scarce or expensive. Once they arrived in the New World, they began to bake at home instead. Even in Massachusetts, where the Pilgrims tended to lay out towns on the European model, most home fireplaces also included an oven. This pattern continued as the settlers moved west. As late as 1900, 95 percent of all flour sold in the United States was being bought by individuals for use in home baking.

Bread would likely be baked no more than twice weekly and because of this, breads made from most American recipes often include an ingredient that will keep the resulting loaf moister than many Continental breads. The majority considered white flour the most desirable because it produced the lightest texture, but "Graham" flour, rye, and cornmeal were also used in breads.

Even while pioneer traditions were fading in the cities, the smell of fresh-baked bread remained imprinted on the national consciousness as the perfume of home.

Bread

AMERICAN HERITAGE WHITE BREAD

These instructions, as the title indicates, make what nineteenth-century Americans pictured when they thought of bread. It is a light yet moist loaf that is good fresh but also keeps well and makes perfect toast. The long rising gives it much more flavor than commercially made breads, which use larger quantities of fast-rising yeast. The original recipe calls for ½ cup of homemade yeast rather than the commercial variety indicated below. If you wish to be very authentic, use Aunt Sarah's Potato Yeast (page 228). Mrs. L. E. Sayre, who contributed the recipe to *The Sun-Flower Cook Book*, adds the helpful note: "My woman kneads it an hour, by the clock, it forms such a smooth paste it scarcely sticks to the hands." In the absence of such help, 15 minutes of kneading will suffice.

1. Combine the mashed potatoes and ⅓ cup of the flour in a medium bowl. Stir in 1 cup boiling water. Let cool to lukewarm, then stir in the yeast. Cover with plastic wrap and let rise at room temperature about 4 hours.

2. Transfer the yeast starter to a large bowl. Stir in 3 cups of lukewarm water, the salt, sugar, and 6 cups of the flour and combine. Transfer the dough to a floured board and knead until smooth and elastic, about 12 to 15 minutes, adding more flour as necessary. Try not to use any more flour than you need to keep the dough from sticking.

3. Place the dough in a large bowl, cover with plastic wrap, and let rise in a cool place overnight.

4. Punch down the dough and form into 2 loaves. Place each loaf in a large (2½ by 4½ by 10 inch) bread pan. Cover lightly with plastic wrap and let rise in a warm place until doubled in bulk, about 1½ hours.

5. Preheat oven to 400°F.

6. Bake the loaves in the middle of the oven until they are puffed and golden and sound hollow when tapped on the bottom.

¾ cup mashed potatoes

6 to 7 cups unbleached all-purpose flour

1 envelope active dry yeast

1½ teaspoons salt

1½ teaspoons sugar

MAKES 2 LOAVES

The Sun-Flower Cook Book by The You and I Club of Lawrence, Kansas

Brown Bread

WHOLE-WHEAT MOLASSES SODA BREAD

Cooks who did not want to wait for yeast to rise often resorted to baking soda when making bread. This brown bread is closely related to the more famous Boston steamed bread. A New England cookbook carried west in a covered wagon gave the recipe for Boston brown bread in rhyme:

> One cup of sweet milk,
> One cup of sour,
> One cup of corn meal,
> One cup of flour,
> Teaspoon of soda,
> Molasses one cup;
> Steam for three hours,
> Then eat it up.

For baking our brown bread, the recipe's author recommends that you use tin cans—more specifically "corn cans [since] they make prettier molds to bake in than any other." Obviously the industrial age was well ensconced in her home in Lawrence, Kansas. If you have trouble finding nineteenth-century corn cans, one 35-ounce tomato can or two 20-ounce cans with the tops and labels removed work nicely. The two smaller cans will take a little less time to bake. The bread tastes better the next day.

1. Preheat oven to 325°F. Generously butter the can(s).

2. Sift together the flour, soda, and salt. In a large bowl, pour ½ cup boiling water over the cornmeal and stir until smooth. Stir in the molasses.

3. Alternating a few tablespoons at a time, stir the flour and buttermilk into the cornmeal mixture. Stir until smooth.

4. Pour into the can(s) and bake until a skewer inserted in the center comes out clean, 1 hour to 1¼ hours depending on the size of the can(s).

The Sun-Flower Cook Book by The You and I Club of Lawrence, Kansas

2½ cups stoneground whole-wheat flour

¾ teaspoon baking soda

¼ teaspoon salt

2 tablespoons cornmeal

5 tablespoons molasses

¾ cup buttermilk

MAKES 2 SMALL OR 1 LARGE LOAVES

Sweetness and Dark

Throughout most of our history, molasses was the most widely used sweetener, not sugar (or corn syrup, today used in many manufactured foods). Molasses was poured over pancakes, added to baked beans, stirred into bread dough, and included in pies, puddings, and cookies. Sugar, from the time it first began coming from the West Indies to the new American colonies to the late nineteenth century, was a luxury that most people reserved for special occasions. On the other hand, molasses, a by-product of sugar refining, was plentiful and inexpensive, in part because the inefficient technology of the day yielded a lot more molasses than it does now. The resulting syrup was likely sweeter and certainly more flavorful than what we can buy in our supermarkets.

Potato Rolls

POTATO DINNER ROLLS

These dinner rolls are particularly moist because of the addition of the potatoes. They are also terrific reheated, even after several days in the refrigerator. You can make the recipe through step 3, then let the dough rise, loosely covered, in the refrigerator overnight.

1 pound baking potatoes, peeled and quartered

1 cup milk

³/₄ cup lard, or substitute butter

¹/₂ cup sugar

1 teaspoon salt

6 to 7 cups unbleached all-purpose flour

1¹/₂ teaspoons active dry yeast

MAKES 32 ROLLS

1. Boil the potatoes until tender. Drain, mash, and measure 1 cup. Bring the milk to a boil, add it to the potatoes in a large bowl. Stir in the lard or butter, sugar, salt, and 1 cup of the flour. Let cool to lukewarm.

2. Dissolve the yeast in ¹/₂ cup lukewarm water, then stir it into the potato mixture, and beat until smooth. Cover with plastic wrap and set aside to rise 2 hours at room temperature.

3. Work 5 cups of flour into the potato mixture. Knead until smooth and elastic, about 10 minutes, adding more flour if necessary. Transfer the dough to a lightly oiled large bowl, cover with plastic wrap, and let rise in a warm place until doubled in bulk, about 1¹/₂ hours.

4. Butter a cookie sheet. Punch down the dough and divide it into 32 pieces. Form each piece into a ball. Place the rolls, barely touching each other, on the cookie sheet. Cover with plastic wrap and let rise in a warm place until doubled in bulk, about 1 hour.

5. Preheat oven to 375°F.

6. Bake until the rolls are golden brown, 20 to 25 minutes. Serve hot.

A Kentucky Woman's Handy Cook Book by Jessie Henderson Colville

Rice Waffles

BREAKFAST WAFFLES WITH RICE

Waffles, like doughnuts, have been with us since the Dutch first settled New Amsterdam. While Old World batters resembled those for plain pancakes, in America waffles were made with sweet potatoes, buckwheat, and cornmeal as well as wheat flour. The Dutch topped them with cream and fruit, whereas Americans used syrup or molasses. This particular recipe comes from Miss Isabella McNear, the principal of the Trinity Parish Cooking School in New York, though it probably originated in the South, as do so many American rice recipes. *The Virginia Housewife* includes a recipe for similar waffles as early as 1824.

1. Cook the rice in 2 cups lightly salted water at a bare simmer until very soft, about 30 minutes. Drain, reserving the cooking water. Measure 1 cup of the rice and ½ cup of the water. Let cool to room temperature.

2. In a medium bowl, sift together the flour, baking powder, and salt. In another bowl, combine the reserved rice, egg yolk, milk, and reserved rice cooking water. Add to the flour mixture and mix until thoroughly combined. Stir in the butter.

3. Beat the egg white until stiff. Fold into the batter.

4. Preheat an oiled waffle iron. Spoon about ⅓ cup of the batter into the iron and cook until golden, about 10 to 12 minutes. (You may need to use more batter depending on the iron.) Make waffles with the remaining batter, oiling the waffle iron as needed.

Cleveland Baking Powder Cookbook

¼ cup white rice

2 cups all-purpose flour

1 teaspoon baking powder

½ teaspoon salt

1 egg, separated

1 cup milk

2 tablespoons butter, melted

Vegetable oil, for waffle iron

MAKES ABOUT 8 WAFFLES

Huckleberry Cake

HUCKLEBERRY LOAF

"The fruits do not yield their true flavor to the purchaser of them, nor to him who raises them for the market," wrote Henry David Thoreau of the native American huckleberry. "There is but one way to obtain it yet few take that way. If you would know the flavor of huckleberries, ask the cow-boy or the partridge." The same is true today—if you want huckleberries you will have to go out and pick them. There is some confusion between native varieties of blueberries and the berries that gave Mark Twain's Huckleberry Finn his name. Both blueberries and huckleberries grow throughout the United States and are often called by each others' names. In general, though, huckleberries tend to be a little smaller and shinier and with fewer but larger seeds. Aficionados claim that the huckleberry's slightly tarter flavor makes it superior to the blueberry in baked goods. However, one can always be substituted for the other. This breakfast cake is best eaten slightly warm with butter.

2½ cups all-purpose flour	1. Preheat oven to 375°F. Butter and flour an 8 by 4 by 2½-inch loaf pan.
1 cup sugar	
2 teaspoons baking powder	2. Sift together the flour, sugar, and baking powder in a medium bowl. In another bowl, stir together the milk, egg, and butter until blended. Add to the flour mixture and stir until just combined. Add the berries and stir again until just combined.
1 cup milk	
1 egg	
6 tablespoons butter, melted	
1½ cups huckleberries or blueberries	
	3. Spoon the batter into the prepared pan. Bake until browned on top and crusty, about 1 hour. A toothpick inserted into the middle of the loaf should come out dry. Cool on a rack for about 30 minutes. To serve, slice and serve warm with butter.
MAKES 1 LOAF	

Mother Hubbard's Cupboard by The Young Ladies' Society

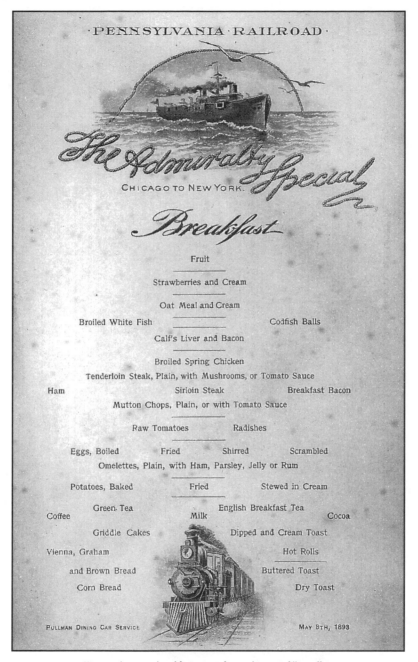

·PENNSYLVANIA·RAILROAD·

The Admiralty Special

CHICAGO TO NEW YORK.

Breakfast

Fruit

Strawberries and Cream

Oat Meal and Cream

Broiled White Fish　　　　　　　　Codfish Balls

Calf's Liver and Bacon

Broiled Spring Chicken

Tenderloin Steak, Plain, with Mushrooms, or Tomato Sauce

Ham　　　　　Sirloin Steak　　　　Breakfast Bacon

Mutton Chops, Plain, or with Tomato Sauce

Raw Tomatoes　　　　Radishes

Eggs, Boiled　　　Fried　　　Shirred　　　Scrambled

Omelettes, Plain, with Ham, Parsley, Jelly or Rum

Potatoes, Baked　　　　Fried　　　Stewed in Cream

Green Tea　　　　English Breakfast Tea
Coffee　　　　　　Milk　　　　　　　Cocoa

Griddle Cakes　　　　Dipped and Cream Toast

Vienna, Graham　　　　　　　Hot Rolls

and Brown Bread　　　　　Buttered Toast

Corn Bread　　　　　　　Dry Toast

PULLMAN DINING CAR SERVICE　　　　　　MAY 8TH, 1893

Nineteenth century breakfasts were often multicourse, filling affairs
as this menu amply illustrates.

African Legacy

The Lasting Influence
of African-American Cooks

Some of America's best food was the product of African-American cooks.

Tennessee, 1890

As Rufus Estes sat down to write his cookbook, *Good Things to Eat*, in 1911, he looked back on a long successful career in the kitchen. Estes was born in 1857, in rural Tennessee, a slave. "After the [Civil] war broke out all the male slaves in the neighborhood for miles around ran off and joined the 'Yankees,'" he writes. "This left us little folks to bear the burdens. At the age of five I had to carry water from the spring about a quarter of a mile from the house, drive the cows to and from the pastures, mind the calves, gather chips, etc." When the war was over, what remained of the family relocated to Nashville, where Rufus, now a teenager, began his life as a cook. He continued his career, one of the few open to a man of color, when he took a position with the Pullman railway company, preparing luxurious American and European meals for those who could afford the fare. As he wrote down his recipes, he was working as a chef for a division of the mighty United States Steel Corporation. Most of the recipes in his cookbook, which he published himself, reflect the cosmopolitan cuisine in vogue in the late nineteenth century, but there are also hints of his rural Southern past. Rufus Estes was in a long tradition of African-American cooks who used their talents and heritage to flavor the food they prepared for Americans of European descent. Estes was able to practice his art more or less of his own free will. The generations that preceded him weren't so lucky.

The renowned culinary achievements of the Old South were the result of the encounter of three peoples. The Europeans, mostly English but also some French in parts of South Carolina and along the Gulf Coast, had freely chosen to settle on foreign shores. The Native Americans who were already here didn't have much to say about the matter. The third group, the Africans, were in the New World as victims of the slave trade. Many were forced to labor in the fields, sometimes on large plantations but more often on smaller farms. A small number were employed in the "Big House" that later loomed so large in the nostalgia of the Southern aristocracy for the antebellum days. Others found themselves in towns like Charleston and Richmond, working as domestics. But everywhere it was the slaves who worked in kitchens, making fires and beating batters, roasting the meats and baking pies, grilling steaks and frying hush puppies, icing birthday cakes and decorating Independence Day cakes. African-Americans cooked Southern food. They cooked Native American, European, and African ingredients in ways they had learned from the Indians and the English slaveholders. They also brought their own heritage to bear, frying meats, fish, and fritters using techniques practiced in West Africa, and cooking stews and rice "pilaus" in ways their great-grandmothers would have recognized.

Foods as well as people traveled between the Old World and the New. Early on, the Portuguese had introduced corn, cassava (a starchy root vegetable), tomatoes, chiles, pineapples, and probably peanuts to Africa. In exchange, foods imported from Africa included sesame seeds, okra, black-eyed peas, watermelons, eggplant, various greens, and rice. By the time Columbus arrived in the Caribbean, rice had already been under cultivation in Africa for two thousand years. When Europeans decided to plant rice in South Carolina, they looked across the southern Atlantic for skilled laborers for this specialized work. During slaving times, part of the West African coast became known as the Rice Coast. In America, Africans experienced in rice growing were a valuable commodity. A 1785 ad in the *Charleston Evening Gazette* publicized the arrival of "a choice cargo of windward and gold coast negroes, who have been accustomed to the planting of rice." Most of the other foods associated with Africa did not gain the reputation that Carolina rice had in the nineteenth century (Escoffier considered it the best the world had to offer), but they did work their way into the core of the Southern repertoire.

The slaves who found themselves in the kitchen of the Big House brought more than a familiarity with a few exotic ingredients. They were also able to draw on a heritage that could enrich that of the Europeans. The Southern penchant for frying appears to have come out of West Africa's fondness for food fried in palm oil. Once in North America, the readily available lard was substituted and used by black cooks to fry everything from chicken to catfish to the corn fritters called hush puppies. Recipes for deep-fried food are few and far between in English cookbooks of the colonial period, whereas they show up regularly in early Southern cookbooks. (See especially Mary Randolph's recipe for fried chicken, page 76).

A similar transatlantic connection can be seen in the favorite African-American dish colloquially called "a mess of greens." In West Africa collard greens (a leafy vegetable of the kale family) are stewed the same way they might be south of the Mason-Dixon line, with one significant difference: In America, smoked pork is substituted for the smoked fish favored along the African coast. It has often been suggested that without the influence of African cooks, the diet of Southern whites, both rich and poor, would have suffered from vitamin deficiencies. Visitors from the North often commented on these exotic "African vegetable preparations." The use of red pepper in the South may also be attributed to the slaves in the kitchen, who, if they did not already know them from their native land, were exposed to chiles in the West Indies, a frequent transit point in the transatlantic slave trade.

Ultimately, though, it wasn't the enrichment of the larder and the repertoire that gave African-American cooks the pivotal role in creating Southern cuisine, it was simply that they were the ones doing the cooking. Naturally, some were more talented than others, though you would hardly know it from the admiration (admittedly often patronizing) expressed by white Americans. "The Negro is a born cook," wrote Charles Gayarre in *Harper's* magazine in 1880. "He could neither read nor write, and therefore he could not learn from books. He was simply inspired; the god of the spit and the saucepan had breathed into him; that was enough." The fact was, the illiterate cook had learned what he or she knew from generations of predecessors. When the white mistress and her successors sought to document the traditions of the South, they had to turn to the black cooks who had been the practitioners of that tradition. The relationship was reciprocal though. Since most slaves were not allowed to learn to read, if a plantation mistress wanted some particularly fashionable recipe prepared she would recite it to her cook. Jefferson apprenticed his cooks to a French chef to learn his tricks of the trade and it was not unheard of for Louisiana slave-owners to send their servants to France to perfect their art. The result led more than one writer to exult in the flavors of the Old South. "The Virginia cook," wrote John S. Wise (he could have been writing of any Confederate state), "and the Virginia cooking of that time were the full realization of the dreams of epicures for centuries."

There were, of course, two very different styles of cooking practiced by American slaves: the aristocratic cuisine of the Big House, where the best ingredients were at their disposal and the preparations were often elaborate, and the cooking in the slave quarters, where they had to cook food, often of very poor quality, under difficult conditions. Nevertheless most slaves did eat as well as, if not better than, poor whites in the rural South (and probably considerably better than European peasants of the time) though there are instances when they were fed little better than livestock. Baily Cunningham, born a slave in 1838, recalled in her nineties the food given out at the plantation where she grew up. Her master was more generous than some.

Rations were given to the field hands every Monday morning. They would go to the smokehouse and the misses would give us some meal and meat in our sack. We were allowed to go to the garden or field and get cabbage, potatoes and corn or any other vegetables and cook in our shanties. We had plenty to eat. We had a large iron baker with a lid to bake bread and potatoes, and a large iron kettle to boil things in. On Saturday morning we would go to the smokehouse and get some flour and a piece of meat with a bone so we could have a hoe-cake dinner on Sunday. Sometimes we had plenty of milk and coffee.

To a greater or lesser extent, most slaveholders permitted their slaves to keep chickens, and sometimes hogs, and to raise vegetables. To the plantation owners, this had the double advantage; it allowed the slaves to improve and vary their diet, while it reduced the cost of maintaining a healthy labor force. In spite of the arduous work in the fields, most women took great pains at securing as tasty a supper as possible.

In their "quarters," they cooked whatever they could get their hands on: fruits and vegetables picked in the garden or in the wild, the cornmeal that was inevitably part of their ration, the parts of the pig that the white people had no use for, chickens, and just about any wild critter that could be caught, netted, snared, or trapped. 'Possum, especially when stewed with sweet potatoes, found a beloved place in the folklore. Whereas most Americans boiled their vegetables (often to excess) and threw away most of the vitamins with the water, African-Americans saved the "pot likker" left over from boiling greens with a ham hock and used corn bread to sop it up. Catfish and perch, considered trash fish by whites, were rolled in cornmeal, fried to a delightful crunch, and often eaten sprinkled with cider vinegar highly seasoned with hot pepper. Squirrels and raccoons were turned into stews and gumbos. Even the pig's small intestine was turned into a palatable dish of chit'lins.

The Civil War brought an end to the distance between the cooking in the quarters and the cuisine in the Big House, but it did not end the predominance of African-Americans in the culinary field. During the conflict, both North and South hired black cooks, and after the war, former slaves trained in the aristocratic culinary tradition of the South found ready employment as cooks on steamships and railways, and in hotels and restaurants across the country. Even before the war, many of the caterers in New York, Philadelphia, and other large cities were African-Americans. Fraunces Tavern, one of George Washington's habitual haunts when he resided in New York, was owned and operated by African-Americans. No doubt the virtual monopoly American blacks had on professional cooking in the nineteenth century was partially due to the trying conditions found in kitchens that depended on firewood and coal to do the cooking and rigorous manual labor to do the rest—nobody else was willing to take the job. There was, however, the culinary reputation blacks enjoyed. Some whites even preferred a black chef to a French one—the ultimate compliment.

A dining car on the Pennsylvania Railroad.

Most of these cooks found themselves slinging hash, as the majority of restaurant cooks do everywhere, but others, like Rufus Estes, cooked for the refined dining rooms of the Pullman company and others like it. A veteran of the railroads later recalled how, in spite of the difficulties of cooking in a small space hurtling at thirty or forty miles an hour, "Everything was first class. The meals were all fresh. The chicken had to be plucked, the fish had to be scaled. Also the peas had to be shelled. It was quite an experience....We used coal and wood-burning stoves and a charcoal broiler for the steaks and chops, and to broil the fish."

A Holiday Spread

A Southern barbecue after emancipation.

Southern slaves had a diet that changed little from day to day for most of the year, except at Christmas. Solomon Northrup, a freeman who was kidnapped and sold into slavery (he escaped after twelve years) reported on a Louisiana holiday spread in *Twelve Years a Slave:*

The only respite from constant labor the slave has through the whole year, is during the Christmas holidays. Epps [the plantation owner] allowed us three—others allowed four, five and six days, according to the measure of their generosity. It is the only time to which they look forward with any interest or pleasure....

It is custom for one planter to give a "Christmas supper," inviting the slaves from neighboring plantations to join his own on the occasion.

The table is spread in the open air, and loaded with varieties of meat and piles of vegetables. Bacon and cornmeal [the usual ration] at such times are dispensed with. Sometimes the cooking is performed in the kitchen on the plantation, at others in the shade of wide branching trees. In the latter case, a ditch is dug in the ground, and wood laid in and burned until it is filled with glowing coals, over which chicken, ducks, turkeys, pigs, and not unfrequently the entire carcass of a wild ox, are roasted. They are furnished also with flour, of which biscuits are made, and often with peach and other preserves, with tarts, and every manner and description of pies, except the mince, that being an article of pastry as yet unknown among them. Only the slave who has lived all the years on his scanty allowance of meal and bacon, can appreciate such suppers.

Though the black chefs were often praised, the job of the professional cook, until very recently, has never been prestigious in the United States. Naturally, African-Americans of any ambition looked to professions where they would find respect. They did retain an affectionate memory for their culinary past, though, even in the years when it wasn't fashionable. As blacks migrated north and west after the turn of the century, they brought Southern cooking with them, so that fried chicken and Southern-style cobblers could be had in Harlem and Watts just as easily as in Nashville. By the late 1960s, with African-Americans looking to their roots, the cooking of poor Southern blacks gained a new sense of cachet when it was reborn as "soul food." In the land of Dixie, this legacy of American black cooks continued to be called Southern cooking.

Down-Home Sunday Dinner

Chicken and Dumplings
(page 183)

Hopping John (page 186)

Collard Greens

Sliced Tomatoes

Corn Bread (page 187)

Peach Pie

Philadelphia Groundnut Cakes
(page 192)

Iced tea

Soul Food

Bob Jeffries writes in his *Soul Food Cookbook,*

When people ask me about soul food, I tell them that I have been cooking "soul" for over forty years—only we did not call it that back home. We just called it real good cooking, southern style. However, if you want to be real technical on the subject, while all soul food is southern food, not all southern food is 'soul.' Soul food cooking is an example of how really good southern Negro cooks cooked with what they had available to them, such as chickens from their own back yard and collard greens they grew themselves, as well as home-cured ham, and bakin' powder biscuits, chit'lins, and dubie [berry cobbler].

John Dabney's Mint Julep

Jacqueline Harrison Smith recounts the story of this version of the renowned Southern libation in *Famous Old Receipts:* "This famous receipt has a history well worth recording of 'the man and his julep.' John Dabney was the famous old negro caterer of Richmond until a few years ago. John was a remarkable character, and in personality most striking, combining as he did some of the Indian with his negro antecedents. He was a slave of a prominent Virginia family, who had consented to set John free some years before the war. John had almost finished paying for his freedom by his thrift and determination when war came. After Mr. Lincoln's proclamation his master said, 'John, you are free,' and wished him good luck, and John started life for himself as a caterer in Richmond."

Mint juleps were a particular favorite of the plantation aristocracy. Many planters drank one before breakfast because it was believed that it gave them protection against malaria. John Dabney's julep is particularly fancy, being garnished with several kinds of fruit, or "Any other little fixings you like," as he expressed it.

Put 1 mint leaf in a tall glass and crush lightly with a spoon. Add 1 tablespoon water and the sugar and stir until completely dissolved. Fill the glass with the ice. Pour in the bourbon and stir well. Top with the remaining mint, the strawberry, cherry, and pineapple slice.

Famous Old Receipts by Jacqueline Harrison Smith

1 sprig mint

2 teaspoons extra-fine granulated sugar

Very finely crushed ice

2 ounces good bourbon

1 strawberry

1 cherry

1 slice of fresh pineapple

MAKES 1 JULEP

Gumbo Soup

CHICKEN AND OKRA GUMBO

The word "gumbo" descends from *ki-ngombo,* the word for okra in an Angolan language. "Okra" itself derives from *nkruma,* in Ghana's Twi language. Though today the dish is most associated with Louisiana, a soup or stew called gumbo was once popular throughout the South. It was always seasoned with red pepper, because poor people could not afford the black pepper imported from halfway across the world. Their taste for red pepper, so familiar in the Caribbean as well as in the southern slave states, may have come from their African past and from a need to enliven the flavor of their plain, and often greasy, food. The African cooks' love of spicy fare eventually migrated to the dining rooms of the English Americans.

¼ cup peanut oil

A 3½-pound chicken, cut into 8 pieces

Salt

Ground black pepper

Cayenne pepper

4 cups sliced okra, cut into rounds ½ inch thick

1 large onion, chopped

½ cup chopped fresh parsley

½ cup chopped celery tops

4 cups chopped peeled tomatoes, fresh or canned, drained

¾ cup dry white wine

SERVES 6 TO 8

1. Heat the oil in a large stewpot over moderately high heat. Season the chicken with the salt, black pepper, and cayenne to taste. Fry the chicken in the fat until golden on all sides. Remove from the pan and set aside.

2. Add the okra to the pan and cook, stirring, for about 5 minutes, until it has lost its bright green color. Remove with a slotted spoon and set aside.

3. Drain off all but 2 tablespoons fat from the pan. Lower the heat to medium and add the onion, parsley, and celery. Sauté until soft, about 5 minutes. Add the tomatoes, the reserved fried chicken, and 7 cups water. Bring to a boil and simmer, uncovered, until the chicken is just cooked through, about 30 minutes. Add the reserved fried okra and continue cooking until the chicken is very tender, about 30 minutes longer.

4. Remove the chicken from the pot, remove the bones, and cut the meat into small pieces. Skim as much fat as possible from the gumbo. Add the chicken meat to the pot with the wine. Season with more salt, pepper, and cayenne. Reheat if necessary. Serve over hot cooked rice.

Housekeeping in Old Virginia edited by Marion Cabell Tyree

Louisiana Cod

COD STEWED WITH TOMATOES AND PEPPERS

When Rufus Estes penned this recipe, he must have been thinking of salt cod, though he doesn't say so. It works beautifully with fresh cod as well, though the cooking time is much shorter. If you do wish to use dried cod, follow the instructions for preparing it on page 273. You will need about a pound, and it will need to bake about one hour.

1. Preheat oven to 325°F.

2. Heat half the butter in a medium saucepan over medium heat. When it just begins to brown, add the flour and stir until smooth. Add 1 cup water, the lemon juice, and salt and pepper to taste. Simmer the sauce, stirring periodically, 5 minutes.

3. Heat the remaining butter in a medium skillet. Add the onion and green pepper and cook until softened, about 5 minutes. Add the sautéed vegetables, tomatoes and bay leaf to the prepared white sauce.

4. Arrange the fish in a shallow casserole. Pour the sauce mixture over it, cover, and set in the oven. Bake until the cod is cooked through, 20 to 30 minutes.

Good Things to Eat by Rufus Estes

3 tablespoons butter

2 tablespoons flour

1 teaspoon lemon juice

Salt

Pepper

1 medium onion, chopped

1 small green bell pepper

1 cup canned tomatoes, passed through a food mill or strainer

1 small bay leaf

1½ pounds cod steaks, cut 1 inch thick

SERVES 4

Crab Meat Delight

SCRAMBLED EGGS WITH CRABMEAT

Mrs. Emma Kelley, who in 1902 founded the Grand Temple, Daughter of Elks, was particularly fond of this dish. Her recipe comes from *The Historical Cookbook of the American Negro*, a volume of old recipes published in the 1950s that was as much about consciousness-raising as it was concerned with food. Each dish was dedicated to a historical personage, often with a rather tenuous connection to the recipe. This "Crab Meat Delight" would be delightful for a large Southern breakfast or brunch.

6 strips bacon
1 medium onion, chopped
1/2 cup chopped green bell pepper
1/4 cup chopped celery
1/2 teaspoon dried marjoram
1/2 teaspoon dried thyme
1 pound crabmeat, picked over
8 eggs, lightly beaten
Salt
Pepper
1 teaspoon chopped fresh parsley
1/4 teaspoon paprika

SERVES 4 TO 6

1. Fry the bacon in a large skillet until crispy. Remove and set aside.

2. Add the onion, green bell pepper, and celery to the bacon fat and sauté until the vegetables are softened, about 5 to 8 minutes. Add the marjoram, thyme, and crabmeat. Cook until just heated through.

3. Add the eggs to the crabmeat mixture and cook, stirring, until they are the consistency of soft scrambled eggs. Season with salt and pepper. To serve, sprinkle with the parsley and paprika and garnish with the bacon, coarsely crumbled.

The Historical Cookbook of the American Negro by The National Council of Negro Women

Chicken and Dumplings
STEWED CHICKEN WITH HERB DUMPLINGS

As originally made, this recipe would have called for an old hen, a bird with lots of taste but in need of three hours of cooking. A modern chicken will cook a lot quicker, but it would be wise to substitute chicken broth for the water called for to make up for the flavor deficit.

1. In a large Dutch oven or flameproof casserole, combine the chicken pieces, onion, carrot, celery tops, parsley sprigs, and peppercorns with the boiling water or broth. Cover, bring to a boil, and simmer until the meat begins to loosen from the bones, about 1 hour. Add salt to taste during the last half hour of cooking. Remove the chicken and vegetables from the broth and skim off the fat. Stir together the butter and flour and whisk into the broth. Bring to a simmer and cook 5 minutes. Return the chicken pieces to the pan.

2. To make the dumplings, stir together the flour, baking powder, salt, parsley, thyme, and marjoram. Using a pastry cutter or your hands, work the shortening into the flour until it is the texture of oatmeal. Stir in ½ cup boiling water, mixing until fully incorporated. The dough will be quite dry. Roll or pat the dough on a surface until it is ½ inch thick. Cut into rounds with a 2- to 3-inch biscuit cutter.

3. Place the dough rounds on pieces of the chicken in the pan. Cover tightly and cook at a low simmer for 15 minutes. Do not lift up the cover while the dumplings are cooking! Serve hot.

The Historical Cookbook of the American Negro by The National Council of Negro Women

A 4- to 5-pound chicken, cut into 8 pieces

1 medium onion, quartered

1 carrot, cut into 1-inch dice

½ cup celery tops, chopped

4 sprigs parsley

20 black peppercorns

3 cups boiling water, or substitute chicken broth

Salt

3 tablespoons butter, softened

4 tablespoons flour

DUMPLINGS

2 cups flour

2 teaspoons baking powder

½ teaspoon salt

3 tablespoons chopped fresh parsley

1 teaspoon fresh thyme leaves

1 teaspoon chopped fresh marjoram

4 tablespoons shortening, or substitute butter or lard

SERVES 4

Sweet Potatoes Stewed
BRAISED CHICKEN WITH SWEET POTATOES

This is a more genteel version of the 'possum and sweet potatoes often eulogized in accounts of the old South. Simon Stokes, born a slave in 1839 and interviewed in the 1930s, was one of many who had fond memories of the dish: "In de fall wen de simmons [persimmons] wuz ripe, me and de odder boys sho' had a big time possum huntin, we alls would git two or three a night; and we alls would put dem up and feed dem hoe-cake and simmons ter git dem nice and fat; den my mammy would roast dem wid sweet taters round them. Dey wuz sho' good, all roasted nice and brown wid de sweet taters in de graby." Though this particular recipe was penned even before he was born, it may nevertheless be more practical for today's city dwellers.

4 medium sweet potatoes (about 2 pounds), peeled

¼ pound ham (preferably Virginia), diced

A 3- to 4-pound chicken, cut into 8 pieces

¼ teaspoon dried marjoram

¼ teaspoon dried thyme

¼ teaspoon dried basil

Salt

Pepper

1 cup chicken broth

1 tablespoon butter, softened

2 tablespoons flour

SERVES 3 TO 4

1. Preheat oven to 350°F.

2. Set the sweet potatoes in the bottom of a Dutch oven or flameproof casserole. Add the ham, the chicken pieces, marjoram, thyme, basil, and salt and pepper to taste. Pour in the chicken broth, cover, and bake about 1 hour, until the chicken and potatoes are tender.

3. Remove the chicken and potatoes from the pan and place in a deep serving dish. Keep warm. Skim off as much fat as possible from the cooking liquid. To thicken the gravy, stir together the butter and flour and mix into the liquid. Bring to a boil and simmer 10 minutes. Adjust the seasonings. Pour the gravy over the chicken and potatoes and serve.

The Virginia Housewife by Mary Randolph

'Possum and Sweet Potatoes

In *A Date with a Dish*, Freda De Knight gives a recipe for 'possum as well as a tale that points out how unfashionable "soul food" was in the 1940's.

Dr. Jeff Fowler of Los Angeles, loves food and could be called a food tester as well as a good family physician. He loves to laugh and a good joke to him is like a good meal!

Dr. Fowler's favorite trick is to wait until one of his elegant friends is among a group of people. Then in his loudest voice he asks the unsuspecting victim if he likes 'Possum and Irish Potatoes! If the person answers, "You mean 'Possum and Sweet Potatoes," he lets out a laugh that can be heard in the next block and exposes the person as really being from the South, despite his cosmopolitan airs. This, of course, amuses the bystanders no end and before the evening is through, he has corralled many a victim. For his sake, here is a fine dish of "'Possum and Sweet Potatoes."

1 'possum
1 tsp. pepper
1 t leaf sage
4–5 slices bacon
2 t salt
1 t paprika
2 cloves garlic
6–8 medium sweet potatoes

Clean, dress, and wash 'possum well. Place overnight in freezing compartment of refrigerator or on ice. Drain and wipe dry. Rub well with a mixture of spices. Lay in a baking pan. Cover with thin slice of bacon and set in slow oven. Bake and baste for 1 to 1½ hours. During the last half hour of baking, arrange sweet potatoes that have been parboiled around meat. Bake until brown, basting with drippings.

A Date with a Dish: A Cookbook of American Negro Recipes by Freda De Knight

Hopping John
RICE WITH BLACK-EYED PEAS AND SAUSAGE

In the Americas, rice and bean dishes are primarily associated with peoples of African ancestry. Jamaicans have "rice and peas;" Cubans have Moros y Cristianos; and Americans have hoppin' John (as it is usually written). Celestine Eustis's recipe comes from an "Uncle John," presumably the cook of one of her South Carolina relatives. Black-eyed peas, sometimes known as cow peas, are more like a bean than a pea, though they aren't closely related to either. They are indigenous to Africa. In the South, hoppin' John is supposed to bring good luck for the New Year, and few would be cynical enough not to have a little as the first of January rolls around. In some families, a coin is buried in the rice and peas just before serving, ensuring a fortunate year for the finder. The addition of sausages is a little unusual, but not unauthentic. Use a spicy smoked sausage like an *andouille*, though even kielbasa will do in a pinch.

1 cup black-eyed peas
1 medium onion, finely chopped
1 bay leaf
1 large sprig parsley
2 slices bacon, chopped
¼ pound smoked sausage, coarsely diced
¼ pound smoked ham, diced
Salt
2 cups long-grain rice
SERVES 8

1. Cover the peas with 3 cups water and soak overnight.

2. Drain the peas. In a large saucepan, combine with 6 cups water, the onion, bay leaf, and parsley. Bring to a boil and continue cooking at a bare simmer until the beans are tender, about 45 minutes. Remove the bay leaf and parsley.

3. In the meantime, fry the bacon until crispy, add the sausage and ham, and fry 2 or 3 minutes longer. Add to the cooked peas.

4. Season the peas with salt. Wash the rice well in a colander. Add to the pan and simmer, covered, 15 minutes. Remove from the heat and let stand to dry out in a warm place 15 minutes longer.

Cooking in Old Creole Days by Celestine Eustis

Our "Aunt Harriet's" Favorite Dish
BUTTERMILK CORN BREAD

Harriet Tubman, the famous escaped slave and abolitionist, was apparently quite enamored of this corn bread. Vivian Carter Mason, the contributor of the recipe, writes:

> My mother and my father loved and revered Harriet Tubman and taught their children to do the same. She would draw us to her side and while we made ourselves comfortable with old pillows on the floor, tell hair-raising stories of her escape from slavery and subsequent returns to the plantations to bring over four hundred men and women to freedom as the chief 'conductor' of the underground railroad. As she talked, her head thrown back and eyes closed, we were in the woods with her tramping at night through stony creeks where the water was cold, hiding in the bush during the day and glad for a piece of corn bread washed down by the water of a hidden spring. Then mother would call us to dinner, and as the lamps cast a bright light on the huge kitchen table, with the steaming bowls of rich soup and the crisp corn bread piled high, it was not hard to imagine that in the darkness outside someone was still searching for Harriet and would take us too.

1. Preheat oven to 425°F. Butter a 9- to 10-inch iron skillet or baking pan.

2. Blanch the salt pork by plunging it into boiling water for 1 minute. Drain and cool. Fry the salt pork (as you would bacon) until very crispy. Finely chop the salt pork and reserve the fat.

3. Sift together the cornmeal, flour, baking powder, baking soda, and salt. Stir together the buttermilk, eggs, and brown sugar.

4. Combine the flour mixture with the buttermilk mixture, and add the chopped salt pork and fat. Stir until just combined. Pour into the prepared pan, set in the oven, and bake 30 to 40 minutes, until the center is firm.

5. Turn the corn bread out onto a warm platter, split it horizontally in half, butter generously, reassemble, then cut in squares and serve immediately.

Butter, for pan

3 slices lean salt pork (about 3 ounces)

1½ cups yellow cornmeal

½ cup all-purpose flour

2 teaspoons baking powder

¼ teaspoon baking soda

½ teaspoon salt

1½ cups buttermilk

2 eggs, lightly beaten

1 tablespoon brown sugar

SERVES 6

The Historical Cookbook of the American Negro by The National Council of Negro Women

Hominy Bread
HOMINY SPOON BREAD

This "bread" is similar to the thick corn puddings called spoon breads in the South. It has an uncommon combination of grits, made from husked corn, and cornmeal, made from the whole kernel.

Salt

¼ cup grits, sometimes sold as hominy grits

2 tablespoons butter

2 eggs, beaten

2 cups milk

½ cup cornmeal

SERVES 6 AS A SIDE DISH

1. Preheat oven to 400°F. Generously butter a deep 10-inch cake pan.

2. Bring 1⅓ cups water to a boil in a saucepan. Add a large pinch salt. Stir in the grits and cook 15 to 20 minutes, until thickened. Stir in the butter until melted.

3. Remove the pan from heat, stir in the eggs, milk, and cornmeal and combine. Spoon into the prepared pan and bake on the bottom shelf of the oven until firm and golden, about 45 minutes.

Housekeeping in Old Virginia
edited by Marion Cabell Tyree

Selling calas

Calas

RICE FRITTERS

The rice fritters called "calas" have all but faded into folklore in New Orleans, but once they were as common as the golden fritters, called *beignets,* are today. According to *The Picayune's Creole Cook Book:*

> The ancient Creole negro women in the French Quarter of New Orleans [sold] a delicious rice cake, which was eaten with the morning cup of Café au Lait. The Cala woman was a daily figure in the streets till within the last two or three years. She went her rounds in quaint bandana tignon, guinea blue dress, and white apron, and carried on her head a covered bowl, in which were the dainty and hot Calas. Her cry, "Belle Cala! Tout Chaud!" would penetrate the morning air, and the olden Creole cooks would rush to the doors to get the first fresh, hot Calas to carry to their masters and mistresses with the early morning coffee.

1. In a medium saucepan, bring 4 cups water to a boil. Add the rice and simmer until very soft, about 40 minutes. Drain the rice, reserving the cooking water. Transfer the rice to a medium bowl. Let the rice and water cool to lukewarm. Stir the yeast into ⅓ cup of the rice water and stir into the rice. Mash the rice with the back of a spoon or pulse briefly in a food processor. It should remain a little lumpy. Cover with plastic wrap and set in a cool place overnight.

2. The next morning, stir the eggs into the rice mixture, along with the flour, sugar, and nutmeg. Beat well until it is the consistency of a thick batter. Cover with plastic wrap and set aside to rise 30 minutes.

3. Fill a heavy deep pan or deep fryer with about 2 inches of peanut oil. Set over moderate heat until the oil reaches 375°F. Drop the batter in heaping tablespoons, a few at a time, into the hot oil and fry until and golden, about 5 minutes. Turn them occasionally so they cook evenly. With a slotted spoon remove and drain well on paper towels. Keep warm in a 200°F oven while you fry the rest. Sprinkle with confectioners' sugar just before serving. Serve hot.

The Picayune's Creole Cook Book

½ cup long-grain rice

1 teaspoon active dry yeast

2 eggs, lightly beaten

1 cup flour

½ cup white sugar

½ teaspoon grated nutmeg

Peanut oil, for frying

Confectioners' sugar, for sprinkling

MAKES ABOUT 20 FRITTERS, SERVING 4 OR 5

Green Tomato Pie

Nothing was wasted in the old days, especially not green tomatoes, which could be fried, or turned into pickles, or made into pie. To modern tastes, green tomato pie tastes as exotic as if it were made from some unknown tropical fruit.

1 recipe pie dough (see page 81)

2 tablespoons butter

2 pounds green tomatoes, sliced paper thin

1 cup sugar

1 tablespoon cider vinegar

1 tablespoon lemon juice

½ teaspoon grated nutmeg

½ teaspoon grated lemon rind

1½ tablespoons flour

1 egg, beaten

SERVES 6 TO 8

1. On a floured work surface, roll out half of the pastry for a bottom crust and fit it into a 9-inch pie pan. Refrigerate.

2. Preheat oven to 425°F.

3. Dot the bottom of the pie with about 2 teaspoons butter. Spread a layer of tomatoes on top, then sprinkle with the vinegar, lemon juice, nutmeg, peel, and flour. Top with a little butter. Make another layer, beginning with the tomatoes and adding vinegar, lemon juice, nutmeg, peel, flour, and butter until all the ingredients are used up.

4. Brush the edge of the dough with the beaten egg. Roll out the remaining piece of dough and place it on top of the filling. Crimp the edges. Cut vent holes in the top crust and brush the top with beaten egg.

5. Set on the bottom shelf of the oven and bake 20 minutes. Reduce the oven temperature to 350°F. Continue baking the pie 50 to 60 minutes, until the crust is golden brown and the filling is bubbling. Cool to room temperature before serving.

Good Things to Eat by Rufus Estes

Calla Lilies

DELICATE CREAM HORNS

These little horns are a near relation to the cookies the French call *tuiles*. They are a little tricky to make, but ever so sophisticated. Be sure to measure all the ingredients very carefully and bake only a few cookies at a time. They are an example of fine European baking as it was adapted through the medium of African-American cooks.

1. Preheat oven to 400°F. Butter a large heavy cookie sheet.

2. To make the cookies, combine the eggs and sugar and beat with a wooden spoon until complete combined. Stir in the flour and lemon extract and beat until smooth.

3. Using a teaspoon measure, drop 4 separate heaping teaspoons of the batter onto the prepared sheet, allowing plenty of room for each one to spread. Using the back of a spoon, spread the batter into 3½-inch circles, leaving about 1 inch in between.

4. Bake in the lower third of the oven until the cookies have a golden brown border about ¾ inch wide, 6 to 8 minutes.

5. Remove the cookies from the oven. Working quickly, scrape each cookie from the sheet with a wide metal spatula, shaping it into a little cone as you remove it. Repeat with the remaining cookies. If they should harden on the sheet, return to the oven for 30 seconds to soften.

6. Scrape the cookie sheet clean, butter it, and repeat steps 3 through 5 until all the batter is used. Let the cookies cool completely.

7. In a large bowl, beat the cream until firm and sweeten to taste with the sugar. Using a piping bag, fill each cookie with a little of the whipped cream. Serve immediately.

Good Things to Eat by Rufus Estes

COOKIES

3 eggs

1¼ cups sugar

⅔ cup flour

½ teaspoon lemon extract

FILLING

1½ cups heavy or whipping cream

Sugar to taste

MAKES ABOUT 2 DOZEN FILLED COOKIES, SERVING 6 TO 8

Philadelphia Groundnut Cakes
PEANUT BRITTLE

The women who compiled the Philadelphia Centennial Exhibition 1876, Women's Centennial Committees, *National Cookery Book* wanted everyone to be represented in their tribute to American cooking. Included were recipes from Native Americans, Jews, and African-Americans. According to the authors, peanut brittle—for that is what this is—came to our shore from Santo Domingo after the Haitian revolution:

> Many Philadelphians old enough to remember the days when neat colored women, in bright madras turbans, sat on low stools at the market corners, with waiters of these cakes for sale before them, may be glad to recall those memories, and perhaps to learn how the cakes so dear to their childhood were made!
>
> Of the numerous families who fled St. Domingo during the massacre of 1791, and took refuge in our city, many brought slaves with them as nurses or attendants. It is to these women, their ready adaptation to new homes and altered circumstances, that we owe the introduction of this small traffic.
>
> The day and generation of this people has passed away. Groundnut cakes—which the little folk called by a less dignified name—are fast becoming myths, and the bright turbans that nodded over the well-stocked waiters are seen no more.

---

1 cup light brown sugar

1²/₃ cups roasted peanuts

MAKES ABOUT 20 CAKES

1. Combine the brown sugar with ½ cup water in a heavy-gauge pan. Bring to a boil and cook until it reads 300°F on a candy thermometer. You can also test it by dropping a little into cold water. It should become brittle when cooled.

2. When the sugar is ready, stir in the nuts. Brush a marble slab or a cookie sheet lined with aluminum foil with water. Drop the hot mixture by heaping tablespoons onto it. Flatten each into a 2- to 3-inch cake. When cool, remove with a flexible metal spatula. Store in an airtight container.

Philadelphia Centennial Exhibition 1876, Women's Centennial Committees,
National Cookery Book

Wild Grape Butter
APPLE GRAPE BUTTER

If you have access to wild grapes, by all means use them, but know that Concord grapes have the appropriate taste. In either case the flavor of this butter will be delicious and the color out of this world.

1. Cut the apples in four but do not peel or core them. Place in a large nonreactive pan, add ½ cup water, cover tightly, and cook over low heat until the apples are very soft, about 30 minutes. Add the grapes and cook, covered, until the grapes are softened, about 10 minutes.

2. Pass the apple-grape mixture through a food mill or press through a coarse sieve. Measure the fruit, then add to it ½ the amount of sugar as there is puree. Return the mixture to the pan and cook over low heat until thick, about 1 hour and 30 minutes.

3. Preheat oven to 300°F. Pour the apple grape butter into a shallow roasting pan and set in the oven. Keep the oven door slightly ajar. Cook, stirring periodically, until the butter is thick enough to spread. (To test for consistency, spoon a little of the butter onto an ice cold plate.) Bottle in preserving jars according to the manufacturer's directions. Store in cool place.

Good Things to Eat by Rufus Estes

3 pounds tart apples

3 pounds Concord grapes

About 3½ cups sugar

MAKES 6 CUPS

Lobsters Uptown, Bagels Downtown

The Heritage of the German Jews

Kosher butcher shops flourished in turn-of-the-century New York.

New York, 1900

The first great wave of Jewish immigrants who crowded into New York's Lower East Side in the 1840s and 1850s had come from the German-speaking parts of Central Europe. They were skilled, highly motivated, and literate, and many prospered. Their food was fundamentally German, though usually modified by the requirements of kosher cooking. Like most immigrants the first generation held on to the old ways, but their well-off sons and daughters who moved uptown were much more concerned with blending into the American mainstream. Many brought along only vague ideas about their Jewish heritage. This was the Gilded Age, and the upwardly mobile looked to champagne to lubricate their rise in society. More traditional Jews looked on with reactions that ranged from horror to bemusement. Esther J. Ruskay, in a turn-of-the-century essay on the Passover holiday, described a seder that said more about the participants' place in society than about their religion:

> One thoroughly well-meaning couple, noted for its propensity of good living, set out invitations for a more than usually sumptuous dinner. Before settling down to the business of the hour, the host arose and expressed himself as extremely gratified to be able, with a number of his co-religionists gathered about the festive board, to dedicate the present occasion to the joyous anniversary of Israel's deliverance from Egyptian misrule and tyranny. Which fact, to be

No Fifth Avenue supper party would be complete without champagne and an oration.

better borne in their vague (upon all subjects pertaining to Judaism) minds, would call for one entire course of the dinner to be given over to matzos and bitter herbs, to be helped down by champagne. "And now," [the host said] to the waitress, "bring on the caviar sandwiches and oysters."

One of the ways the immigrants sought to integrate into Protestant America was to adopt a milder, reformed Judaism. Whereas in 1850 there were 200 Orthodox congregations and eight Reform ones in the United States, by 1880, the situation was almost precisely opposite, with 200 Reform and six Orthodox synagogues. The reform congregations no longer required head coverings for men and some even changed the Sabbath to Sunday. And they abolished the Jewish dietary laws. By 1883, when a group of American Reform rabbis was ordained in Cincinnati, the banquet — served by a Jewish caterer — served shrimp and oysters, both forbidden by Jewish tradition. The occasion caused quite a stir but apparently only two participants walked out. The reality was that most of the time, American Jews were already cooking and eating like Americans, even while reserving certain specialties for festive occasions.

The cookbooks from the late nineteenth century provide a vivid snapshot of the middle-class Jewish approach to the culinary arts. The first Jewish cookbook published in the United States was the *Jewish Cookery Book* of 1871. It came out of an established European tradition in which food that was technically kosher was cooked in the same style as the fashionable cuisine of the Continental gentry. Esther Levy, the author, was seeking to educate the daughters of immigrants in the English-American tradition, though she also included a sprinkling of German recipes that would have been familiar to her readers. Trying to head off criticism from those who wished to assimilate further, Levy wrote, "without violating the precepts of our religion, a table can be spread, which will satisfy the appetites of the most fastidious. Some have, from ignorance, been led to believe that a repast, to be sumptuous, must unavoidably admit forbidden food. We do not venture too much when we assert that our writing clearly refutes that false notion." Her book, however, was to be virtually the only example of a kosher American cookbook written before the First World War.

Kaffee Klatch Menu

Oysters on Half Shell.

Hot Rolls. Butter. Soft Shell Crabs.

Roast Turkey.

Mushroom and Sweetbread Salad.

Aspic (Sultz). Veal Patties. Kuchen.

Neapolitan Ice-cream. Fruits. Nuts.

Coffee.

Aunt Babette's Cook Book by "Aunt Babette"

Much more typical—and popular—was *"Aunt Babette's" Cook Book,* first published in 1889 and in print thereafter for twenty-five years, with at least eleven editions. The volume is almost indistinguishable from an Anglo-American cookbook of the same period, except that it does eschew lard, contains a number of German specialties, and includes a section called "Easter" dishes— devoted to Passover. Mrs. Bertha F. Kramer, the "Aunt Babette" of the title, was unapologetic in her desire to keep up with the Joneses. Not only did her cookbook contain recipes for all-American pies and roast turkey with oyster dressing, but she also had instructions on organizing the theme meals so popular during the Gay Nineties. Her advice on putting together a Pink Tea must have been indispensable to her trendy readers. "'Pink Teas,' just now so fashionable," she writes, "are rather novel if carried out to the letter, and an expensive way of entertaining, too; yet, as the old saying is, one might as well be dead as out of fashion. So all those who wish to be fashionable come and listen and I will give you a few hints in regard to getting up a 'Pink Tea.'" First, the host needed to secure serving containers: "Serve the creams and ices in novel designs made of pink paper, such as baskets, boxes, buckets, freezers, cups and saucers, shells, wheelbarrows, vases, etc....you may procure these and many more beautiful designs at almost any fashionable caterer's." The table itself was to be a pink-tinted jungle of frilly doilies, flowers, napkins, ribbons, and dishes, all illuminated by pink lamps. The charlotte russe, the guests' boutonnieres, and even the cap and gown worn by the waitress was to be pink! Naturally, it was assumed that the reader had a maid to take care of the preparations.

Increasingly after 1880, though, a new wave of Jewish immigrants made the affluent German Jews a minority. Where 200,000 Jews had arrived in the United States in the mid-eighteen hundreds, the so-called Russian Jews who arrived from Poland, Russia, Romania, and other parts of Eastern Europe after 1880 numbered over two and a half million. Many of the uptown Jews wanted nothing to do with the newcomers, whom they regarded as uncouth and uncivilized. The remainder wanted to make sure the arrivals who were now crowding the Lower East Side would be assimilated into the modern American way of life as quickly as possible, in part from philanthropic motives, but also in part so that they would not cause embarrassment.

Vocational schools and settlement houses were organized to instruct the immigrant girls in American standards of hygiene, housekeeping, and cookery, and numerous cookbooks were published to help finance these ventures. Many of the new immigrants were, in fact, anxious to become American. Trying to impress a young man who made known his preference for the culinary ways of his adopted homeland, a character in an Anzia Yezierska novel set in the Lower East Side of the early twentieth century, heads to the settlement house: "Mashah found that Jacob liked American cooking, like salad and spinach. And right away Mashah joined the cooking class in the settlement, one evening a week, to learn the American way of cooking vegetables and fixing salads. And soon we all had American salad and American cooked vegetables instead of fried potato latkes and the greasy *lokshen kugel* [noodle pudding] that Mother used to make."

The difference between the cooking of the mostly observant Jews in the crowded tenements and the dishes served on starched linen in the middle-class Jewish-American homes could not have been greater. Downtown, there were lox and bagels, knishes and latkes, pastrami and garlic pickles, while uptown they were eating fried oysters, fillet of sole à la Mouquin, German-style pot roast, and ham sandwiches. All the early cookbooks published in English reflect this latter repertoire of American and German dishes interspersed by trendy French preparations. Lobsters, oysters, frogs' legs, caviar, and even ham and bacon, all foods forbidden by traditional Jewish law, are notable by their presence in these books written by and for Jews. In an index entry on "trefa" (foods that violate the laws of ritual purity) Aunt Babette writes, "Nothing is 'trefa' that is healthy and clean." Nevertheless, she does make concessions to the kosher reader, admonishing that "whenever the word lard occurs it refers especially to cotton seed lard, which is entirely free from hog fat, and is strictly kosher, pure and wholesome and economical as well." While Reform Jews may not have followed Orthodox food practices, they found certain foods like uncured pork and lard aesthetically repugnant.

By the time World War I ended, the downtown Jews had begun to publish cookbooks of their own, first in Yiddish, then in English for the children. What we generally recognize today as Jewish cooking in America is, like those masses who passed through Ellis Island, fundamentally from Eastern Europe. Pastrami originated in Romania, borscht in Russia, bagels in Poland. The foods that characterize the distinct heritage of the German Jews have been absorbed into the general culture or they have disappeared. Their culinary culture now exists only on the pages of those old cookbooks, and in an occasional holiday dish passed down through the generations.

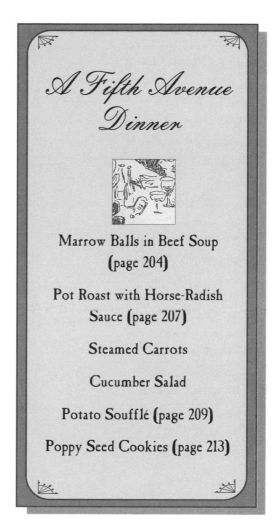

A Fifth Avenue Dinner

Marrow Balls in Beef Soup
(page 204)

Pot Roast with Horse-Radish
Sauce (page 207)

Steamed Carrots

Cucumber Salad

Potato Soufflé (page 209)

Poppy Seed Cookies (page 213)

Tomato Soup with Meat Balls

Mrs. Henry Leiter and Miss Sara Van Bergh's *Flower City Cook Book* is a well written, comprehensive volume that is very typical of its time and milieu. It differs from English-American cookbooks of the era by including numerous German- and Hungarian-style recipes. Uncured pork and lard are absent from the dishes, but ham and shellfish certainly are not. One common, and very idiosyncratic, trait that shows up in almost all German-Jewish cooking is the trio of salt, pepper, and ginger used as a seasoning in much the same way we would use salt and pepper alone. In other respects the cooking of the German Jews was much like their gentile German contemporaries, with the lard subtracted. Soup with meat dumplings is certainly very German.

2 tablespoons chicken or duck fat, or butter

1 onion, finely chopped

1 large celery rib, finely chopped

4 cups chicken broth

4 cups canned plum tomatoes with juice, passed through a strainer or food mill

$\frac{1}{2}$ teaspoon ground ginger

Large pinch cayenne pepper

Salt

2 tablespoons flour

1 recipe Meat Balls (recipe follows)

SERVES 6

1. Heat the fat in a large saucepan. Add the onion and celery and sauté, stirring, until softened, about 5 minutes. Add the broth and tomatoes. Bring to a boil and simmer 20 minutes.

2. Add the ginger and cayenne and season with salt to taste. Ladle about $\frac{1}{2}$ cup of the soup into a bowl and allow to cool briefly. Stir in the flour and return to the saucepan. Bring to a simmer, stirring occasionally. Add the meat balls and continue to simmer 15 minutes.

Meat Balls

1. Heat 1 tablespoon of the oil in a small skillet, add the onion, and sauté until softened, about 5 minutes. Set aside.

2. Soak the bread in water, then squeeze it as dry as possible. Combine the beef, bread, onion, egg, parsley, and ginger in a bowl. Season with salt and pepper to taste. Stir until thoroughly mixed. Using lightly oiled hands, form the mixture into meat balls the size of marbles.

3. Heat the remaining oil in a large skillet over moderate heat. Add the meat balls in batches, if necessary, and cook until browned and cooked through, about 8 to 10 minutes. Use as garnish for soup.

The Flower City Cook Book by Mrs. Henry Leiter and Miss Sara Van Bergh

$1/4$ cup vegetable oil

1 small onion, finely chopped

2 slices stale white bread

$1/2$ pound ground beef

1 egg, beaten

1 tablespoon chopped fresh parsley

$1/4$ teaspoon ground ginger

Salt

Pepper

MAKES 20 TO 30 SMALL MEAT BALLS, SERVING 6

Eating Kosher

In Jewish tradition, cooking has to observe the laws of kashrut which stem from biblical and later rabbinical texts. Observant Jews are forbidden specific foods such as pork, rabbit, shellfish, and scaleless fish. Certain foods may not be eaten in combination; meat, in particular, may not be eaten in the same meal with milk products. Other foods, like fish, eggs, and vegetables are considered neutral and thus can be eaten with any other food. Furthermore, there are regulations regarding the way meat is prepared and slaughtered. At one time, New York had almost 4,000 kosher butcher shops to serve the Jewish community.

Marrow Balls

MATZOH BALLS WITH BEEF MARROW

Like matzoh balls (normally made with chicken fat), these dumplings are made with the crumbs of the unleavened bread called "matzoh" (or "matzah"), traditionally eaten at Passover. Matzoh was first produced commercially by Jacob Horowitz when he opened a bakery in New York in 1883. A few years later, Dov Behr Manischewitz, a Lithuanian Jew, opened a shop with machines that eventually produced fifty thousand pounds of matzoh a day. He made a fortune shipping it to England, New Zealand, France, Hungary, Egypt, and even Japan.

In the days when beef soup was made with real bones instead of coming from cans, marrow was easy enough to come by. Today, you will need to ask a butcher for marrow bones. Have them cut into pieces so you can scoop out the fatty marrow. You will need about a pound of bones to extract 2 or 3 tablespoons of marrow. Serve the dumplings in beef soup.

---

2 tablespoons beef of veal marrow

3 eggs, beaten

1 teaspoon finely chopped fresh parsley

Large pinch ground ginger

Salt

White pepper

¾ cup matzoh meal

6 to 8 cups veal or beef broth

MAKES 25 TO 30 DUMPLINGS, SERVING 4 TO 6

1. Rub the marrow to a creamy consistency with a wooden spoon in a medium bowl. Gradually stir in the eggs, then the parsley, ginger, and salt and pepper to taste. Stir in the matzoh meal. Rub until well incorporated. Refrigerate ½ hour. Using lightly greased fingers, form the mixture into balls the size of marbles.

2. Cook the dumplings by carefully dropping them into barely simmering veal or beef broth. Cover and cook 30 to 40 minutes. Serve the marrow balls in the broth.

The Practical Cookbook by The Sisterhood of the West End Synagogue

Tongue with Sauer Kraut
SMOKED BEEF TONGUE BRAISED WITH SAUERKRAUT

Smoked beef tongue is one of the great glories of Jewish *charcuterie*, though you may find it hard to come by unless you live near a good butcher. The tongue is cooked in the same manner as the famous Alsatian casserole of cured pork, sausages, and sauerkraut called *choucroute garnie*. The sauerkraut absorbs the flavor of the smoked meat as it slowly cooks.

1. Cover the tongue with cold water and soak overnight.

2. The next day, drain the tongue, set it in a saucepan, cover with cold water, bring to a boil, and simmer 30 minutes. Drain. Trim off the fat from the root end.

3. Drain the sauerkraut and rinse it under cold running water. Combine the sauerkraut, onions, parsley, cloves, chicken broth, and carrots in a large stewpot. Add the tongue, cover, and simmer slowly for 3 to 4 hours, until the tongue is tender. Peel the skin off the tongue while it is still warm.

4. Discard the parsley and cut the carrots into slices. Slice the tongue. To serve, arrange the sauerkraut in the middle of a platter, place the sliced tongue on top of it, and arrange the carrots around the edge.

Jewish Cookery Book by Esther Levy

1 smoked beef tongue, about 4 pounds

2 pounds sauerkraut (about 6 cups)

2 onions, sliced

1 small bunch parsley, tied together

10 whole cloves

2 cups chicken broth

2 large carrots, peeled

SERVES 4 TO 6

Fillet of Sole à la Mouquin
BAKED SOLE WITH SPINACH AND CHEESE

Here is an elegant dish that is essentially identical to the classic French recipe called *sole à la florentine*. The combination must have had some popularity since the same recipe appears again in *The Jewish Cookbook* from 1931.

1½ pounds spinach, cleaned and washed	1. Preheat oven to 500°F.
Salt	2. Steam the spinach until just wilted. Drain, let cool, and press out as much liquid as possible. Chop fine. Season with salt and pepper.
Ground white pepper	
1 small onion, sliced	3. Combine the onion, parsley, lemon slice, and bay leaf with 4 cups water in a saucepan, and season with salt and pepper. Bring to a boil and simmer 10 minutes.
1 sprig parsley	
1 thick lemon slice	
1 small bay leaf	
1¼ pounds flounder, sole, or halibut fillets	4. Arrange the fish fillets in one layer in a flameproof dish. Pour the flavored liquid over them and poach over low heat until just cooked through, about 3 minutes.
Cream Sauce (p. 211)	5. Arrange the chopped spinach in an ovenproof dish. Using a slotted spatula, remove the fish from the poaching liquid and arrange on the spinach. Stir the Parmesan into the cream sauce and spoon over the fish. Set the dish on the top shelf of the oven and cook until lightly browned, 5 to 10 minutes.
2 tablespoons grated Parmesan cheese	
SERVES 4	

The Practical Cookbook by The Sisterhood of the West End Synagogue

Pot Roast with Horse-Radish Sauce
POT-ROASTED BRISKET WITH HORSERADISH SAUCE

Brisket is a particular favorite in Jewish cooking. Long cooking makes it tender while bringing out its flavor. The horseradish is a Central European touch.

1. Season the brisket with the ginger and about 1 teaspoon each salt and pepper. Cover and refrigerate 3 to 4 hours.

2. Heat the oil in a Dutch oven. Add the brisket and brown on both sides. Add 1 cup boiling water, the onion, carrot, celery, and tomatoes. Cover and cook at a bare simmer until tender, about 3 hours.

3. Remove the brisket to a warm platter, cover, and keep warm. Strain the sauce through a sieve in a saucepan, pressing down on the vegetables. Stir the flour together with about 2 tablespoons cold water. Stir into the sauce, bring the mixture to a boil, and simmer 15 minutes. Stir in the horseradish and parsley. Adjust the seasonings and serve the sauce on the side.

The Flower City Cook Book by Mrs. Henry Leiter and Miss Sara Van Bergh

A 4-pound lean beef brisket

1 teaspoon ground ginger

Salt

Pepper

1 tablespoon vegetable oil

1 onion, sliced

1 carrot, sliced

1 celery rib, sliced

1 cup canned plum tomatoes with juice

3 tablespoons flour

3 tablespoons freshly grated horseradish, or to taste

1 teaspoon chopped fresh parsley

SERVES 6

Pot Roast Breast and Legs of Goose

Season the breast and legs of goose with salt, pepper, ginger, and if desired, a little finely cut garlic, and let stand overnight. Heat about 4 tablespoons goose fat in iron spider, add goose and brown on both sides, then add a very little hot water or soup stock, cover closely and cook slowly until tender.

The Flower City Cook Book by Mrs. Henry Leiter and Miss Sara Van Bergh

To roast a chicken

ROAST CHICKEN WITH GINGER

Roast chicken is as fundamental to Jewish cooking as chicken soup. The method of dusting the chicken with a little flour is strictly Victorian, but the distinctive addition of ginger sets the dish apart from the English-American mainstream.

½ pound fresh bread crumbs, made from day-old bread, about 4 cups

1 tablespoon chopped fresh parsley

½ teaspoon dried thyme

½ teaspoon dried marjoram

¼ teaspoon cayenne pepper, or to taste

2 tablespoons grated onion, plus 1 small onion, cut in half

1 egg, beaten

2 teaspoons ground ginger

Chicken fat, melted, or substitute vegetable oil

Salt

A 5-pound roasting chicken, giblets and neck reserved

2 tablespoons flour

SERVES 6

1. Preheat oven to 450°F.

2. Stir together in a large bowl the bread crumbs, parsley, thyme, marjoram, cayenne, grated onion, egg, 1 teaspoon of the ginger, 2 tablespoons of the chicken fat or oil, and salt to taste. Fill the chicken cavity with the stuffing and truss the chicken.

3. Set the chicken on a rack in a roasting pan, sprinkle it with the remaining 1 teaspoon ginger, 1 tablespoon of the flour, and salt to taste. Place in the oven and roast 20 minutes. Reduce the oven temperature to 375°F and continue roasting until the juices from the thigh meat run clear when pierced, about 1½ to 2 hours total. While the chicken is roasting baste it every 15 minutes with chicken fat or oil.

4. Combine the giblets (but not the liver) and chicken neck with the halved onion and 3 cups water in a saucepan. Simmer about 2 hours or until the roast chicken is cooked. Strain.

5. When the chicken is cooked, remove as much fat from the roasting pan as possible. Stir together 1 tablespoon flour with 2 tablespoons water. Stir into the giblet broth. Pour the mixture into the roasting pan and return the pan with the chicken in it on the rack to the oven. Continue roasting 10 more minutes, basting the chicken 3 or 4 times with the gravy.

6. Remove the chicken from the pan, set breast side down on a serving platter, cover loosely with aluminum foil, and let stand in a warm place. Season the gravy with salt if necessary.

7. To serve, set the chicken breast side up on the platter and serve the gravy on the side.

Jewish Cookery Book by Esther Levy

Potato Soufflé

Though the Germans adopted the potato quite late in their history, nowhere will you find a nation more fanatical about it. When the German Jews arrived in the New World they had a thing or two to teach Americans about this New World tuber.

1. Preheat oven to 400°F. Butter a 4-cup baking dish.

2. Cook the potatoes in lightly salted boiling water to cover until tender. Drain well, mash, and measure 2 cups. In a small saucepan heat the cream together with the butter until the butter melts.

3. Using an electric mixer, beat the potatoes until fluffy. Beat in the cream mixture and then the yolks. Season with salt and pepper. Whip the egg whites until stiff. Fold into the potatoes, then transfer to the buttered baking dish.

4. Bake until puffed and golden, about 20 minutes. Serve at once.

The Flower City Cook Book by Mrs. Henry Leiter and Miss Sara Van Bergh

1½ pounds potatoes, peeled and quartered

½ cup heavy cream

2 eggs, separated

2 tablespoons butter

Salt

White pepper

SERVES 4 TO 6

Celery Timbales

CELERY ROOT CUSTARDS

Celery root, fundamentally a peasant's vegetable, is transformed here into a creamy, elegant, opulent dish. Reformed Jews would have served it with roast meats, even ham. You may feel that adding the cream sauce gilds the lily, but after all the recipe *is* from the Gilded Age.

1 large celery root (celeriac), about 2 pounds, peeled and cut into 1-inch pieces

Butter

4 eggs, beaten

1 cup heavy cream

Salt

White pepper

Cream Sauce (recipe follows)

SERVES 6

1. Cook the celery root in lightly salted boiling water until tender, about 30 minutes. Drain well, mash, and press through a coarse sieve or purée in a food processor. Measure 2 cups.

2. Preheat oven to 350°F. Butter six 6-ounce pudding cups.

3. Stir the eggs and cream into the celery purée and season with salt and pepper. Divide the mixture evenly among the prepared pudding cups.

4. Set the cups in a deep pan large enough to hold all of them. Pour boiling water into the pan so that it reaches halfway up the sides of the cups. Set in the oven and bake until the timbales are firm to the touch, about 30 to 40 minutes. Remove from the oven and the pan.

5. To unmold, run a small thin knife around the inside of each cup and turn the timbale upside down onto a plate. Serve as a side dish with Cream Sauce.

Cream Sauce

Melt the butter in a small nonreactive saucepan over moderate heat. Add the flour and cook, stirring, 1 minute. Add the cream, bring to a boil, and cook at a bare simmer 15 minutes. Add the mace or nutmeg and season with salt and pepper.

The Flower City Cook Book by Mrs. Henry Leiter and Miss Sara Van Bergh

1 tablespoon butter

1 tablespoon flour

1 cup light cream

Pinch ground mace or grated nutmeg

Salt

White pepper

MAKES 1 CUP

Chestnut Croquettes

In Germany as in America, chestnuts were often reserved for winter festivities. Because peeling chestnuts is a chore, they were served as a treat at special dinners. These croquettes go well with roast chicken or turkey.

1 pound chestnuts

2 eggs, separated

2 tablespoons heavy cream

1 tablespoon sherry

2 teaspoons sugar

Pinch salt

Flour

1 egg, beaten

Bread crumbs

Peanut oil, for deep frying

MAKES 12 CROQUETTES, SERVING 4 AS A SIDE DISH

1. Using a serrated knife, make an X in the skin of each chestnut. Bring about 6 cups water to a rapid boil and add the chestnuts. Boil for 20 to 30 minutes. Drain the chestnuts and with the aid of a small paring knife remove both the exterior shell and the interior skin. (The hotter the chestnuts are, the easier they are to peel.) Measure 1 cup firmly packed chestnuts.

2. In a food processor, purée the chestnuts with the 2 egg yolks, cream, sherry, sugar, and salt. Beat the 2 egg whites until firm and stir into the mixture. Refrigerate at least 1 hour, or until thoroughly chilled.

3. Using well-floured spoons, form the chestnut mixture into about 12 oblong croquettes, each about 1 by 2 inches. Refrigerate until ready to use.

4. Fill a deep skillet with about 1 inch of the oil. Set over moderate heat.

5. Dip the croquettes, one at a time, into the remaining egg and then into bread crumbs. Fry in the hot oil until golden, about 5 minutes. Remove with a slotted spoon and drain on paper towels. Serve hot.

The "Best by Test" Cook Book by Mrs. Alfred Loeb

Poppy Seed Cookies

These delightful little cookies are close cousins to standard shortbread, but much more fun.

1. Preheat oven to 375°F. Dust 2 or 3 cookie sheets lightly with flour.

2. Cream the butter and sugar together in a large bowl until smooth and light. Sift together the flour, cinnamon, and baking soda. Gradually mix the flour mixture into the creamed butter. Knead until smooth.

3. On a floured board, roll out the dough ⅛ inch thick. With a 2½-inch cookie cutter, cut out rounds and set them on the prepared cookie sheets. Brush the rounds with the beaten egg, sprinkle with poppy seeds, and press one almond in the middle of each. Set in the oven and bake until a pale gold, about 12 to 15 minutes. Cool on wire racks.

The "Best by Test" Cook Book by Mrs. Alfred Loeb

1¼ cups butter, softened

¾ cup brown sugar

3 cups flour

1 teaspoon ground cinnamon

Large pinch baking soda

1 egg, beaten

2 to 3 tablespoons poppy seeds

About 60 blanched almonds (about ¾ cup)

MAKES 4 TO 5 DOZEN COOKIES

Schnecken
RAISIN AND ALMOND DANISH

Schnecken are usually sweet buns shaped into a snail-like roll. But not here. The dough, called *kuchen* dough, is made in the traditional way, even the filling is the usual filling, but somewhere along the way, the pastry became a square, like a Danish. If you want to make snail shaped sweet-bread, cover the entire surface of the rolled-out dough with the filling, then roll it tightly, and cut the roll into 1-inch slices. Proceed according to the recipe.

Once schnecken arrived in the United States from Germany, they were transformed into irresistible pecan rolls and sticky buns, often baked in muffin tins.

In a large city like New York, a housewife could avail herself of a bakery operated along the precepts of her faith.

1. To make the dough, in a saucepan heat the 2 cups milk to lukewarm. In a large bowl combine it with the 1 teaspoon sugar and salt. Stir in the yeast and 1½ cups of the flour. Set aside to rise 15 minutes.

2. Cream the softened butter and the 1 cup sugar together. Stir in the egg yolks. Beat the egg whites until stiff, then stir into the butter mixture. Add the lemon rind and juice. Stir into the yeast mixture, then add the remaining flour until a dough forms. Cover with plastic wrap and let rise in a cool place overnight.

3. Lightly butter a large cookie sheet.

4. To fill the dough, using as little flour as possible, pat or roll the dough out on a floured board into a rectangle about 12 by 18 inches and ½ inch thick. Brush with the melted butter. Sprinkle half the dough with the raisins, currants, slivered almonds, citron, lemon peel, and cinnamon. Fold the uncovered part over and press down on the edges. Roll out the dough to about ¾ inch thick. Cut into 3-inch squares and, again, press down on the edges. Set the squares on the prepared cookie sheet just barely touching.

5. To top the Schnecken, stir together the egg yolk and milk and brush the mixture on the tops of the squares. Crumble together the sugar, chopped almonds, butter, and cinnamon. Sprinkle on top of the dough.

6. Cover the dough loosely with plastic wrap and set in a warm place to rise until doubled in bulk, about 1 hour.

7. Preheat oven to 375°F.

8. Bake the pastries in the oven until golden, about 30 to 40 minutes. Serve warm.

The Flower City Cook Book by Mrs. Henry Leiter and Miss Sara Van Bergh

DOUGH

2 cups milk

1 cup plus 1 teaspoon sugar

Pinch salt

1 envelope active dry yeast

5 cups all-purpose flour, plus additional flour for rolling

¾ cup butter, softened

3 eggs, separated

1 teaspoon grated lemon rind

2 tablespoons lemon juice

FILLING

2 tablespoons butter, melted

½ cup golden raisins

½ cup dried currants

½ cup slivered almonds

¼ cup diced citron

1 teaspoon grated lemon peel

½ teaspoon ground cinnamon

TOPPING

1 egg yolk

2 tablespoons milk

⅓ cup sugar

½ cup chopped almonds

4 tablespoons butter

1 teaspoon ground cinnamon

MAKES 15 PASTRIES

Quince Marmalade

Quinces and quince marmalade were very common throughout Europe and the United States until the twentieth century. Today the fruit, edible only when cooked, is available from specialized growers at farmers' markets and fancy food stores.

4 pounds quinces

2½ cups sugar

1 cup orange juice

MAKES ABOUT 8 CUPS

1. Wash the quinces. Peel, quarter, and core them, reserving the trimmings and cores. Put the fruit in a bowl and cover with cold water until ready to use.

2. Put the peelings and cores in a saucepan and cover with 5 cups water. Bring to a boil and simmer until very soft, about 30 minutes. Strain the quince water into a large heavy saucepan or preserving pan. Add the quinces, cover, and simmer 20 minutes. Uncover, add the sugar and orange juice, and simmer, stirring periodically, until thick, about 1½ hours. Ladle into canning jars, and process according to the manufacturer's directions. Store in a cool place.

The Flower City Cook Book by Mrs. Henry Leiter and Miss Sara Van Bergh

A Tasteful Passover

In *Hearth and Home Essays*, Esther Ruskay described an elegant turn-of-the-century house in preparation for the Passover, the holiday commemorating the Jewish exodus from Egypt. In preparation for the holiday, the house has to be meticulously cleaned and special dishes have to be prepared.

The week just preceding Passover is a busy one for Jewish house-keepers. Those among us who assert that Passover entails upon observing Jews a week of self-denial of many of the necessaries of life should take a peek on the day before Passover into the pantries and closets, the cupboards and larders of those who have infused their soul and spirit into all this preparation, into every detail of the House Beautiful. Row upon row—on lace-edged shelves or newly oil-clothed ones—stands ranged the special Passover service of china, polished until it gives back the sun's rays, and near by the burnished coppers and shining tins vie with the quaint old silver on the dining-room sideboard, tankards, bowls, loving cups of gold and silver taken out in honor of the occasion. The linen-closet, too, upstairs, which is to yield up its finest patterned table-cloths, doylies [*sic*], and napkins to the decking of the table for the Seder nights, is quite in keeping with the rich smell and spicy fragrance that ascends and penetrates from the well-stocked larder below. Just why Passover stores of sugar and coffee, of tea, raisins, lemons, dried fruit, honey cake, wine and spices, should have this distinct holiday flavor, is one of the things to be forever unex-plained. It is, nevertheless, an incontrovertible fact that, whether due to the renewal of everything in the house or to the special care taken in their manufacture and packing, all these ordinary, every-day necessities of life have a decidedly appetizing taste during the gala festival week.

From a
Dutch Oven

Breads and Cakes from
the Golden Age of the
Pennsylvania Dutch

Bucks County, 1905

The first thing to welcome Mary when she got out of the buggy at her Aunt Sarah's farm in Schuggenhaus, Pennsylvania, was a well-scrubbed table covered with an array of breads and pastries. "The day preceding that of Mary's arrival at the farm was a busy one for Aunt Sarah, who, since early morning, had been preparing the dishes she knew Mary enjoyed," writes Edith Thomas in *Mary at the Farm and Book of Recipes*, an account of a summer visit to Pennsylvania Dutch country in the years preceding World War I. There were "pans of the whitest, flakiest rolls, a large loaf of sweetest nut-brown, freshly-baked 'graham bread', of which Mary was especially fond and an array of crumb-cakes."

Mary, who had grown up as an orphan and was now working in Philadelphia as a kindergarten teacher, had come to the farm with a mission. She was nineteen, engaged to be married, and yet, due to her motherless youth, entirely unschooled in the domestic arts. "Quite time I think, she should learn housekeeping, something every young girl should know," her uncle commented. "We should hear of fewer divorces and a less number of failures of men in business, had their wives been trained before marriage to be good, thrifty, economical housekeepers and, still more important, good homemakers."

Edith Thomas's semi-fictional book is full of such wisdom, intending to instruct at least as much as to entertain. Recipes are included as a part of the young heroine's education. Her teacher and model was to be Aunt Sarah, the kind of super-housewife who rarely exists outside the sentimental realms of turn-of-the-century fiction. Aunt Sarah "had developed a fine character by her years of unselfish devotion to family and friends. She never failed to find joy and pleasure in the faithful performance of daily tasks, however insignificant." She was a

Aunt Sarah

proponent "of fresh air, fruit and clear spring water…never ate to excess, and frequently remarked: 'I think more people suffer from over-eating than from insufficient food.'" Nevertheless, she instructed her favorite niece in how to make "good wholesome food, and plenty of it."

Aunt Sarah, like most of her neighbors, was Pennsylvania Dutch, descended from German immigrants of the eighteenth and early nineteenth centuries. ("Dutch" is a contortion of "Deutsch," the word for German in its native tongue.) Most of the settlers had come from the Rhineland Palatinate, where a combination of religious intolerance and lack of opportunity made news of the New World sound sweet. Most were farmers, peasants, and agricultural workers who found in Pennsylvania fertile soil for their crops and culture. When travelers from other parts of the young United States visited eastern Pennsylvania, they found the area more German than New England was English. Nowhere was this more evident than in the food. George Washington became fond of

A Pennsylvania farm.

Pennsylvania German cooking when he used Pennsylvania Dutch
soldiers as messboys, and later brought Pennsylvania Dutch cooks
back to Mount Vernon.

Although Pennsylvania Dutch cooking would later become
known for its abundance, the first German settlers lived quite
frugally. Theophile Cazenove, after a visit to Pennsylvania in 1795,
reported: "they live on potatoes, buckwheat cakes, instead of bread.
They deny themselves everything costly." Even in the early days,
though, the Protestant feast days of baptisms, weddings, and
funerals were occasions of general revelry. The old pastors were
always railing against the indulgence evident at these holidays.
Aunt Sarah recalled how in "old times" on these occasions
sumptuous feasts were provided for relatives and friends. One
witness describes a funeral custom: "while the people were coming
in, good cake cut into pieces is passed around on a large tin plate to
those present, each person receives then, in a goblet, a hot West
India rum punch into which lemon, sugar, and juniper berries are

put, which gives it a delicious taste. After that sweet cider, heated, is passed." Also invariably served at times of bereavement was raisin, or rosina, pie, also known as funeral pie.

Between the Civil War and the outbreak of World War I, the family farms of the Pennsylvania Germans experienced a golden age. The Pennsylvania Dutch were (and continue to be) superior farmers, and the wives turned the abundant grain, fruit, vegetables, milk, and meat into food for the family and help.

Pennsylvania Dutch cooking was influenced by American ways just as other groups' cooking had been. Here, however, the core was German rather than English, French, or African. Some foods, such as pretzels, sauerkraut, dumplings, and rye bread, were made the same as in the Old World. Another example was apple butter *(lattwaerrich)*, made the same way a plum conserve was made in the Rhineland. Making apple butter was a festive occasion at which the neighbors would sit around and socialize while they pared and cored apples. The fruit was then boiled in large kettles of cider until it cooked down to a thick, sweet purée.

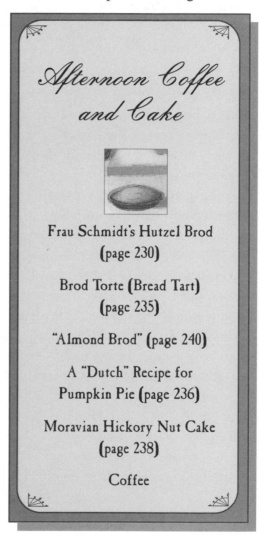

Afternoon Coffee and Cake

Frau Schmidt's Hutzel Brod
(page 230)

Brod Torte (Bread Tart)
(page 235)

"Almond Brod" (page 240)

A "Dutch" Recipe for
Pumpkin Pie (page 236)

Moravian Hickory Nut Cake
(page 238)

Coffee

One typical Pennsylvania dish that has only tenuous links to its European past is *Schnitz un Gnepp* (also spelled *Knepp*), a stew of dried apples with ham and dumplings. Better known is scrapple, made by combining scraps of meat (thereby the name), meat broth, and cornmeal or buckwheat flour. Once firm, loaves of scrapple are cut into slices and fried. Fried scrapple was a frequent White House breakfast during the administration of Herbert Hoover, a descendant of Pennsylvania Dutchmen.

The cooking of Pennsylvania Germans, while certainly hearty and filling, would not have won many prizes for delicacy. The baking, however, is another story. Cooks were known for turning out delicate rolls, hearty breads, toothsome cakes, and flavorful pies of every description. Though they do not have even a crumb of German ancestry, pies became a trademark of Pennsylvania Dutch baking. In Bucks County, a young girl's education was considered incomplete without an encyclopedic knowledge of pie-making. Edith Thomas writes: "The Pennsylvania German farmers' wives, with few exceptions, serve the greatest variety of pies at a meal of any class of people I know; not alone as a dessert at twelve o'clock dinner, but frequently serve several different varieties of pie at breakfast and at each meal during the day." The most common varieties of pies were *Rivel Kuchen*, a pie crust covered with a mixture of sugar, butter, and flour crumbled together; *schnitz* pie, made with either stewed and mashed dried apples or peaches and covered with a lattice-work of pastry; cheese pie, made of *smier Kase* (similar to cream cheese); as well as egg custard, and pumpkin and molasses pie. Best known is shoofly pie, made by combining streusel with molasses (or sorghum syrup) in the pastry crust. The pie is supposedly so good you have to shoo the flies away while it cools.

By the end of the nineteenth century, a Pennsylvania Dutch housewife often had not only an outdoor, wood-fired oven but a smaller oven in her coal-burning stove. The outdoor oven was still preferred for bread, but since it was no simple task to fire it, bread was usually baked only once a week. The breads, often many varieties, were usually baked Friday so that they would be fresh for the weekend. Coffee cakes and pies might also be baked in the outdoor oven but fancier baking—wedding cakes, for example—was usually done indoors.

By the end of the summer, Mary knew enough to make any Pennsylvania hausfrau proud. She returned to Philadelphia with a hope chest filled with a handmade quilt and rugs, jars of fruit, dried sweet corn, homemade soap, crocks of apple butter, jellies, jams, and canned vegetables, and, most importantly, Aunt Sarah's recipes.

Bucks County Hearth-Baked Rye Bread

Edith Thomas writes in *Mary at the Farm:* "The bread baked from this recipe has the taste of bread which, in olden times, was baked in the brick ovens of our grandmother's day, and that bread was unexcelled. I know of what I am speaking, having watched my grandmother bake bread in an old-fashioned brick oven, and have eaten hearth-baked rye bread, baked directly in the bottom of the oven, and know, if this recipe be closely followed, the young housewife will have sweet, wholesome bread. Some Germans use Kummel or Caraway seed in rye bread." She adds that Aunt Sarah's loaves always won a blue ribbon at country fairs and farmers' picnics.

The Many Uses of Stale Bread

The Pennsylvania Dutch were even more renowned for their thriftiness than they were for their pies. Aunt Sarah was full of advice to Mary on using leftover bread. "Never waste stale bread, as it may be used to advantage in various ways. The young housewife will be surprised at the numerous good, wholesome and appetizing dishes which may be made from stale bread." Here are some of her suggestions.

Take a half-dozen slices of stale bread of equal size and place in a hot oven a few minutes to become crisped on the outside so they may be quickly toasted over a hot fire, a delicate brown. Butter them and for breakfast serve with a poached egg on each slice.

Serve creamed asparagus tips on slices of toast for luncheon.

Loaves of bread which have become stale can be freshened if wrapped in a damp cloth for a few minutes, then remove and place in a hot oven until heated through.

For a change...put the stiffly-beaten white of an egg on the center of a hot, buttered slice of toast, carefully drop the yolk in the center of the beaten white and place in hot oven a few minutes to cook. Serve with a bit of butter on top, season with pepper and salt. Serve at once.

1. Heat the milk to lukewarm in a saucepan, and pour into a large bowl. Stir in the butter, sugar, salt, 4 cups of the rye flour, and finally the yeast. Beat thoroughly. Cover with plastic wrap, and set in a warm place until doubled in bulk, about 3 hours.

2. Stir in the remaining 4 cups rye flour and the all-purpose flour. Turn out onto a well-floured board and knead until smooth and elastic, about 10 to 20 minutes. Form the dough into a ball. Sprinkle liberally all over with flour. Fold a kitchen towel or napkin in four, set it in the bottom of a large bowl and sprinkle it liberally with flour. Set the dough on top of the towel in the bowl. Cover with plastic wrap and set in a cool place to rise overnight.

3. Preheat oven to 375°F. Sprinkle a large baking sheet with flour and set it in the oven to heat for 5 minutes.

4. Remove the sheet from the oven. Carefully turn the bowl with the bread upside down onto the hot baking sheet. Carefully remove the bowl and towel and immediately set the baking sheet on a shelf set in the bottom ⅓ of the oven. Bake about 1 hour, until the bread sounds hollow when the bottom is tapped, and a skewer inserted comes out dry and clean.

5. While still hot, brush the top crust with melted better. Wrap the entire loaf in a barely damp cloth, set the loaf on a rack, and let cool.

Mary at the Farm and Book of Recipes by Edith M. Thomas

3 cups milk

2 teaspoons butter, melted

1½ tablespoons sugar

2 teaspoons salt

8 cups rye flour

¾ cup Potato Yeast (page 228), or 1½ teaspoons active dry yeast dissolved in ½ cup lukewarm water

1 cup unbleached all-purpose flour, plus additional flour for kneading

Melted butter

MAKES A 2½-POUND LOAF

Aunt Sarah's Potato Yeast

Until the late 1800s, commercially made yeast was unavailable, so everyone made their own. Of the many methods, the simplest was to make a thin dough of flour and water and leave it out to collect the wild yeasts that are naturally present in the air. This is the sourdough starter that gives San Francisco sourdough its tang. Once the yeast was "captured," it had to be fed. The baker would use the yeast as necessary to make the bread and then would add a little more flour and water paste to the starter to keep it going. As pioneers moved west, a little jar of yeast was often one of their most valued provisions. Cooked potatoes often replaced part of the flour, as they do here, because potato yeast lasts longer and does not sour as quickly.

Breads made with homemade yeast are much tastier than those made with commercial yeast, in part because they need to rise longer, which allows the flavor of the bread to develop. However, they do make the result less predictable. Rising times will vary from batch to batch because the yeast will have a different strength each time.

You can make the initial batch of potato yeast by using a little commercial active dry yeast. If you can't use the potato yeast within ten days, it can be frozen for several months. One cup of potato yeast is roughly equivalent to one envelope of active dry yeast.

1 pound potatoes, peeled

4½ teaspoons sugar

4½ teaspoons salt

½ cup potato yeast, or 1 teaspoon active dry yeast

MAKES ABOUT
3½ CUPS YEAST

1. Bring 4 cups water to a boil in a medium saucepan. In the meantime, grate the potatoes.

2. When the water boils, add the potatoes to it with the sugar and salt. Cook the potatoes at a bare simmer, stirring occasionally, until they fall apart, about 40 minutes. Let cool to lukewarm and pour into a medium bowl. Stir in the potato yeast (or, if using the active dry yeast, dissolve it first in ¼ cup lukewarm water and then add it to the potato mixture).

3. Cover the bowl loosely with plastic wrap. Let stand in a warm place for 3 to 4 hours, until foamy and doubled in volume. Stir it down. Ladle the yeast into glass jars, cover, and refrigerate until needed. The yeast will keep about 10 days.

Mary at the Farm and Book of Recipes by Edith M. Thomas

Kartoffel Twist
BRAIDED POTATO BREAD

Potatoes flavor and lend moisture to this lovely braided loaf (*Kartoffel* means potato). It will be even tastier if you use Potato Yeast (page 228) — if you do so, reduce the milk to ½ cup.

1. Cook the potatoes in boiling water until very tender. Drain, reserving the cooking water. Measure ½ cup of the water. When it has cooled to lukewarm, dissolve the yeast in it.

2. Mash the potatoes. Measure 1 cup and place in a large bowl. Stir in 2 tablespoons of the butter, the sugar, salt, the lukewarm milk, and 2 cups of the flour. Stir in the yeast mixture. Beat together thoroughly with a wooden spoon. Cover with plastic wrap and set in warm place to rise until doubled in bulk, about 1 hour.

3. Stir the egg into the dough and work in about 3½ cups more of the flour. Knead the dough on a floured board until smooth and elastic, about 10 minutes. Put back in the bowl, cover again with plastic wrap, and let rise in a warm place until doubled in bulk, about 1 hour.

4. Punch down the dough. Set aside ⅓ of it. Divide the remaining ⅔ into 3 pieces. On a lightly floured board, roll each into an 18-inch-long strip. Braid the strips, then set the braid on the diagonal on a cookie sheet. Divide the remaining dough into 3 pieces and braid in the same way. Lay the smaller braid on the larger one. Brush with the remaining 2 tablespoons butter. Cover the braid lightly with plastic wrap and let rise until doubled in bulk, about 1 hour.

5. Preheat oven to 400°F.

6. Set the bread on the cookie sheet in the oven and bake 10 minutes. Lower the heat to 350°F and continue baking until the loaf is golden and sounds hollow when the bottom is tapped, about 45 minutes. Cool on a wire rack.

Mary at the Farm and Book of Recipes by Edith M. Thomas

¾ pound Russet potatoes, peeled and quartered

1 envelope (2 teaspoons) active dry yeast

4 tablespoons butter, melted

1 tablespoon sugar

1½ teaspoons salt

1 cup lukewarm milk

About 6 cups unbleached all-purpose flour

1 egg, beaten

MAKES A 3-POUND LOAF

Frau Schmidt's Hutzel Brod

PEAR BREAD

Dried fruit—apples, pears, and peaches—was a central element in Pennsylvania Dutch cooking. It might be stewed with meat or made into desserts. Dried fruit pies were very common. Here, dried pears flavor a sweet bread that might have been served with afternoon coffee. A mid-afternoon break for coffee and "coffee cake" was as typical of the Pennsylvania Germans as it was for the cousins in the old country. It's also tasty for breakfast. The author notes, "This bread will keep well several weeks, if kept in a tin cake box."

Dried pears can be found in health food stores.

Pebble Dash or Shoo-Fly Pie

Aunt Sarah made these to perfection and called them Pebble Dash pie. They are not really pies, they resemble cakes, but having a crust we will class them with pies. She lined three small sized pie tins with rich pie crust. For the crumbs, she placed in a bowl 3 cups flour, 1 cup brown sugar and ³/₄ cup of butter and lard, mixed and rubbed all together with the hands, not smooth, but in small rivels or crumbs. For the liquid part she used 1 cup baking molasses, 1 cup hot water, 1 teaspoonful baking soda dissolved in a few drops of vinegar and stirred this into the molasses and water. She divided the liquid among the three pans, putting one-third in each crust, over which she sprinkled the crumbs. Bake one-half hour in a moderate oven. These have the appearance of molasses cakes when baked.

Mary at the Farm and Book of Recipes by Edith M. Thomas

1. Place the dried pears in a medium saucepan, and cover with water. Cover the pan and simmer until the pears are just tender but not mushy, about 20 minutes. Drain the pears, reserving the liquid. When cool, cut the pears into ½-inch dice. Measure 1½ cups of the pear cooking liquid. Reserve the remainder.

2. When the 1½ cups of pear juice is lukewarm, pour it into a medium bowl and dissolve the yeast in it. Beat in 1½ cups flour and the salt. Cover with plastic wrap and let rise overnight.

3. Cover the raisins with the remaining pear cooking liquid. If necessary, add water so that they are entirely covered. Let soak overnight. Drain.

4. The following morning, dissolve the baking soda in 1 teaspoon water and stir into the dough.

5. Cream together the butter and sugar. Beat in the egg.

6. In a large bowl, beat together the dough and the sugar mixture. Stir in the diced pears, raisins, cinnamon, and fennel seeds. Stir in enough flour to make a moderately stiff dough, about 3 to 4 cups. Turn the dough out on a floured board and knead it until elastic, about 12 minutes. Set the dough in a lightly oiled large bowl. Cover with plastic wrap and set in a warm place until doubled in bulk, about 3 hours.

7. Lightly butter two 8 by 4 by 2½-inch loaf pans. Cut the dough into 2 pieces and form into loaves. Place each piece in a prepared pan, brush with a little butter, cover lightly with plastic wrap, and let rise until doubled in bulk, about 2 hours.

8. Preheat oven to 350°F.

9. Bake the loaves for about 45 minutes, until a toothpick inserted in the center comes out clean. Cool on a wire rack.

Mary at the Farm and Book of Recipes by Edith M. Thomas

2 cups dried pears (about ¾ pound)

1 teaspoon active dry yeast

4½ to 5½ cups unbleached all-purpose flour

Pinch salt

8 ounces (1¼ cups) raisins

Large pinch baking soda

6 tablespoons butter, slightly softened

6 tablespoons brown sugar

1 egg

1 teaspoon ground cinnamon

½ teaspoon fennel seeds

Melted butter

MAKES 2 LOAVES

Aunt Sarah's Rhubarb Pudding
RHUBARB COBBLER WITH VANILLA SAUCE

In other parts of the United States this would be called a cobbler, the common name for fruit baked with a topping of biscuit dough. The same recipe can be made with any other seasonal fruit such as peaches, blackberries, or plums. Here, the biscuit topping is just barely sweetened since the sauce is very sweet. As Edith Thomas points out in *Mary at the Farm and Book of Recipes*, "[T]he combined flavor of rhubarb and vanilla is delicious."

2 pounds rhubarb stems
½ cup plus 1 tablespoon sugar
1⅓ cups all-purpose flour
1 teaspoon baking powder
Pinch salt
3 tablespoons butter, cut into small pieces
1 large egg
6 tablespoons milk
Vanilla Sauce (recipe follows)

SERVES 6

1. Peel the rhubarb by stripping off the fibrous outside layer. Cut into ½-inch pieces. Combine with the ½ cup sugar and 2 tablespoons water in a small saucepan with a tightly fitting lid. Set over moderate heat and cook until the rhubarb is soft, about 15 minutes. Remove the lid and continue cooking until thickened slightly, about 5 minutes. Spoon the rhubarb into a 10-inch round or oval baking dish.

2. Preheat oven to 425°F.

3. Sift together the flour, the remaining 1 tablespoon sugar, baking powder, and salt. Add the butter and, using your fingers, break it up until the mixture has the texture of oatmeal. Stir together the egg and milk. Add to the flour mixture and stir briefly to combine. Do not overmix.

4. Drop spoonfuls of the batter over the hot rhubarb. Set the dish in the oven and bake until the crust is light brown, about 40 minutes.

5. Serve in individual dishes, spooning a couple of tablespoons of vanilla sauce over each portion.

Vanilla Sauce

½ cup heavy cream
1 cup light brown sugar
1 teaspoon vanilla extract

MAKES 1 CUP

Using an electric mixer, beat the cream until light and foamy. Add the sugar and continue beating until smooth and light. Beat in the vanilla extract.

Mary at the Farm and Book of Recipes by Edith M. Thomas

Apple Johnny Cake
SWEET APPLE CORN BREAD

The Pennsylvania Germans transformed the dense corn pancakes, known as johnnycakes in Rhode Island, into a dessert that is half cake, half pudding. Serve it hot with plenty of rich cream poured over each portion along with a sprinkle of sugar. It is also good with a scoop of vanilla or cinnamon ice cream. The author mentions that the apples could be replaced by raisins; if you do this, first plump 1 to 2 cups raisins by soaking them in boiling water for 15 minutes.

1. Preheat oven to 350°F. Butter a large loaf pan (10 by 4½ by 3 inches), using about 1 teaspoon of the melted butter.

2. Sift together the cornmeal, flour, sugar, baking soda, and salt. Stir in the buttermilk and remaining butter. Fold in the apples. Spoon into the prepared pan and bake until firm and a toothpick inserted in the center comes out clean, about 45 minutes.

3. To serve, cut into slices while still hot. Let each person spoon some cold cream and sugar over each portion.

Mary at the Farm and Book of Recipes by Edith M. Thomas

2 tablespoons butter, melted

1 cup cornmeal

⅔ cup flour

3 tablespoons sugar

1 teaspoon baking soda

¼ teaspoon salt

1 cup buttermilk

1 pound tart apples, such as Granny Smiths or Rhode Island Greenings, peeled, cored, and cut into thin slices

Heavy cream, for serving

Brown sugar, for serving

SERVES 6

Aunt Sarah's
Walnut Gingerbread

This is a classic encounter of the Old World with the New. This gingerbread has the slightly dry, spicy quality that Germans favor in their coffee cakes. Black walnuts, on the other hand, are indigenous to America.

The gingerbread tastes better after a day or two, when the black walnut flavor has penetrated the entire loaf. If you cannot find black walnuts, instead of using the English ones, use raisins dusted with flour (so they don't sink in the batter).

½ cup butter, softened

1 cup light brown sugar

½ cup molasses

3½ cups flour

2 teaspoons baking soda

½ teaspoon ground ginger

½ teaspoon ground cinnamon

½ teaspoon ground cloves

2 eggs

¾ cup chopped black walnuts

MAKES 1 LARGE LOAF OR
2 SMALLER LOAVES

1. Preheat oven to 350°F. Butter and flour one large loaf pan (10 by 4½ by 3 inches) or 2 standard-size bread pans (8 by 4 by 2½ inches).

2. Using an electric mixer, in a large bowl beat the butter until light. Gradually beat in the sugar, and then the molasses. Add 1 cup boiling water and stir to combine.

3. Sift together the flour, baking soda, ginger, cinnamon, and cloves. Stir into the molasses mixture until just barely mixed. Stir in the eggs, one at a time, then finally add the black walnuts. Spoon the batter into the prepared pan and bake until a toothpick inserted in the center comes out clean, about 1½ hours for the large loaf and 1 hour for the smaller ones. Cool on a wire rack. Store tightly wrapped.

Mary at the Farm and Book of Recipes by Edith M. Thomas

Brod Torte

CHOCOLATE AND RYE TORTE

This torte was devised by the thrifty Germans to use up stale rye bread.

1. Butter and flour an 8-inch cake pan. Preheat oven to 375°F.

2. Melt the chocolate in a bowl set over hot water. Let cool slightly.

3. Combine the yolks and sugar in a bowl and beat with an electric mixer until thick and light colored. Gradually beat in the chocolate and then the allspice and cloves.

4. In a clean bowl beat the whites along with the salt until soft peaks form. Fold $1/3$ of the whites into the yolk mixture, then fold in the remainder. Fold in the bread crumbs.

5. Spoon the batter into the prepared pan. Bake about 45 to 60 minutes, until a toothpick or skewer inserted into the cake comes out clean. Cool on a cake rack. Serve topped with lots of whipped cream.

Mary at the Farm and Book of Recipes by Edith M. Thomas

4 ounces unsweetened chocolate, broken into pieces

6 eggs, separated

1 cup sugar

1 teaspoon ground allspice

$1/2$ teaspoon ground cloves

Large pinch salt

1 cup finely ground bread crumbs, made from stale rye bread

Whipped cream

SERVES 8 TO 10

Black Walnuts

Black walnut trees were once plentiful all along the East Coast. Sadly, most of them were cut down to make furniture and few have been replanted. Black walnuts have a winey perfume that seems a distillation of the autumn woods; they have very little in common with "English" walnuts.

If you can find black walnuts shelled, buy them that way because they are tricky to extract from their rock-hard shells. It is easiest to crack them with a vise, though a hammer will do in a pinch. Keep the shelled nuts in the freezer because they quickly grow rancid.

A "Dutch" Recipe for Pumpkin Pie

Unlike almost every other American pumpkin pie recipe, this does not begin with a pumpkin purée. Rather, it is made like an apple pie, with thin slices of pumpkin cooking slowly as the pie is baked. Be sure to use a cooking pumpkin. Most of the large, pretty pumpkins sold in the United States are bland and watery and best suited for jack-o'-lanterns. Cooking pumpkins or "sugar pumpkins" are much smaller and more flavorful. The so-called "cheese pumpkins" are best; they have a squat shape and beige skin, and inside they are a brilliant orange. You can also substitute Hubbard or butternut squash.

1. On a floured surface, roll out half the pastry for a bottom crust and place in a 9-inch pie pan. Refrigerate.

2. Preheat oven to 425°F.

3. Cut the pumpkin in half. Scoop out the seeds, cut the flesh into large pieces, and slice them into long pieces 1 inch wide. Peel these with a vegetable peeler or paring knife. Slice the peeled pumpkin crosswise into ⅛-inch-thick pieces. Toss the pumpkin with the sugar, vinegar, flour, cinnamon, nutmeg, and cloves. Arrange in the pastry-lined shell.

4. Brush the edge of the dough with the beaten egg. Roll out the remaining dough and place on top of the filling. Crimp the edges. Cut vent holes in the top crust and brush with the egg.

5. Set the pie in the middle of the oven and bake 20 minutes. Reduce the oven temperature to 350°F and continue baking until the crust is golden brown and the pumpkin offers no resistance to a knife or skewer, about 1 hour more. Cool at least 2 hours before serving. Serve at room temperature or slightly warm.

Mary at the Farm and Book of Recipes by Edith M. Thomas

1 recipe pastry pie dough (page 81)

A 2½-pound cooking pumpkin

¾ cup dark brown sugar

2 tablespoons cider vinegar

2 tablespoons flour

½ teaspoon ground cinnamon

Large pinch grated nutmeg

Large pinch ground cloves

1 egg, beaten

SERVES 6 TO 8

Moravian Hickory Nut Cake

Hickory Pound Cake

The Moravian Brothers was one of the many sects that was driven out of Central Europe and settled in Pennsylvania. When they arrived here, they substituted hickory nuts for their familiar walnuts or hazelnuts. If you cannot locate hickory nuts, substitute their close relative, the pecan.

This is a classic pound cake enriched with brandy. In the days when the recipe was written, it would take at least an hour of continual beating by hand to make a pound cake. We are lucky to have electric mixers.

2 cups finely chopped hickory nuts (about ½ pound)

2 cups flour

1 cup butter, softened

2 cups sugar

7 eggs

¾ cup brandy

Serves 8 to 10

1. Preheat oven to 325°F. Butter and flour a 10-inch bundt pan.

2. Stir together the hickory nuts with ½ cup of the flour.

3. Using an electric mixer, in large bowl beat the butter until light. Add the sugar and continue beating until very light and creamy, at least 10 minutes. Add the eggs, one at a time, alternating with 1 tablespoon flour. Beat at least 2½ minutes after each addition. Fold in the remaining flour, then the hickory nuts and finally the brandy. Combine well.

4. Spoon the batter into the prepared pan. Set in the middle of the oven and bake 1½ hours, until a toothpick inserted in the center comes out clean. Cool on a wire rack.

Pennsylvania Dutch Cook Book of Fine Old Recipes by William Dorman and Leonard Davidow

Oatmeal Cookies

A German, Ferdinand Schumacher, first popularized oatmeal as a breakfast dish when, in 1856, he started his mill near Akron, Ohio. Up until then, most Americans of English extraction fed oats to horses or used them as medicine. At one time, oats were dispensed by the ounce, not at the grocer's, but at the apothecary, usually upon a doctor's prescription.

1. Beat the butter and sugar in a medium bowl until creamy. Beat in the egg. Sift together the flour, salt, cinnamon, cloves, soda, and nutmeg. Stir the dry ingredients into the butter mixture. Add the oats. Refrigerate the dough about 1 hour, or until firm enough to roll.

2. Preheat oven to 375°F.

3. On a well-floured board, roll out the dough slightly thicker than ⅛ inch. Using a round cookie cutter, cut into 2-inch cookies. Set the cookies on an ungreased cookie sheet, place in the middle of the oven, and bake until golden, 10 to 12 minutes. Cool on wire racks.

The Art of German Cooking and Baking by Lina Meier

¾ cup unsalted butter, softened

½ cup brown sugar

1 egg

1 cup flour

½ teaspoon salt

½ teaspoon ground cinnamon

¼ teaspoon ground cloves

¼ teaspoon baking soda

Large pinch grated nutmeg

1 cup rolled oats

MAKES ABOUT
3 DOZEN COOKIES

Almond Brod

ALMOND COOKIES

These are not bread (*Brod* in German), but little biscuits similar to Italian biscotti. The presence of olive oil in the recipe points to an origin in Southern Europe, even if the recipe did arrive on our shores by way of Germany. Like *biscotti*, these cookies keep well and are terrific for dunking.

³/₄ cup sugar

3 eggs

3 tablespoons olive oil

¹/₄ teaspoon almond extract

2¹/₂ cups flour

1¹/₂ teaspoons baking powder

Pinch salt

1¹/₂ cups almonds

MAKES ABOUT 30 COOKIES

1. Preheat oven to 400°F. Lightly sprinkle a cookie sheet with flour.

2. Beat the sugar and eggs together in a medium bowl. Beat in the olive oil and almond extract. Sift together the flour, baking powder, and salt. Stir the flour mixture into the egg mixture, mixing until smooth. Stir in the almonds.

3. Divide the dough into 4 pieces. Using lightly oiled hands, roll out each piece into a 15-inch-long roll. Set the rolls about 2 inches apart on the cookie sheet and bake until light brown, about 20 minutes.

4. While still warm, cut the rolls into 2-inch pieces. Cool. Store in an airtight container.

Mary at the Farm and Book of Recipes by Edith M. Thomas

Ginger Snaps

Beginning in the middle of the nineteenth century, ginger snaps were one of America's favorite cookies. This version has a little more spice than the average English-American recipe, but otherwise the recipe is much the same.

This recipe is from the Midwest rather than Pennsylvania. Mrs. Lina Meier wrote the bilingual *The Art of German Cooking and Baking* in Milwaukee and included the basics of both German and American cooking. The culinary heritage of these recent immigrants was much the same as that of the Pennsylvania Dutch.

1. In a medium bowl beat the butter and sugar until creamy. Gradually beat in the egg, molasses, and buttermilk. Sift together the flour, ginger, cinnamon, baking soda and cloves. Gradually stir into the butter mixture and mix until smooth. Gather into a ball, wrap in plastic wrap, and flatten slightly. Refrigerate about 1 hour, or until firm enough to roll.

2. Preheat oven to 400°F.

3. On a lightly floured board, roll out the dough very thin (less than ⅛ inch thick). Cut out cookies, using a plain or fancy cookie cutter. Set on ungreased cookie sheets and bake in the middle of the oven until golden, 8 to 10 minutes. Cool on wire racks.

The Art of German Cooking and Baking by Lina Meier

6 tablespoons butter, softened

⅓ cup light brown sugar

1 egg

⅓ cup unsulphured molasses

2 tablespoons buttermilk

2¼ cups flour

1½ teaspoons ground ginger

1 teaspoon ground cinnamon

¾ teaspoon baking soda

¼ teaspoon ground cloves

MAKES 6 TO 8 DOZEN
1½-INCH COOKIES

puntan las
as para los
eles.

Est

e demuestra donde se hizieron los banquetes, y se pu
esto dieron los naturales, á que assistió el Valiente Nam
os del gran Caltzontzi, y concurrieron los demas Cabos en

Dinner on the Range

Mexican Foods and Cowboy Ways

Many of the foods we associate with the Southwest were first encountered by the Spaniards when they met the native people of what we now call Texas.

Texas, 1925

While Texas may seem big today, it seemed even bigger in the days before railroads and interstates. In the past, long days and even weeks of dusty travel separated places with distinctive ways of cooking and eating. Folks in east Texas did not eat the same as they did down in Austin, and cowboys in central and north Texas sat down to different grub than did the Mexicans in El Paso. There were no dishes that we would recognize as Texan until well after the Civil War.

Yet centuries before, distinct ways of cooking existed throughout the territory, and cooking in Texas has a long and colorful history. The first Spanish missionaries who arrived in the sixteenth century were hosted by Native Americans who entertained them with dances and fed them tamales and cornmeal mush. Though the record does not mention it, chiles, beans, and game were sure to have been on the menu as well. When the Spanish conquered the territory, they established Santa Fe as their provincial capital. There, Spanish families set up haciendas where they tried to maintain their European ways, importing sugar, wine, olive oil, spices, and other luxuries in mule caravans from Mexico City over the long and tortuous Chihuahua Trail. But this wasn't a practical option for most of the population in this part of New Spain, especially in towns like El Paso and San Antonio, a long way from the governor's fashionable dinner parties. The people, culture, and food intermarried, intermingled, and were blended into what Mexicans call mestizo—part native and part conquistador. The resulting cuisine incorporated Spanish cheeses, pork, beef, and imported spices into the local diet of corn, chiles, beans, and tomatoes.

It was this Mexican style of cooking that pioneers from the newly formed United States encountered when they ventured into Texas, Arizona, California, and the other territories ruled from Mexico City. It is not difficult to guess the reaction of Anglo-Americans to the local food. We can take the opinion of a later northern visitor, touring Reconstruction-era Texas, as speaking for the earlier group: "[The Mexicans eat] various savory compounds," wrote Edward King in 1874, "swimming in fiery pepper, which biteth like a serpent; and the tortilla, a smoking hot cake, thin as a shaving, and about as eatable, is the substitute for bread."

However, few Americans got the chance to compare their pioneer rations of salt pork, molasses, and corn bread with tortillas and chiles, since most pioneers were entering from the east while the main Mexican settlements were in the south and west. The homesteaders' diet could certainly have used a little enriching. Frederick Law Olmsted, before taking up the career of landscape architect (his work was to include Central Park in New York City), traveled through the new state of Texas in the 1840s and was less than thrilled with the food he was served. In *A Journey Through Texas*, he describes one of his first encounters with pioneer hospitality: "[The hostess] placed upon the table a plate of cold, salt, fat pork; a cup of what to both eye and tongue seemed lard, but which she termed butter; a plate of very stale, dry, flaky, micaceous corn-bread; a jug of molasses and a pitcher of milk." He didn't do much better during the rest of his trip.

Yet while Olmsted was grumbling about his diet of salt pork and molasses in the backcountry, the port of Galveston offered restaurant menus rich with cakes and pies, shops selling platters of oysters, both raw and cooked, and confectioners serving up candies and ice cream. Just down the Gulf of Mexico, Corpus Christi had 200 barrooms in 1845 selling mostly whiskey and brandy but also imported gin, champagne, claret, and port.

In spite of Olmsted's reports, there was no shortage of meat on most Texas tables. Not only was there plenty of venison, buffalo, bear, wild turkeys, and assorted smaller birds, but the plains were home to numberless longhorn cattle and mustangs, originally from Spanish stock, but now thoroughly wild.

Most of the folks who arrived in east Texas came from the southern United States—Tennessee, in particular—but also Alabama, Louisiana, Georgia, and the Carolinas. With them, they brought the hybrid of African, Indian, and English cookery that had evolved into Southern cooking. Some years later, John Wayne crooned the praises of east Texas food in the movie *Rio Grande*, with a song about black-eyed peas, mustard greens, corn pone, and "chicken fried with a golden hide." What he—and real cowboys— remembered as they moved west was plantation food, as it had been cooked for generations by black cooks throughout the South.

Working a herd of longhorns.

In 1836, Texas became independent of Mexico (Americans outnumbered Mexicans four to one by that date), and by the late 1840s all of the Southwest had been seized by the United States. The Chihuahua Trail, which had connected Santa Fe to the Mexican capital, was replaced by the Sante Fe Trail, which led to Missouri. Annexation to the United States meant that a huge market was suddenly opened to Texas beef. To enterprising ranchers, the cattle were there for the roping. Spanish longhorn cattle had survived and prospered in the unforgiving climate of the Texas prairie because they were tough and resourceful at finding pasture and water. This hardiness made it possible to drive them on foot for thousands of miles to market. Before railroads and cattle cars shortened the cattle drives, Texas longhorns even walked as far as New York, with only a few stops along the way to fatten them up! Needless to say, the beef was far from fork-tender. Chicken fried steak—a piece of meat that is whacked until it is reasonably edible before being shallow fried—was one recipe developed to make those tough old longhorns palatable.

While the longhorns scrounged on the prairie, the cowboys brought along the chuck wagon, supplied with the pioneers' usual rations and manned by cooks who, on occasion, could summon up a bit of imagination. Many of the cooks were Mexican or black (as were the cowboys). The chuck wagons would go in advance of the cattle. When they set up camp, the cooks would often stew beef with beans and chile and bake sourdough biscuits in a Dutch oven. If the cook was ambitious, leftover dough might be made into a pudding, or dried apples reconstituted to make a pie.

The stews cooked on the trail were similar to chili con carne, one dish everyone agrees is Texan through and through. No lesser person than LBJ suggested that chili be made the state food of Texas. (Mexicans actively disavow it.) The first documentary evidence of chili appears in 1828, when it was described as "a kind of hash with nearly as many peppers as there are pieces of meat." Nevertheless, even after the Civil War the taste for chili was not universal. Writing in 1885, Alexander Sweet, a Texas journalist, gave a tongue-in-cheek description of a chili experience in San Antonio:

After the shades of night have begun to fall, the visitor who strolls around that ancient [Military Plaza], that has so oft resounded to the clash of arms between Spanish cavaliers and the Indian hordes, will observe campfires. He will see an array of tables and benches, and he will be assailed by the smell of something cooking. At the fire are numerous pots and kettles, around which are dusky female figures, and faces that are suggestive of "the weird sisters" whose culinary proclivities were such a source of annoyance to MacBeth [sic].

These are the chile con carne stands, at which this toothsome viand is sold to all who have the money and inclination to patronize them.

Chile con carne is a dish which literally means "pepper with meat". …There is nothing hotter than these little red chile peppers with which the Mexican seasons everything he eats.

There is a refreshing candor displayed in calling this Aztec symposium "pepper with meat," for the pepper is the most conspicuous feature of the entertainment. The innocent stranger who takes a mouthful of chile con carne never inquires what the other ingredients are. His only thought is how to obtain the services of the fire department to put out the fire in the roof of his mouth. The incandescent glow is almost as heated as is the language he uses after his mouth has sufficiently cooled down to enable him to use it for conventional purposes.

Mexican supper on the San Antonio Military Plaza around 1890.

To relish chile con carne when eaten for the first time, it is indispensable that the would-be junketer have his throat lined with some uncombustible substance, and a ceiling of fire-proof bricks inserted in the roof of his mouth.

And yet there are many Americans and others, who become accustomed to this kind of diet, and absorb it into their systems without exhibiting any more emotion than is visible at an ice cream festival, and who send up their plates for more.

Just a few years later, this "toothsome viand" represented Texas at the 1893 Columbian Exposition in Chicago. In 1908, chili hit the national market when William Gebhardt started putting it into cans.

It was only after the First World War that recipe collections in Texas began to have a distinctively regional voice. Even then what you ate depended on where you ate it: The east retained its Southern heritage of fried chicken and pecan pies, the west its cowboy traditions of the chuck wagon and barbecue, and the south its Mexican foodways. The last gave birth to a way of cooking that would later be called Tex-Mex, a mixture of American and northern Mexican influences. A similar style could be found throughout the Southwest (and is still found today in

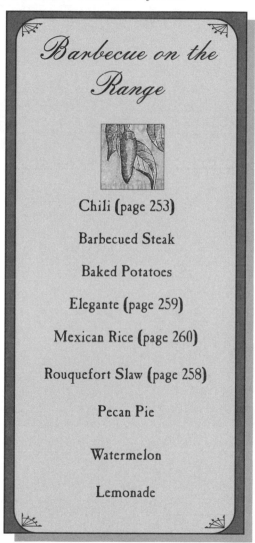

Barbecue on the Range

Chili (page 253)

Barbecued Steak

Baked Potatoes

Elegante (page 259)

Mexican Rice (page 260)

Rouquefort Slaw (page 258)

Pecan Pie

Watermelon

Lemonade

restaurants in cities across the country). In the 1920s and '30s, we see for the first time Mexican-style recipes in cookbooks from Houston to Hollywood. To most Anglos, though, chili and enchiladas remained special-occasion foods or foods that you ate at the local Mexican joint. Folks in Texas, or for that matter through-out the Southwest ate, like the majority of Americans, a day-to-day diet of steak and potatoes, with strawberry shortcake for dessert. Of course in the longhorn state, the steak was Texas-size.

Shrimp Balls with Cactus Leaves
POTATO SHRIMP BALLS WITH NOPALITOS

The portrait Arthur and Bobbie Coleman give of regional Texas cooking in *The Texas Cookbook* was way ahead of its time. They were sticklers for authenticity and refused to make allowances for the fact that chiles and other local ingredients were totally unavailable outside of the Southwest in the 1940s. Today, foods like cactus leaves *(nopalitos)* and Mexican husk tomatoes *(tomatillos)* are readily available across the country, not only in Hispanic markets but even in many fancy food stores—but imagine how outlandishly exotic they would have seemed in most of the United States just after World War II!

1. Cook the potatoes in lightly salted boiling water to cover until soft. Drain and mash; cool. Stir in the shrimp, butter, egg, and cream. Season with salt and pepper to taste. Chill in the refrigerator until firm, at least 30 minutes. Using well-floured hands, roll the potato mixture into about 20 balls, each the size of a golf ball. Roll in flour.

2. To make the sauce, heat 1 tablespoon of the lard or oil in a small saucepan, add the onion, and sauté it until soft and transparent. Add the tomatoes and nopalitos and simmer 5 minutes.

3. To fry the shrimp balls, heat the remaining lard or oil in a large skillet over moderately high heat. When hot, add the balls and fry until brown on all sides, about 8 to 10 minutes. Drain on paper towels.

4. Meanwhile, toast the pumpkin seeds by placing them in a small skillet over moderate heat and tossing them until lightly browned.

5. To serve, pour the sauce over the shrimp balls and sprinkle them with the toasted pumpkin seeds.

The Texas Cookbook by Arthur and Bobbie Coleman

1½ pounds Russet potatoes, peeled and quartered
1 cup dry shredded shrimp (available in Hispanic and Asian markets)
3 tablespoons butter, melted
1 egg, beaten
1 tablespoon heavy cream
Salt
Pepper
Flour, for dredging
½ cup lard, or substitute peanut oil
½ cup chopped onion
1 cup drained canned tomatoes, chopped
1 cup chopped canned nopalitos, drained (available in Hispanic markets)
2 tablespoons pumpkin seeds

SERVES 4

Tamale Pie

CORNMEAL SAUSAGE PIE

Tamale pie is as authentically Tex-Mex as chili con carne. There are numerous variations on this casserole of cornmeal and meat, some using chili as a base, others using the same masa meal that Mexicans use for real tamales. Either way, it is a homey meal that may lack the complexity of tamales steamed in corn husks, but then again it does not take hours to prepare.

1 teaspoon vegetable oil
¹/₂ pound sausage meat or Mexican *chorizo*, crumbled
¹/₂ pound ground beef
2 tablespoons chili powder
1 large garlic clove, minced
¹/₂ cup cornmeal
1 cup milk
¹/₂ cup tomato juice
2 eggs
¹/₄ teaspoon salt

SERVES 4 TO 5

1. Preheat oven to 375°F.

2. Heat the oil in a large skillet over moderately high heat. Add the sausage and beef and cook until browned and cooked through, about 8 to 10 minutes. Add the chili powder and garlic and cook 1 more minute. Drain off any excess fat. Spoon into a 9-inch pie plate.

3. Combine the cornmeal, milk, tomato juice, eggs, and salt and stir until smooth. Pour over the meat mixture. Set in the oven and bake until firm and golden, about 30 minutes. Serve hot.

Favorite Recipes of Colfax County Club Women compiled by the Colfax County Home Demonstration Clubs

Chili

By the 1920s, the spicy stew called chili con carne was already a Lone Star State institution. There is no end to the arguments about what does and does not belong in chili. Today, some purists insist that only chili powder and meat (with perhaps a grace note of onions and garlic) should ever enter the recipe. They insist that the frequent addition of both beans and tomatoes is inauthentic. They might be surprised to know that every one of the half-dozen recipes for chili that appeared in *The Junior League of Dallas Cook Book* in the 1930s has beans in it. Some of the recipes use ground beef, others finely cubed beef, another source of great controversy among "chili heads." Most of the recipes use tomatoes in one form or another.

This particular chili is unique in that the beans are fully cooked separately from the meat and the beef is cooked only briefly. Mrs. Devereux Dunlap, who contributed the recipe, recommends cutting the meat into small pieces, using kitchen scissors.

1. Cover the dried beans with water and soak overnight. Drain.

2. The following day, fry the bacon in a deep saucepan until crisp. Pour off the fat and reserve. Add the beans, and cover with 5 cups fresh water and the tomato soup. Cook until the beans are tender, about 1 hour. Add the chili powder, cumin, and garlic and continue cooking 10 more minutes.

3. Cut the steak into ¼-inch pieces. Season with salt and dredge lightly in flour. Heat the reserved bacon fat in a large skillet, add the meat, in two batches, and fry until well browned. Set aside.

4. Add the onions to the skillet and cook until golden. Add the reserved meat and onions to the beans, season with salt and cayenne pepper to taste, bring to a boil, and simmer 10 minutes.

The Junior League of Dallas Cook Book compiled and edited by Members of the Dallas Chapter of the Association of Junior Leagues of America

1½ cups dried pinto beans

½ pound lean bacon, diced

One 10¾-ounce can condensed tomato soup

3 tablespoons chili powder

2 tablespoons ground cumin

1 large garlic clove, minced

2 pounds round steak

Salt

About 4 tablespoons flour, for dredging

2 medium onions, finely chopped

Cayenne pepper

SERVES 6

Enchiladas in Green Sauce

Tomatillos are used frequently in Mexican cooking. Resembling small green tomatoes enclosed in papery husks, they are usually cooked before they are added to a recipe. To cook, simply remove the husks, place the fruit in a saucepan, cover with water, and bring to a boil. Turn off the heat and let stand in the hot water for 10 minutes. You can substitute canned *tomatillos*, available in most Hispanic markets, with little loss of flavor.

¼ cup olive oil

12 corn tortillas

1 pound ground pork

1 medium onion, cut in half

1 cup cooked whole *tomatillos* (see introduction to recipe)

1 cup cooked spinach, chopped

3 canned green chiles, coarsely chopped (one 4-ounce can)

2 garlic cloves, chopped

1 cup chicken broth

1 teaspoon dried oregano

Salt

Pepper

1 cup grated Monterey Jack cheese

SERVES 4

1. Heat the oil in a large skillet over moderately high heat. When hot, add the tortillas, one at a time, frying each for about 10 to 12 seconds per side. Soften all the tortillas in this way, blotting them on paper towels as they are done. Wrap in foil and keep warm.

2. Add a little more oil to the skillet if necessary. Add the pork and fry until light brown. Drain well. Reserve the pork and keep warm.

3. While the pork cooks, combine half the onion, coarsely chopped, the *tomatillos*, spinach, chiles, garlic, chicken broth, and oregano in a blender and blend until puréed. Pour the sauce into the pan, bring to a boil, and cook at a gentle simmer for 20 minutes.

4. Chop the remaining half onion. Mix half of the chopped onion with half of the cheese and add to the pork. Season with salt and pepper.

5. To serve, dip the tortillas, one at a time, into the green sauce. Fill with ¹/₁₂ of the pork filling along with a tablespoon of the sauce. Roll the tortilla up and set on a warm platter. When all of the tortillas have been filled and rolled, cover them with the remaining sauce and sprinkle with the remaining cheese and onion. Serve hot. (The enchiladas can be heated for 10 to 15 minutes in a 400°F oven.)

Fashions in Foods in Beverly Hills compiled by the Beverly Hills Woman's Club

Spanish Chicken

CHICKEN STEWED WITH TOMATOES AND CHILES

According to *Fashions in Foods in Beverly Hills*, Spanish chicken was the favorite dish of silent screen stars Mary Pickford and Constance Bennett. This version comes from Miss Bennett.

1. Preheat oven to 350°F.

2. Stir together the flour, salt, pepper, and thyme. Dredge the chicken in the seasoned flour. Heat the oil in a large flameproof casserole over moderately high heat. Add the chicken pieces and fry until browned on all sides. Pour off the fat. Add the onions, parsley, celery, garlic, and chile to the pan. Add ¾ cup water. Cover, set in the oven, and bake until the chicken is tender, about 45 minutes.

3. Remove the cover, arrange the tomatoes over the chicken, and sprinkle with the cheese and paprika. Place the casserole, uncovered, in the oven and bake 15 minutes longer. Serve hot.

Fashions in Foods in Beverly Hills compiled by the Beverly Hills Woman's Club

½ cup flour

1 teaspoon salt

1 teaspoon pepper

1 teaspoon powdered thyme

A 3½-pound chicken, cut into 8 pieces

¼ cup olive oil

3 small onions, peeled and cut in half

1 tablespoon chopped fresh parsley

1 tablespoon chopped celery

2 garlic cloves, minced

1 dried New Mexican or Anaheim chile, stemmed, seeded, and crumbled fine

1 large tomato, sliced

1 cup grated Monterey Jack cheese

½ teaspoon paprika

SERVES 3 TO 4

Guisado de Cabrito
SPICY KID STEW

Baby goat, or kid, is very popular in northern Mexico, where it is often spit-roasted or barbecued. It is also found north of the Rio Grande. The flavor of young goat is similar to lamb, though real Texans will probably tell you that it is a whole lot tastier. This dish is essentially a chili con carne, and another meat such as lamb or beef could be substituted, though with some loss of flavor. The recipe's authors suggest that the two pounds of meat "ought to do for two or three." Non-Texans might be inclined to make the portions a little smaller.

1 tablespoon lard, or substitute peanut oil

2 pounds boneless stewing kid, cut into 1-inch pieces

1 cup tomatillos, husked and chopped (for procedure see page 254)

2 medium onions, chopped

2 Ancho chiles, ground, or ¼ cup chili powder

1 large garlic clove, minced

½ teaspoon ground cumin

Large pinch dried oregano

Salt

SERVES 3 TO 4

Heat the lard in a large flameproof casserole over high heat. Add the kid and cook until browned on all sides. Add 2¼ cups of water, the *tomatillos*, onions, ground chile, garlic, cumin, oregano, and salt to taste. Bring to a boil and simmer, uncovered, until the meat is very tender, about 1½ hours.

The Texas Cookbook by Arthur and Bobbie Coleman

Spanish Meat Loaf

MEAT LOAF WITH CHILE

In her *Mexican Cookbook*, Erna Fergusson describes a New Mexico of old Spanish families and traditional ways that, in 1934, were already disappearing. Much of her book pays homage to typical Mexican dishes like tamales and *buñuelos* (Mexican doughnuts), but other recipes, like this meat loaf, show a blend of Anglo and Mexican traditions.

1. Roast the chile over an open flame until charred but not too burnt all over. Place in a plastic bag and let steam for 15 minutes. Peel and wash. Remove the stem and seeds. Purée in a blender or food processor.

2. Heat the vegetable oil in a small skillet. Add the onion and garlic and sauté until softened, about 5 minutes. Do not brown.

3. Preheat oven to 400°F. Lightly butter a deep roasting pan.

4. Combine the ground beef and pork, onion and garlic mixture, beaten egg, bread crumbs, milk, and puréed chile in a large bowl. Add salt and pepper to taste. Cut off about ¼ inch of each end of the hard-boiled eggs. Fit the eggs end to end and wrap with the meat mixture. Form into a long loaf.

5. To make the biscuit dough, stir together the flour, baking powder, and salt. Add the butter and, using a knife, cut it into the flour until it is in very small pieces. Add the milk and stir until the dough just combines. Roll the dough out on a lightly floured board until it is about ¼ inch thick. Wrap the meat loaf in the dough, and set it seam side down in the prepared pan.

6. Bake the meat loaf 10 minutes, then reduce the heat to 350°F. Cover loosely with foil and continue baking until cooked through, about 1½ hours.

Mexican Cookbook by Erna Fergusson

---

1 large fresh Ancho or Anaheim chile

1 tablespoon vegetable oil

1 onion, finely chopped

1 garlic clove, minced

1 pound ground beef

¾ pound ground pork

1 egg, lightly beaten

1 cup bread crumbs

¼ cup milk

Salt

Pepper

3 hard-boiled eggs, shelled

BISCUIT DOUGH

2 cups flour

4 teaspoons baking powder

½ teaspoon salt

2 tablespoons butter

¾ cup milk

SERVES 6 TO 8

Rouquefort Slaw
COLESLAW WITH BLUE CHEESE DRESSING

Mrs. Earl Hulsey, who contributed this coleslaw to *The Junior League of Dallas Cook Book*, notes that it is excellent with chili. She knew her stuff.

½ head cabbage, finely shredded

1 cup mayonnaise

¼ pound Roquefort cheese, at room temperature, in pieces

1 garlic clove, chopped

2 tablespoons lemon juice

½ teaspoon paprika

Salt

SERVES 6 TO 8

1. Cover the cabbage with ice water and soak ½ hour, or until crisp.

2. Combine the mayonnaise, Roquefort, garlic, lemon juice, and paprika in a blender and blend until smooth. Season with salt.

3. Drain the cabbage well, pressing out the water. Toss with the dressing. Serve immediately.

The Junior League of Dallas Cook Book compiled and edited by Members of the Dallas Chapter of the Association of Junior Leagues of America

Barbacoa de Armadillo

¼ cup celery seed
¼ cup paprika
½ teaspoon sesame seed
6 dried chiletipines [a type of chile]
1 tablespoon chili powder
2 tablespoons salt

Mix ingredients well, put into a large shaker, and use as needed. Dress the armadillo and place on the grid. Sear. Sprinkle with barbecue mixture several times while it is cooking. When done, remove from the fire. Pour 2 tablespoons of hot catsup over each serving. This mix is equally good with spareribs.

The Texas Cookbook by Arthur and Bobbie Coleman

Elegante

CHILE AND SQUASH STEW

Like the succotash of the East Coast, this vegetable stew probably has a Native American source. Use a dry goat cheese such as *ranchero seco*, if you can get it; otherwise, feta will give a similar salty bite.

1. Roast the chile over an open flame until charred but not too burnt all over. Place in a plastic bag and let steam for 15 minutes. Peel and wash. Remove the stem and seeds. Purée in a blender or food processor.

2. Heat the oil in a large saucepan over moderate heat. Add the onion and garlic and sauté 2 minutes. Add the squash and continue sautéing 2 more minutes. Add the chile purée, corn, tomato, mint, and coriander and continue cooking 6 minutes. Add the milk and cook, uncovered, at a bare simmer until the squash is very tender and the sauce is thickened, about 40 minutes. Stir occasionally. Stir in the goat cheese. Season with salt.

Mexican Cookbook by Erna Fergusson

---

1 small fresh ancho or Anaheim chile

1 tablespoon peanut oil

1 small onion, chopped

1 garlic clove, minced

2 pounds summer squash, cut into 1-inch dice

½ cup corn kernels

1 large ripe tomato, peeled and diced

1 teaspoon chopped fresh mint

1 teaspoon chopped fresh coriander

1 cup milk

¼ cup dry goat cheese, crumbled

Salt

SERVES 4 TO 6

Mexican Rice

TOMATO RICE WITH CHORIZO

Fashions in Foods in Beverly Hills credits Ramon Novarro for this dish. The actor, best known for his starring role in the first *Ben Hur*, was born in Mexico.

1 tablespoon lard, or substitute peanut oil

1 cup long-grain rice

1 cup tomato juice

Salt

Pepper

½ pound Mexican *chorizo*

Sliced pimiento, for garnish

Chopped parsley

SERVES 4 AS A SIDE DISH

1. Heat the lard or oil in a small saucepan over moderate heat. Add the rice and sauté, stirring, until golden, about 2 minutes. Add the tomato juice and 1 cup water. Season with salt and pepper to taste. Bring to a boil, cover, reduce the heat, and simmer until all the water is absorbed, about 15 minutes. Let rest 10 minutes.

2. Crumble the *chorizo* and in a small skillet and fry it until browned. Drain.

3. To serve, spoon the rice into a dish and top with the *chorizo*. Garnish with the pimiento and parsley.

Fashions in Foods in Beverly Hills compiled by the Beverly Hills Woman's Club

Honey Fudge
CHOCOLATE HONEY FUDGE

As settlers moved into Texas from the East, they brought with them their favorite recipes for desserts and candy. Honey makes this fudge slightly chewy.

1. Combine the sugar, chocolate, honey, and cream in a heavy saucepan over low heat. Stir until the chocolate has melted and the mixture is smooth. Continue cooking until the mixture reaches 236°F on a candy thermometer, or forms a soft ball when dropped into cold water.

2. Butter an 8-inch square baking pan.

3. Transfer the fudge to a large bowl. Stir occasionally until it starts to thicken, then beat with a wooden spoon until thick and creamy. Stir in the nuts. Pour into the prepared pan, spreading it evenly. Chill. When firm, cut into small squares. Store in an airtight container.

Favorite Recipes of Colfax County Club Women compiled by the Colfax County Home Demonstration Clubs, Colfax County, New Mexico

2¼ cups sugar

1½ ounces unsweetened chocolate, broken into pieces

½ cup honey

1 cup light cream

1 cup pecans, coarsely chopped

MAKES ABOUT
2 POUNDS OF FUDGE

Quick Chocolate

NEW MEXICAN HOT CHOCOLATE

Chocolate was popular as a drink long before it was a candy or ice cream. Cortez reported that the Aztec elite drank chocolate. The Spaniards added sugar and other spices to the potion. It took the Americans to add marshmallows.

4 cups milk

1½ ounces unsweetened chocolate, broken into pieces

4 tablespoons sugar

¼ teaspoon ground cinnamon

Large pinch ground nutmeg

Very small pinch salt

6 marshmallows, cut into quarters

¼ teaspoon almond extract, or ¼ teaspoon vanilla extract

SERVES 4

1. Bring the milk to a boil.

2. In a separate pan, bring ½ cup water to a boil. Add the chocolate, sugar, cinnamon, nutmeg, and salt and simmer, stirring, until dissolved.

3. Combine the hot milk with the chocolate mixture, marshmallows, and almond or vanilla extract. Beat until the marshmallows are dissolved. Serve immediately.

Mexican Cookbook by Erna Fergusson

Texas Barbecue

While Texans hold no monopoly on barbecue, they have a great passion for it. Arthur and Bobbie Coleman, in *The Texas Cookbook*, pay tribute to the Lone Star State's love for the grill.

Wherever it started, barbecue as a food and barbecuing as an art and the barbecue as a social function have been carried to their highest development in Texas. Anyone who cares to risk his life arguing the point is free to do so. Whenever in Texas an individual or a group want to celebrate something, a barbecue is forthcoming. It may be a politician running, or just thinking about running, for office. It may be a rancher who has finally paid off the mortgage. It may be a church trying to raise funds. It sometimes is a house-warming. On occasion it is simply a bunch of city fellers and their girls having a picnic. Or it could be a real-estate outfit opening a new subdivision. And if there is nothing to celebrate, it may be a couple or two sweating over a "barbecue pit"—anything from a hole in the ground with some chicken wire over it to an elaborate, "scientifically" built brick structure or a fancy high-priced steel contraption that folds up at night—because they are hungry for barbecue.

Big feeds used to be free, and a rare one still is. The affairs were pretty elaborate, too—some of them more so than today. At a barbecue at Marble Falls, on the Colorado, in July, 1854, [an eyewitness] found that "some of the Mormon ladies who were famous cooks had prepared the bread. Old man Hirston...was put down of a wagon load of roasting ears....Other farmers brought loads of watermelons and cantaloupes, together with such vegetables as were on hand. Huntsmen brought in venison and wild turkeys, and beef and pork galore were advanced....There were wild grape pies and dewberry pies and wild plum pies." The ground "was carpeted with sawdust" and the people danced till the next morning.

Food for Sale

Premium Cookbooks and Their Legacy

The Story of Crisco encouraged the young to introduce their elders to modern ways.

Cincinnati, 1927

In 1912, the Procter & Gamble Company of Cincinnati, Ohio—until then best known as the manufacturer of Ivory, "the soap so pure that it floats"—unveiled "An Absolutely New Product. A Scientific Discovery Which [would] Affect Every Kitchen in America. Something that the American housewife had always wanted." The company had developed hydrogenated vegetable shortening, better known as Crisco.

For Crisco to succeed, the manufacturer had to convince American cooks to give up the lard they had cooked with for generations. And Procter & Gamble did it. Using every marketing technique then available, they actually changed an essential component of the American diet.

The company knew from the start that it would take more than magazine ads to change the way people cooked. So as soon as Crisco came on the market, you could send away for a free copy of *Tested Crisco Recipes*, a pamphlet of a hundred recipes and "the interesting story of Crisco's discovery and manufacture." A year later, in 1913, the pamphlet was expanded to 250 recipes and entitled *The Story of Crisco*. For ten cents, consumers could get a deluxe cloth-bound edition that featured an additional 365 days' worth of menus, and recipes to go with each. The introduction to

The Story of Crisco predicted a glorious destiny for hydrogenated vegetable shortening:

> Crisco has been a shock to the older generation, born in an age less progressive than our own, and prone to contend that the old fashioned things are good enough. But these good folk, when convinced, are the greatest enthusiasts. The modern woman is glad to stop cooking with expensive butter, animal lard and their inadequate substitutes.

> And so the nation's cook book has been hauled out and is being revised. Upon thousands of pages, the words "lard" and "butter" have been crossed out and the word "Crisco" written in their place.

Though promotional cookbooks were the cornerstone of Procter & Gamble's strategy, they did not stand alone. The company sought the endorsements of celebrity chefs, home economists, and nutritionists. In *The Story of Crisco,* two authorities were quoted extolling the virtues of fat, specifically in the form of Crisco. "Girls, especially, show at times a dislike for fat," they wrote. "It therefore is necessary that the fat which supplies their growing bodies with energy should be in the purest and most inviting form and should be one that their digestions welcome, rather than repel." The concept of calories had recently become widely known, and the consensus was that children could seldom have enough of them. And since fat had the greatest concentration of calories, it was the most desirable food. Mothers were assured that "[Children] may eat Crisco doughnuts or pie without being chased by nightmares [since] sweet dreams follow the Crisco supper." Even religious authority was invoked: Rabbi Margolies of New York was quoted stating that "the Hebrew Race has been waiting 4,000 years for Crisco."

Although Procter & Gamble may have been exaggerating the place of their product in history, it is true that new packaged foods of all kinds were causing a revolutionary change for the American cook. Previously, almost all food was made at home from scratch or purchased locally. In the late 1800s you could buy a limited number of foods at a grocery store. There were no supermarkets, no national brands, and virtually no packaged goods. Flour was sold

The Boston Cooking School

When the Woman's Education Association founded the Boston Cooking School in 1879, they just wanted to introduce a little modernity and science into the home. They could not have dreamed of the influence the institution would have on American cooking. (One of the Association's other projects was to open the doors of Harvard and MIT to women.) At first the school was intended to inculcate working-class women and domestics in "rational" cookery, that is, a system of preparing food based on careful measurement and nutritional theory (as it was then understood) and certainly not on the frivolous basis of taste. But the courses became so popular that most were being filled by ladies of "the better classes."

The school built a national following through its "Normal" courses designed to graduate cooking teachers. These classes offered a taste of modern science—a field denied to most Victorian women. The six-month program included Psychology, Physiology and Hygiene, Bacteriology, Foods, Laundry Work, and the Chemistry of Soap, Bluing and Starch. Another two classes focused on teaching. Only one course, called Laboratory Practice, involved actual cooking. The students weren't even allowed to eat the food because that would have been considered indelicate. They were, however, grudgingly permitted to taste the recipes they had made.

The graduates were in great demand all over the country. As they founded schools, they spread the Boston Cooking School ideology throughout America. Many graduates went to work for schools, hospitals, and prisons; others chose to lecture. But those who were to have the greatest influence went to work for the large Midwestern food manufacturers, developing their recipes, holding public demonstrations, and, in general, convincing the public to use their employer's products in recipes derived from their alma mater. Many Boston Cooking School instructors had lucrative careers endorsing products.

The school became even more famous when Fannie Farmer took over the helm in 1893. Farmer, who combined an enthusiasm for cooking with a very modern, precise approach (she is considered the mother of level measurement), later wrote one of the best-selling cookbooks of all time; her *Boston Cooking School Cookbook*, first published in 1896, had sold over 360,000 copies by the time she died in 1915. Some 3 million copies have sold since.

out of great bins. Oats were simply called oats, cornmeal was cornmeal. The wary shopper would examine a product, smell it, taste it, and, if satisfactory, buy the desired quantity. With the coming of the railroads, this began to change. National wholesalers set up shop, mostly in the burgeoning Midwest, and started selling food all over the country. Canned goods appeared on the shelves of grocery stores. The ubiquitous biscuit barrel now contained brand-named Uneeda biscuits; a shopper could request Purina flour.

The manufacturers had to figure out a way to imprint their brand names on the public's consciousness. They tried all kinds of gimmicks. At the 1904 St. Louis World's Fair, for example, the Quaker Company introduced Quaker Puffed Rice by shooting it from eight bronze cannons. A more conventional approach was to place food ads in the women's magazines and on billboards. In addition, the companies offered an assortment of promotions for both consumer and shopkeeper. Various premiums, especially premium cookbooks, were a huge hit. An early pamphlet, *The Vital Question Cook Book*, produced by the Shredded Wheat Company, had sixteen editions of 250,000 copies each by 1902.

Similar promotional techniques had been used by patent medicine peddlers for at least two generations. Self-help cures made of questionable if not dangerous ingredients were wildly popular in the late 1800s. (The most successful of these, Coca-Cola, contained both alcohol and cocaine in one of its earliest incarnations. It was initially marketed as a cure for hangovers and headaches.) Cookbooks often served as a medium for advertising assorted brands of snake oil—even if the product had nothing to do with food and was not used in the recipes. For example, in *The Family Cookbook* from the Kickapoo Indian Medicine Company, a recipe for blueberry cake on one page is next to testimonials that "Kickapoo Indian Sagwa cures General Debility, Female Diseases, Nervousness, Sleeplessness, Melancholy, Malaria, Fever and Ague...." The potion had as little to do with cooking as it did with Indians or medicine.

"The Home of Shredded Wheat" in Niagara Falls.

At first, the food companies imitated the patent medicine cookbooks, publishing pamphlets that included popular recipes of the day whether they used the company's product or not. That soon changed. In *The Story of Crisco,* every single recipe prominently featured vegetable shortening. The book even uses Crisco as a verb, instructing readers to "Crisco" a sheet tin. By the 1920s, there were thousands of cookbooks promoting everything from chocolate and baking powder to hot sauce and marshmallows. Some of them were good, others weird, and many have had a tremendous impact on what Americans have cooked and eaten ever since.

The better premium cookbooks were written by prominent cooking teachers, many of whom were associated with the new home economics (or domestic science) schools that were in vogue. Seeing an opportunity, the manufacturers were often the money behind these institutions. However, it would be unfair to characterize the women who promoted domestic science as entirely in the pay of the large food companies. The teachers genuinely believed that mass-manufactured food was better because, to them, it signified progress, modernity, and science. They saw the Armour canned meat, Heinz pickles, Fleischmann's yeast, Cleveland baking powder, Kellogg's Corn Flakes, and Crisco shortening that came from factories in Chicago, Pittsburgh, Cleveland, Cincinnati, and Battle Creek, Michigan, as critical ingredients in making the home a more economical and rational place. They envisioned a day when, with the aid of industrial America, women would be freed from the drudgery of the kitchen.

Nevertheless, not everyone was enthusiastic about the new packages on their grocers' shelves, and often with good reason. For decades, many mass-marketed products had been adulterated and colored with poisonous chemicals. Even when public pressure convinced Congress to pass a pure food bill in 1906, many people did not trust food they couldn't examine or taste. As late as 1912 a grocers' magazine claimed that "many people are afraid of canned goods because of sensational stories which are repeatedly printed about them."

It was also at this time that germs were beginning to get attention, though most people did not know what they actually were. To allay their customers' fears, companies organized tours of their establishments. Many a honeymoon couple rounded out their visit to Niagara Falls by touring the Shredded Wheat Factory, the "cleanest, most hygienic food

A Cincinnati Luncheon

Shrimp Salad

Rabbit Pudding (page 274)

Macaroni and Cheese (page 277)

Creamed Spinach

Lettuce Salad

Astor House Rolls (page 278)

Apricot Ginger Upside-Down Cake (page 282)

Pear Marlow (page 290)

Coffee, Soft Drinks

factory in the world," as a souvenir postcard described it. By 1907, 100,000 visitors were touring the facility annually. *The Story of Crisco* describes Procter & Gamble's factory for hydrogenated vegetable shortening in words appropriate for a temple:

> It would be difficult to imagine surroundings more appetizing that those in which Crisco is manufactured. It is made in a building devoted exclusively to the manufacture of this one product. In sparkling bright rooms, cleanly uniformed employees make and pack Crisco.
>
> The air for this building is drawn in through an apparatus which washes and purifies it, removing the possibility of any dust entering.
>
> The floors are of a special tile composition; the walls are of white glazed tile, which are washed regularly. White enamel covers metal surfaces where nickel plating cannot be used. Sterilized machines handle the oil and the finished product. No hand touches Crisco until in your own kitchen the sanitary can is opened, disclosing the smooth richness, the creamlike, appetizing consistency of the product.

The results of marketing campaigns like Procter & Gamble's must have outpaced even their most ambitious goals. For not only were women in Maine and Maryland no longer rendering lard for their apple pie crust, but as far away as Alaska, Yup'ik and Inupiaq women were now using Crisco instead of caribou fat or seal oil to make the berry confection known as *akutaq*.

"Now, Bridget, here were a lot of 'left-overs' going to waste in your refrigerator"
—a lesson in household management from Durkee's salad dressing.

Salt Cod, Southern Style
SALT COD STEWED WITH PEPPERS

In spite of the fondness Mrs. Rorer shared with her generation for white sauce (she once advised immersing a boiled chicken in a bed of popcorn and smothering the entire creation in white sauce), she allowed herself to dally in the exotic world of spice when it came to her Tabasco sauce project. Not only did she include hot sauce in savory dishes like this one, she even managed to add a few drops of Tabasco to sweets.

1. Wash the cod, cover with cold water, and soak overnight in the refrigerator to remove excess salt. Drain.

2. Heat the olive oil in a medium flameproof casserole over moderate heat. Add the onion and green and red peppers and sauté, stirring, until softened, about 5 minutes. Add the wine, potatoes, ½ cup water, Tabasco, and salt cod. Cover, bring to a boil, and simmer gently until the fish is tender, about 40 minutes.

McIlhenny's Tabasco Sauce Recipes by Sarah Tyson Rorer

1 pound salt cod, cut into 2-inch squares

2 tablespoons olive oil

1 onion, chopped

1 green bell pepper, cored, seeded, and chopped

1 red bell pepper, cored, seeded, and chopped

1 cup dry white wine

1 pound red-skinned potatoes, peeled and cut into ¾-inch dice

10 drops Tabasco, or more to taste

SERVES 3 TO 4

Rabbit Pudding

RABBIT POT PIE

Sarah Tyson Rorer of the Philadelphia Cooking School was a one-person promotional whirlwind, not only penning a cookbook for McIlhenny's Tabasco sauce from which this recipe is adapted, but also assembling recipe collections for a meat grinder and ice-cream manufacturer, a patent egg-beater company, Shredded Wheat, and Wesson Oil. She endorsed numerous products as a food columnist and popular lecturer.

This is a classic pot pie recipe made with rabbit (the terms pie and pudding were often used for similar dishes in the nineteenth century). It is just barely enlivened with a little hot sauce; your contemporary palate may wish to increase the Tabasco. The dish can also be made with chicken, skinned and cut into 2-inch pieces.

The Triumph of the Can-Opener

By the 1920s, canned food had replaced whole categories of comestibles. Writing in 1924, an early historian of the canning industry was thrown into rapture in contemplation of the can-filled pantry:

Canning gives the American family—especially in cities and factory towns—a kitchen garden where all good things grow, and where it is always harvest time. There are more tomatoes in a ten-cent can than could be bought in city markets for that sum when tomatoes are at their cheapest, and this is true of most other tinned foods. A regular Arabian Nights garden, where raspberries, apricots, olives, and pineapples, always ripe, grow side by side with peas, pumpkins, spinach; a garden with baked beans, vines and spaghetti bushes, and sauerkraut beds, and great caldrons of hot soup, and through it running a branch of the ocean in which one can catch salmon, lobsters, crabs and shrimp, and dig oysters and clams.

1. Place the rabbit in a flameproof casserole, and cover with the milk and 1 cup water. Cover and simmer for 45 minutes. Drain. Measure 2 cups of the cooking liquid and reserve. Melt 1 tablespoon of the butter in a skillet over high heat, add the mushrooms, and sauté until they are soft and stop giving off liquid, about 5 minutes.

2. Preheat oven to 400°F.

3. On a well-floured board, roll out half the dough into a circle about 14 inches in diameter. Line a 9-inch deep-dish pie pan with the dough. Arrange the rabbit pieces over the dough, sprinkle with salt, the mushrooms, ham, onion, and parsley.

4. Stir together the remaining 2 tablespoons butter with the flour. Mix into the reserved rabbit cooking liquid. Bring to a boil, and simmer 5 minutes. Add the Tabasco and pour over the rabbit pieces.

5. Brush the outside edge of the bottom crust with water. Roll out the remaining dough on a well-floured board into a circle large enough to cover the pie plate. Fold in half, center over the filling, and then unfold over the pie. Trim and crimp the edges. Cut a steam vent in the middle.

6. Set the pie on the bottom shelf of the oven. Bake 20 minutes, reduce the heat to 325°, and continue cooking 40 minutes. Serve hot.

McIlhenny's Tabasco Sauce Recipes by Sarah Tyson Rorer

---

1 small rabbit (about 2½ pounds), cut into 2-inch pieces

1 cup milk

1 recipe pie dough (pages 81 or 285)

3 tablespoons butter, softened

2 cups sliced mushrooms

Salt

½ cup chopped smoked ham

1 tablespoon finely chopped onion

1 tablespoon chopped fresh parsley

2½ tablespoons flour

10 drops Tabasco, or more to taste

SERVES 4

Costillas Rellenas
Pork Chops with Chile

A German by the name of William Gebhardt began the Tex-Mex food industry in 1896 when he packaged a chili blend under the label Eagle Brand. In the 1930s, the company published a cookbook to try to expand its national audience. Gebhardt's Chili Powder Company promised the exotic in its *Mexican Cookery for American Homes,* but the accent was definitely on "American Homes" rather than "Mexican." It would be another fifty years before most Americans outside of the Southwest were ready for a really spicy dose of Mexican cooking.

FILLING

2 tablespoons butter

3 tablespoons chopped onion

1 cup bread crumbs

½ teaspoon chili powder

Salt

⅓ cup milk

4 thick pork chops, about 10 ounces each

CHILI BUTTER

3 tablespoons butter, softened

1 teaspoon chili powder

1 small garlic clove, finely chopped

2 tablespoons lemon juice

Chopped parsley, for serving

SERVES 4

1. Preheat oven to 450°F.

2. To make the filling, heat the butter in a medium skillet over moderate heat. Add the onion and sauté until softened. Add the bread crumbs, chili powder, and salt and continue sautéing until the crumbs begin to brown. Stir in the milk. Let cool briefly.

3. Using a small sharp knife, make a pocket in each chop, cutting into the meat side of the chop. Fill each pocket with crumb stuffing and secure with toothpicks.

4. To make the chili butter, stir together the softened butter, chili powder, garlic, lemon juice, and salt to taste. Spread all over the chops.

5. Place the chops, side by side, in a roasting pan. Set in the oven and roast, turning once, until they are just cooked through, about 30 to 40 minutes. Sprinkle with chopped parsley and serve.

Mexican Cookery for American Homes by Gebhardt's Chili Powder Company

Macaroni with Cheese

Macaroni and cheese has been an American dish at least since Mary Randolph's *Virginia Housewife*. By the late nineteenth century, macaroni and cheese had been standardized into something we would easily recognize today. Yet pasta was still considered more gourmet than everyday food. Mrs. Rorer wrote in 1886: "In this country, "[macaroni] is a sort of luxury among the upper classes; but there is no good reason, considering its price, why it should not enter more extensively into the food of our working classes." She should have been working for Kraft. Macaroni and cheese was primarily a side dish at this time.

1. Preheat oven to 375°F.

2. Bring a large pot of water to a boil, season generously with salt, add the macaroni, and cook until just tender. Drain and cool under cold running water. Drain well.

3. Heat 1 tablespoon of the butter in a small saucepan over moderate heat. Add the flour and cook, stirring, 1 minute. Add the milk, bring to a boil, and simmer 5 minutes.

4. Sprinkle the bottom of a 6-cup casserole with ⅓ of the cheese. Add half the macaroni, half the sauce, another ⅓ of the cheese, the remaining macaroni, and then the remaining sauce. Finish with a layer of cheese, the crumbs, and finally with the remaining 2 tablespoons butter, cut into little bits.

5. Bake in the top third of the oven until golden and crusty, about 20 to 25 minutes.

Cleveland Baking Powder Cookbook

¼ pound macaroni, elbow or other (about 1½ cups uncooked)

Salt

2 tablespoons butter

1 tablespoon flour

1½ cups milk

1 cup grated cheddar cheese (¼ pound)

2 tablespoons bread crumbs

SERVES 4 AS A SIDE DISH

Astor House Rolls

BUTTERY DINNER ROLLS

Much like the patent medicine premium cookbooks it was imitating, the *Cleveland Baking Powder Cookbook* was a general cookbook that included many recipes that didn't use baking powder. It is especially peculiar that this recipe for yeast-leavened dinner rolls appeared in a cookbook promoting baking powder! The booklet contains endorsements from all the bigwig cooking teachers of the time, as well as some of their recipes. The name of these rolls comes from one of the most famous nineteenth-century New York hotels, the Astor House.

2 cups milk

1/4 cup plus about 4 tablespoons butter, softened

2 tablespoons sugar

1/4 teaspoon salt

1/2 envelope (1 teaspoon) active dry yeast

5 cups all-purpose flour

MAKES 30 TO 36 ROLLS

1. Bring the milk to a boil in a small saucepan. Pour into a large bowl, stir in the butter, sugar, and salt. Let cool to lukewarm. Stir in the yeast. Stir the mixture into the flour, combine, turn the dough out on a lightly floured board, and knead until smooth and elastic, about 3 to 5 minutes.

2. Place the dough in a lightly greased bowl, cover with plastic wrap, and let rise in a warm place until doubled in bulk, about 1 hour. Punch down the dough and knead briefly.

3. Roll out the dough to a thickness of about 1/2 inch. Cut out rounds with a 2 1/2-inch biscuit cutter. Spread each of these with about 1/3 teaspoon butter. Fold over into a half-moon shape, squeeze the edges and flatten slightly.

4. Butter a cookie sheet. Place the rolls, barely touching each other, on the prepared cookie sheet. Cover with plastic wrap and let rise in a warm place until doubled in bulk, about 1 hour.

5. Preheat oven to 375°F.

6. Bake until the rolls are golden brown, about 12 to 15 minutes. Serve hot.

Cleveland Baking Powder Cookbook

Peanut Biscuits
PEANUT BAKING POWDER BISCUITS

During both world wars, government, industry, and patriotic organizations published cookbooks to help the public reduce consumption of commodities seen as vital to the war effort. In a letter reprinted in *Best Wartime Recipes,* a cookbook promoting Royal Baking Powder, the government gives its blessing to breads made with baking powder: "…the use of baking powder breads made of corn or other coarse flours instead of patent wheat flour is recommended by the Conservation Division of the Food Administration. The wheat needed for export is thus conserved, and at the same time healthful food for our own people is provided. The circulation of recipes providing for these uses would be of assistance in carrying out our plans." Here, part of the flour and butter normally found in dinner biscuits is replaced by peanuts, a food deemed inessential for the war effort, but ironically higher in protein. These are very peanuty, and if you like peanuts, you'll definitely enjoy them.

1. Preheat oven to 425°F. Lightly butter a cookie sheet.

2. Grind the peanuts fine in a food processor.

3. Sift together the flour, baking powder, and salt in a medium bowl. Stir in the peanuts. Using a pastry cutter or your hands, work the butter into the flour until it has the texture of oatmeal. Stir in the milk until just combined.

4. Roll out the dough ³/₄ inch thick on a lightly floured surface. Cut the dough into biscuits with a 2- to 3-inch biscuit cutter. Place the biscuits on the prepared cookie sheet and bake until golden brown, 12 to 15 minutes. Serve warm.

Best Wartime Recipes, Royal Baking Powder Company

2 cups roasted unsalted peanuts

2 cups all-purpose flour

4 teaspoons baking powder

1 teaspoon salt

2 tablespoons butter, cut into small pieces

³/₄ cup milk

MAKES 10 TO 15 BISCUITS

Chocolate Cup Cakes

This is the quintessential chocolate cupcake recipe, the staple of generations of bake sales. No doubt, it owes part of its popularity to books such as *My Party Book of Tested Chocolate Recipes*, a General Foods pamphlet devoted to chocolate.

2 ounces unsweetened chocolate, broken into pieces

1½ cups bleached all-purpose flour

1½ teaspoons baking powder

½ teaspoon salt

⅓ cup butter, softened

1 cup sugar

2 eggs, beaten

1 teaspoon vanilla extract

½ cup milk

Chocolate Wonder Frosting (recipe follows)

Chopped nuts, tiny colored candies, or coconut, for decoration

Makes 18 cupcakes

1. Preheat oven to 350°F. Line 18 paper muffin cups with cup liners or butter the pans.

2. Melt the chocolate in a small bowl set over very hot (but not boiling) water. Sift together the flour, baking powder, and salt.

3. With an electric mixer, beat the butter until light and fluffy. Gradually add the sugar and eggs and continue beating until light and creamy. Beat in the vanilla and melted chocolate. Gradually beat in the flour mixture, alternating with the milk. Beat until smooth.

4. Fill each of the prepared muffin cups ⅔ full of the batter. Bake until a toothpick inserted in the center comes out clean, about 20 to 30 minutes. Cool on a rack. Ice with Chocolate Wonder Frosting and decorate with nuts or candies.

Chocolate Wonder Frosting

A chocolaty, creamy frosting.

1. Melt the chocolate in a small bowl set over very hot (but not boiling) water. In a bowl, beat the cream cheese with the milk and salt until light. Beat in the sugar, 1 cup at a time. Add the chocolate and beat until smooth.

2. Use to frost cakes and cup cakes.

My Party Book of Tested Chocolate Recipes by General Foods

2 ounces unsweetened chocolate, broken into pieces

½ cup cream cheese, at room temperature

2 tablespoons milk

¼ teaspoon salt

2 cups confectioners' sugar

MAKES ENOUGH TO ICE 24 CUPCAKES OR A 2-LAYER 8-INCH CAKE

Gingerbread Upside-Down Cake
APRICOT GINGER UPSIDE-DOWN CAKE

While many of the cookbooks promoting products have been either derivative or bizarre, occasionally there is a gem like *Brer Rabbit's Modern Recipes for the Modern Hostess*. The booklet's author combined a profound knowledge of Southern cooking with a sprightly inventiveness. This variation on the classic pineapple upside-down cake is a lovely example. The recipe calls for canned apricots, a fragile fruit that until recently was available fresh for only a few weeks each year. You can substitute fresh apricots, just make sure they are ripe; you will need about 12 to 15, depending on their size. For the syrup, substitute ½ cup apricot nectar.

4 tablespoons butter, softened
¾ cup sugar
Two 17-ounce cans apricot halves
2 cups flour
2 teaspoons baking powder
½ teaspoon baking soda
1 teaspoon ground ginger
½ teaspoon salt
1 cup unsulphered molasses
½ cup vegetable shortening, or substitute butter
1 egg, beaten
Whipped cream, for topping

SERVES 8 TO 10

1. Preheat oven to 350°F.

2. Cream the 4 tablespoons butter with ½ cup of the sugar. Spread over the bottom of a 10-inch round cake pan. Drain the apricots, reserving the syrup, and arrange cut side down on the butter mixture. Measure ½ cup of the syrup and stir into the molasses. Sift together the flour, baking powder, soda, ginger, and salt.

3. Using an electric mixer, beat the ½ cup shortening or butter with the remaining ¼ cup sugar until light and creamy. Beat in the egg. Gradually beat in the flour mixture, alternating with the molasses mixture.

4. Pour the batter over the apricot halves, set the pan in the oven, and bake until a toothpick inserted in the center comes out clean, about 1 hour. Let cool no more than 10 minutes before unmolding.

5. To unmold, run a small knife around the edge of the pan to loosen the cake. Set a serving plate on top and quickly turn the cake pan over. Serve slightly warm or at room temperature with whipped cream.

Brer Rabbit's Modern Recipes for the Modern Hostess

Lemon and Apple Tart

It could be said that apple pie—an invention of the English—wasn't eligible for its naturalization papers until its crust was made with an all-American shortening.

1. On a floured surface roll out half of the pastry to form the bottom crust and place in a 9-inch pie pan. Refrigerate.

2. Preheat oven to 425°F.

3. Peel, core, and grate the apples. Measure 2 cups. Toss immediately with the lemon juice so that they do not discolor. Stir together the sugar, eggs, shortening, salt, lemon rind, and cream. Stir in the apples.

4. On a floured surface, roll out the remaining piece of dough ⅛-inch thick. Cut into plain or serrated ¾-inch strips. Pour the filling into the lined pie pan. Moisten the edges of the crust. Using the strips of dough, make a lattice top on the pie: this is done by starting at one edge, and interweaving the strips as you set them down. Lightly moisten any place where the strips overlap. Press down on the edges to adhere them to the bottom crust and trim the excess dough.

5. Set the pie on the bottom shelf of the oven. Bake 20 minutes. Lower the temperature to 350°F. Continue baking until the top is golden and the custard has set, about 40 minutes longer.

A Modern Manual of Cooking by Marion Harris Neil

1 recipe New Crisco Pastry (page 285)

1½ pounds baking apples, such as Northern Spy, Baldwin, or Golden Delicious

3 tablespoons fresh lemon juice

1¼ cups sugar

2 eggs, beaten

2 tablespoons vegetable shortening, or substitute butter, melted

½ teaspoon salt

1 teaspoon grated lemon rind

1 cup light cream

SERVES 6 TO 8

On Making Pie Dough

One of the most important legacies of the domestic science movement is the standard recipe with thorough instructions. This essay on making pastry by former *Ladies' Home Journal* editor Marion Harris Neil is an admirable example of her "science" and is as valid today as it was then. It comes from the introduction on pastry making in *The Story of Crisco*.

With pastry, a good deal always depends on the mixing. The best way is to measure out the average quantity of liquid, to pour about three-quarters of this gradually into the flour, at the same time stirring this briskly with a knife, so as to get it evenly moistened, and then add, in very small quantities at a time, as much more water as may be needed. To see, in this way, when the flour has been moistened enough is easy. By the time the first three parts of water have been put in, most of it will have stuck together in little separate rolls; if on pressing these they should not only cling together, but readily collect about them whatever loose flour there may be, sufficient moisture will have been added; but so long as the mixture, when pressed, remains to some degree crumbly, it is a sign that a little more water is required. When done, the paste should stick together, but should not adhere to the hands or the basin.

To roll out, flour the pastry board slightly, lay the dough on it, and form into a neat, flat oblong shape. Press it out a little with the roller, and roll with short quick strokes to the thickness required. Always roll straight forwards, neither sideways nor obliquely. If the paste wants widening, alter its position, not the direction of the rolling. At the beginning of each stroke, bring the roller rather sharply down, so as to drive out the paste in front of it, and take especial care in rolling always to stop just short of the edges.

[The pastry] should be handled and rolled as little as possible and when carefully made it should not be in the least leathery or tough....Make pastry in a cool atmosphere and on a cool surface.

The New Crisco Pastry

The invention of Crisco in 1911 had a profound impact on that quintessential American institution, the pie. Until then, the shortening used almost universally to make pastry in the United States was lard. (In Britain, beef suet was often used; in Continental Europe, butter was preferred.) Hydrogenated vegetable shortening has many of the same characteristics as lard, but lacks a distinguishing flavor. This latter quality was promoted as a virtue by Marion Harris Neil in *The Story of Crisco*. The book went through at least twenty-six editions between 1912 and 1925.

The acidity of the lemon juice makes the dough a little less crumbly and as a result somewhat flakier.

1. Sift the flour with the salt into a medium bowl. Add the shortening. Using one or two well-floured knives, cut the shortening into the flour until the mixture is about as fine as rolled oats.

2. Stir together the egg, lemon juice, and 2 tablespoons ice water. Sprinkle over the flour and toss to mix. Add 1 to 3 more tablespoons ice water and toss with the flour to make a dough that just barely sticks together. Do not overmix. Gather the dough together, divide into 2 even pieces, and wrap each in plastic film. Refrigerate at least 2 hours before rolling out.

The Story of Crisco by Marion Harris Neil

2 cups flour

³/₄ teaspoon salt

³/₄ cup vegetable shortening

1 egg, lightly beaten

1 tablespoon lemon juice

MAKES ENOUGH DOUGH TO MAKE 2 SINGLE-CRUST PIES OR 1 DOUBLE-CRUST PIE

Crisco Brownies

MOLASSES BROWNIES

The brownie, that much-loved confection that is part cake and part cookie, began to appear regularly in cookbooks at the turn of the century. According to the *Oxford English Dictionary*, the term "brownie" was first used in a Sears & Roebuck catalog in 1897, which makes it certain that this American confection was already familiar at the time.

Brownies usually included chocolate but not always, as this recipe shows. The author suggests baking the brownies in a large cake pan and then cutting them up, just as we do now. She also suggests an alternate method in which the brownies are baked in individual fancy tins.

⅓ cup sugar

⅓ cup vegetable shortening

¼ teaspoon salt

2 eggs, beaten

⅓ cup molasses

½ teaspoon vanilla extract

1 cup all-purpose flour

1 cup coarsely chopped nuts
(walnuts or pecans)

MAKES 12 BROWNIES

1. Preheat oven to 350°F. Grease an 8- by 8-inch square baking pan.

2. Beat the sugar and shortening in a medium bowl until creamy. Gradually beat in the salt, eggs, molasses, and vanilla extract. Stir in the flour and nuts.

3. Spoon into the prepared pan. Bake about 30 minutes, until firm. Cut into 12 bars.

The Story of Crisco by Marion Harris Neil

Brownies, from *The Story of Crisco*.

Shredded Wheat Cookies

Shredded wheat was invented by Henry D. Perky in the early 1890s and introduced as a health food to calm troubled stomachs. Along with Kellogg's Corn Flakes and Post's Grape Nuts, it was part of a health food craze that swept the country around the turn of the century. At first, Perky didn't think of his little pillow-shaped biscuits as specifically breakfast food. The first promotional pamphlet, *The Vital Question Cook Book,* included recipes for Raspberries in a Bisquit Basket, Poached Egg on Shredded Wheat Bisquit, and Creamed Spinach on Shredded Wheat Bisquit Toast, among others. By 1925, though shredded wheat had become an integral part of the nation's breakfast selection, the premium cookbook, *Health in Every Shred,* was still offering suggestions for shredded wheat in every course. Giving her seal of approval was author Alice Bradley, the principal of Fannie Farmer's Boston Cooking School at the time.

These cookies are best eaten slightly warm. Coarsely chopped walnuts or pecans can be substituted for the coconut.

1. Preheat oven 350°F. Lightly butter several cookie sheets.

2. Using a rolling pin, crush the Shredded Wheat biscuits. Sift together the flour and baking powder.

3. Cream together the butter and sugar. One by one, beat in the 2 egg yolks and then the vanilla. Stir in the coconut, crushed Shredded Wheat, and flour mixture. Beat the egg whites until firm and glossy. Stir into the batter.

4. Using 2 spoons, form the batter into 1-inch balls. Drop these about 2 inches apart on the prepared cookie sheets. Bake until puffed and golden, 20 to 25 minutes.

Health in Every Shred by The Shredded Wheat Company

3 Shredded Wheat biscuits

1 cup all-purpose flour

2½ teaspoons baking powder

5 tablespoons butter, softened

1 cup sugar

2 eggs, separated

½ teaspoon vanilla extract

½ cup shredded unsweetened coconut

MAKES 3 TO 4 DOZEN COOKIES

Walnut Wafers

These "wafers" bridge the gap between a cookie and a praline.

2 eggs

1 cup brown sugar

1/2 teaspoon salt

1/4 teaspoon baking powder

3 tablespoons flour

1/2 pound walnuts, broken into pieces, but not chopped

MAKES 3 TO 4 DOZEN COOKIES

1. Preheat oven to 350°F. Butter and flour 2 cookie sheets.

2. Using an electric mixer, in a medium bowl beat the eggs until light. Add the brown sugar and beat until light and creamy. Add the salt, baking powder, and flour and beat until smooth. Lastly, stir in the walnuts.

3. Drop the mixture by heaping teaspoonfuls, leaving about 2 inches between each cookie, onto the prepared sheets and spread them out slightly. Bake in the middle of the oven until light brown and no longer glossy, 12 to 15 minutes. Remove the wafers with a flexible metal spatula as soon they come out of the oven. Cool.

Cleveland Baking Powder Cookbook

Chocolate Pudding
CHOCOLATE PUDDING WITH CHOCOLATE MERINGUE

Although this recipe comes from a Carnation Milk promotional pamphlet from 1941, its meringue topping is typical of the late nineteenth century, the heyday of all sorts of puddings and custards. The pudding can be made in four individual dishes or in a single 10-inch pan; in the latter case, increase the cooking time by 15 to 20 minutes.

1. Preheat oven to 325°F.

2. Bring the milk to a boil, remove from heat, then stir in the chocolate. Let melt.

3. Beat the egg yolks together with the salt and 6 table-spoons sugar until light. Gradually stir in the hot chocolate mixture. Pour into four wide, shallow 8-ounce ramekins. Set in a baking pan. Place the baking pan in the oven and add boiling water to come halfway up the sides of the ramekins.

4. Bake until the pudding is thickened, about 30 to 40 minutes. Remove the pan from the oven and the ramekins from the pan; let cool to room temperature, then refrigerate until cold.

5. Preheat oven to 425°F.

6. Beat the egg whites until firm. Add the remaining 4 tablespoons sugar and beat until stiff and glossy; beat in the cocoa. Top each of the puddings with some of the meringue. Set the ramekins in the top third of the oven and bake until firm and lightly browned, about 6 to 8 minutes.

The Carnation Cook Book by Mary Blake

2 cups evaporated milk

2 ounces unsweetened chocolate, coarsely chopped

6 egg yolks

Large pinch salt

10 tablespoons sugar

4 egg whites

4 teaspoons cocoa

SERVES 4

Pear Marlow

MARSHMALLOW PEAR MOUSSE

"Marlows are first cousins to the mousses," write the authors of *How Famous Chefs use Marshmallows*, "they both use gelatin as their stiffening 'agent.' Only, in the case of marlows, gelatin is introduced by means of marshmallows, while in mousses it is added in dissolved granulated form." This unintentionally wacky pamphlet features pictures of chefs from across the land smiling at their magnificent marshmallow creations. Today, using marshmallows as a thickening and aerating agent in mousses may be worth a second look since raw egg whites are now considered a health risk.

The recipe calls for syrup obtained from preserved ginger. Should you not have preserved ginger on hand, you can make a similar syrup by combining ⅓ cup sugar with ⅓ cup water and about 1 tablespoon coarsely chopped ginger. Bring this to a gentle simmer and cook 15 minutes. Strain and measure the necessary quantity.

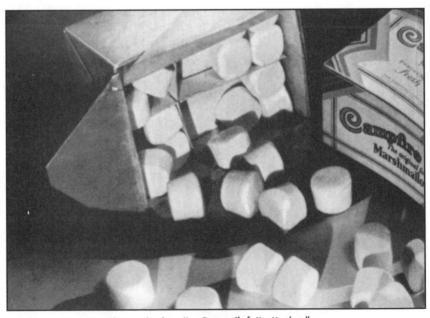

Glamour shot from *How Famous Chefs Use Marshmallows*.

1. Drain the pears, reserving the juice. Pour ¼ cup of the juice into a medium metal bowl. Purée the drained pears and measure 1 cup.

2. Add the marshmallows to the pear juice, set over a pan of simmering water, and heat, stirring occasionally, until the marshmallows have melted (it will take about 10 to 15 minutes). Remove from the heat, stir in the puréed pears, ginger syrup, and lemon juice. Cool to room temperature and then chill until the mixture is slightly stiffened, 20 to 30 minutes.

3. Whip the cream until stiff. Fold into the marshmallow mixture. Spoon into 1 large or 4 individual serving bowls. Refrigerate until firm.

How Famous Chefs use Marshmallows by Angelus-Campfire Co.

One 16-ounce can pears

18 marshmallows

3 tablespoons syrup from preserved ginger

1 tablespoon lemon juice

1 cup heavy or whipping cream

SERVES 4

Cocktails
and Casseroles

Cooking in the Suburbs

The dream kitchen of the fifties was sleek, modern, and convenient.

Pasadena, 1955

In 1951, when the Gallup organization asked married women who was a better cook, they or their mothers, a mere 23 percent considered themselves more skilled. Indeed, there is a great deal of evidence that when it came to American cooking, the fifties may have been, as Norman Mailer has called them, "one of the worst decades in the history of man." Though it wasn't for lack of trying. As a matter of fact, that may have been the problem.

Women were now cooking in a new American place — suburbia. Across the country, American families were leaving their crowded inner-city apartments for tracts, subdivisions, and other developments that sprawled across the countryside. By 1960, a quarter of the population had moved to the suburbs.

In California, suburbia meant street after street of ranch-style homes with front lawns garnished with orange trees and backyards equipped with patios and sprinkler systems. These towns were given romantic names like "Villa Serena" and "Tierra Vista," and were connected by freeways. The first freeway to open in Los Angeles was the Pasadena Freeway, which allowed passage to downtown in a magical twelve minutes. Everybody wanted to live in California, the land of convertibles and drive-ins, beaches and backyard barbecues. Even Lucy followed the sun when *I Love Lucy* abandoned New York for the Golden State in the mid-fifties.

While her husband commuted to work, the model fifties housewife was left home alone to prepare meals with foods and devices undreamed of by her mother. Her kitchen had an electric toaster (to toast the Wonder Bread purchased at the supermarket), a freezer (to store the bounty brought home in the station wagon), an electric can opener (to more easily open the canned vegetables, condensed soup, luncheon meat, and tuna so essential to casseroles), an electric carving knife (to shred the defrosted turkey), an electric mixer (facilitating mixing a batch of cake mix), a blender (for making an exotic cocktail on hubby's return from the office), a dishwasher, and, of course, Tupperware for the leftovers.

According to the polls, which for the first time in history gave us some sense of what regular people thought, most women actually enjoyed cooking. The trouble was, they did not know what to cook. In 1945, when *Good Housekeeping* interviewed its readers, most declared that "the most bothersome problem in cooking" was "getting more variety into meals." The young housewife was justifiably insecure about her skills. She was an offspring of the Depression, a time when getting enough to eat at the lowest possible price was much more important than culinary finesse; she had grown up during the war, when rationing made imitation foods like oleomargarine an acceptable substitute for the real thing; and she was living in a home isolated from the traditional community she had grown up in.

The women's magazines, especially their advertisers, were more than happy to fill the gap with their culinary advice. *Family Circle,* with a circulation of over four million in 1955, was one of the foremost proponents of the open-a-can and defrost-the-package school of cooking. During the fifties, it was often difficult to differentiate between the recipes included in ads to promote a product and the magazine copy. Features named "Take-it-easy Meals," "Lazy-day Baking" and "Six Cheers for Canned Peaches" live up to all the clichés about the fifties. To assemble "Savory Hash Bake," you start with a can of pineapple, a can of corned-beef hash, and a bottle of chili sauce; "Marshmallow Brownie Pudding" is

The pièce de résistance in the fifties: a gelatin salad.

homemade from canned chocolate-flavor syrup, marshmallows, and devil's food cake mix. In an article called "It's the Added Flavor That Counts When…", gravy coloring is spread on hamburgers, MSG is sprinkled over shirred eggs, seasoned salt flavors a mixture of dry breakfast cereal and nuts, and steak sauce is drizzled over cream cheese ("The meat sauce blends with the cheese as you dip into it to spread crackers"). Although the recipes written for the distinctly more upmarket *Ladies Home Journal* ask the reader to make everything from scratch, the recipes in the full-color advertisements are much more seductive in their elegance and simplicity than the magazine recipes. Who could doubt a 1955 ad that announced "A Jell-O salad *makes* the meal"? And who could resist such an architectural wonder of transparent green in which gravity-defying bits of onion, canned pimiento, and raw cauliflower float in ethereal, shimmering lime Jell-O?

Though advertising had been used to sell food in this country since the late nineteenth century, it was now everywhere, most notably on the new device that no suburban house could do without, the television. Some early shows even incorporated the promotion directly into the script. On the "George Burns and Gracie Allen Show," sponsored by Carnation, the program moved seamlessly into the commercial. As Gracie Allen stands by, her friend Mamie pours a cup of coffee.

"Ummm, this is delicious," she croons.

"I use Carnation, you know," the ever cheerfully oblivious Gracie replies.

"Oh, by the way," her friend adds helpfully, "I sent in thirty-five cents and got that wonderful Carnation cookbook with your autograph."

"The recipes are delicious, aren't they?" counters Gracie.

"Yes, and so economical too. Do you know that one can makes enough muffins for 24 people?"

"Really? And I've been throwing those cans away," Gracie answers ingenuously, and the show goes on.

Promotional cookbooks were put out not only by food companies but also by kitchenware manufacturers like Pyrex. Independent authors also wrote cookbooks that took advantage of the new appliances. For example, a blender cookbook told how to make everything from soups to turkey stuffings in the new-fangled device.

The California lifestyle, exemplified by cocktail parties on the patio and Sunday backyard barbecues, inspired cookbooks as well. Some specialized in barbecuing, others in a hundred and one burger variations. One of the more attractive examples was Helen Evans Brown's *Patio Cook Book*. She had direct experience, living in Pasadena, the prototypical suburban paradise.

In *The Cocktail Hour*, Louis P. De Gouy offered over six hundred cocktail recipes for that pre-meal, post-war institution, as well as instructions for hors d'oeuvres that ranged from tasty to grotesque. Among the latter is an overly creative recipe for

"Griddled Banana Snacks": brush bananas with a mixture of butter, anchovies, and parsley, brown on a griddle, arrange them on "finger toast," and finally brush with peanut butter.

Louis P. De Gouy was not only the author of *The Cocktail Hour, The Burger Book,* and many other books, but one of the main contributors to the original *Gourmet* magazine. The "journal of good living" picked an inauspicious time to premiere when it began publication in 1941. With Europe under occupation, *Gourmet* presented articles on travel to Canada and South America, but its culinary predilections were firmly planted in France. It also ran recipes reflecting old-fashioned regional American cooking, as well instructions for dishes like tomato and cantaloupe ball aspic salad (which is even worse than it sounds) alongside the genuine classics of French cuisine.

By the late forties, though, the magazine began reflecting something altogether new in American cooking. For the first time, writers for *Gourmet* took to the road searching out authentic international recipes. Not only did they feature the kind of restaurant cooking that would have been familiar to Escoffier, they also sought out provincial French, Italian, German, Scandinavian, and even Lebanese dishes. *Gourmet*'s readers could sit back in their E-Z recliners and take part in the grand tour that was bringing numberless Americans to Europe. They could read recipes for pesto and *carciofi alla romana,* prepare authentic smorgasbord, and even purée "hommous b'tahani" and "babba gnougge" in their blender. They were told that "The greens for a salad should be almost anything but iceberg lettuce. Boston lettuce, romaine, escarole, field salad, curly endive, Belgian endive, watercress are all good." There were cookbooks that followed suit, led by *Gourmet's* own *Bouquet de France,* which enjoyed over 100,000 readers.

Even *Ladies Home Journal* jumped on the gourmet bandwagon, printing recipes for the likes of "canneloni con vongoli," which required you to make homemade pasta. Seeing a trend, General Foods set up a gourmet food division for a while in the late fifties.

By 1962, with Julia Child on television and the Kennedys in the White House making fine cooking trendy for the first time in several generations, it seemed a new page had been turned in the American cookbook.

But had it really? Was there ever more than a tiny minority who made *boeuf à la bourguignonne?* On the other hand, was everyone part of the suburban cocktail party circuit? And was anybody actually getting pleasure from eating casseroles made with canned tuna, canned tomato soup, canned mushroom soup, all topped with a rubbery layer of American cheese studded with potato chips?

In 1953, when Gallup asked men and women what provided the real test of a woman's ability to cook, their answer was pie, roasts, bread, steak, and cake. President Eisenhower was more typical of his nation's eating habits than the Kennedys would be. Though he employed a French chef for formal occasions, he preferred American food, such as hash, which he often consumed on a tray in front of the TV. Ike's favorite was beef steak, preferably 1½ to 2 inches thick. In 1963, when servicemen were polled, their food preferences, much like those of their former commander-in-chief, hadn't changed much since the thirties. Topping their list was steak, French fries, corn on the cob, sliced tomatoes, hot rolls or

Backyard Barbecue Etiquette

Helen Evans Brown gives lots of advice on outdoor entertaining in her Patio Cook Book. To those harassed as they sweat over the grill she offers these words:

Let there be but one [cook], at least but one at the grill. Whenever possible let it be a man. No smart woman ever officiates at a broiler in male company. If she knows the subject well she'd best keep her knowledge to herself—the only thing a man resents more than being told by another man how best to cook a steak is to be directed by a woman. To a cook of either sex, harassed by kibitzers, try this remedy: hand over your apron to the unofficial adviser with a "Here, do take over."

biscuits, and strawberry shortcake.

They probably would have agreed with the dissatisfied reader of *Gourmet* magazine who wrote: "Your choice magazine wandered into our tiny apartment—quite by chance, I assure you—and we were amazed at some of the so-called "receipts" therein. We are firm believers in simple home-cooked meals, without sauce, without incredible mixtures as you suggest in you epicurean journal….Can you deny that after a day at the office you all go home to a dinner of baked beans and frankfurters?"

Although the gourmet revolution came slowly, come it did over the next decades. As airplane travel became more affordable, numerous Americans, young and old, experienced European food firsthand. Immigrants to the United States opened restaurants serving authentic Asian food—the spicy vegetarian stews of India, the incendiary curries of Thailand, the complex cuisines of China, and the refined flavors of Japan. Restaurants serving reasonably authentic foods like Greek and northern Italian opened in cities

Couples like this one, on board Air France in 1952, brought home a taste for new cuisines.

across the country, while cookbooks were published about Mexican, Tuscan, and Moroccan food. Regional American food was rediscovered. American chefs began to combine Asian and French techniques with local ingredients, just as early Americans once adapted European methods to indigenous foods.

But another food trend still with us had its roots in the fifties, too—the commercialization of the food we eat. The first McDonald's opened in 1954, and the fifties gave us the TV dinner. With fast food, take-out, convenience food, cake mixes, and "family restaurants," fewer people cook their own food each year.

Today, when people make the time to cook, it is often a passion: an act intended for sharing with family and friends, for celebrating holidays and special occasions, for providing both the sustenance and the spice for everyday life. In this, we share a great deal with the generations of American cooks who sat around the American table before us. By cooking some of the recipes that were once special to them, we can stand for a brief time in their kitchens, taste their food, and learn something of who they were.

Dinner Party on the Patio

Park Avenue Watermelon Cooler (page 302)

Port and Cheddar (page 305)

Cold Cucumber Soup (page 307)

Barbecued Hamburgers

Asparagus and Bacon Salad (page 312)

Potato Salad with White Wine (page 313)

Pecan Torte (page 315)

Park Avenue Watermelon Cooler

WATERMELON CHAMPAGNE COCKTAIL

Louis P. De Gouy had an unlikely background for writing a book about that thoroughly American institution, the cocktail. The son of French parents in Austria, he had trained with chefs all over Europe in classical French techniques including, apparently, the renowned Escoffier. Once he got to this side of the Atlantic, though, he realized that Americans were not necessarily enamored of Continental ways. In *The Cocktail Hour,* he catalogued recipes for over 600 mixed drinks along with numerous cocktail party nibbles. This cocktail recipe, made with bubbly, is especially fun.

1 small watermelon

1 bottle chilled champagne or sparkling wine

6 lemon twists

MAKES 6 DRINKS

1. Using a melon baller, scoop out 24 melon balls. Pick out the seeds. Set in a bowl, cover, and refrigerate until ready to use.

2. Fill 6 shallow champagne glasses with the wine, and add 4 melon balls to each glass and a lemon twist.

The Cocktail Hour by Louis P. De Gouy

Gin Fizz

RASPBERRY GIN FIZZ

This fizzy aperitif was served at the old Albemarle Hotel in New York.

In a shaker, combine the ice, sugar, lemon juice, raspberry syrup, and gin. Shake well. Strain into a small tumbler. Add a splash of seltzer.

The Cocktail Hour by Louis P. De Gouy

3 tablespoons finely cracked ice

$\frac{1}{2}$ teaspoon extra-fine granulated sugar

1 tablespoon lemon juice

1 teaspoon raspberry syrup

1 jigger (1$\frac{1}{2}$ ounces) good gin

Seltzer

MAKES 1 DRINK

The Cocktail Hour

Here are just three of the thirty-six pointers on serving cocktails given by Louis P. De Gouy in *The Cocktail Hour:*

- When serving cocktails or other beverages, always give napkins to the ladies. Men need them too but they are inclined to put them in their pockets, finding it difficult to dispose of them when not in use. The ladies really want them.
- Never serve a drink in a chipped glass.
- The hostess should know that some cocktails are fast and some slow in action. If dinner is to be served immediately, a fast cocktail is in order. If not, the slow should be served. Many a dinner has been ruined through passing around too many cocktails of the wrong kind, with the result that the guests are other than food conscious when dinner is announced. Too many cooks spoil the broth, and too many cocktails spoil the dinner. Generally speaking, tart or dry cocktails are fast; sweet cocktails are slow. In the fast category are the Martini and the daiquiri. In the slow class are the cocktails containing grenadine and other sweetening ingredients. At any rate, cocktails, slow or fast, should be sipped slowly, never gulped.

Vegetable Cocktail

Ruth Ellen Church got her blender to do just about anything. In her introduction to *Mary Meade's Magic Recipes for the Electric Blender* she gives a little background on this new gadget: "Originally developed as a drink mixer, for turning out exotic frozen daiquiris, fresh pineapple drinks and malted milks, the early blenders were greeted with glee by health food fans who found they could now have their daily portion of fresh carrot juice with parsley and green pepper without going to any trouble at all." In addition, she notes that a "blender may be a luxury, but some women are beginning to regard it as a necessary luxury; and so will you, too, when you've really learned to know your blender." As far as this recipe goes, she has only a few choice words: "A real tantalizer!"

2 cups tomato juice
1 small celery stalk, with leaves, cut up
1 tablespoon coarsely chopped fresh parsley
Two ¼-inch-thick slices lemon, with peel
One ¼-inch-thick slice green bell pepper
One ⅛-inch-thick slice small red onion
½ teaspoon sugar
¼ teaspoon salt
1 cup cracked ice
SERVES 4

Place all the ingredients in a blender and blend until completely liquefied. Pour into glasses and serve.

Mary Meade's Magic Recipes for the Electric Blender by Ruth Ellen Church

Port and Cheddar

PORT AND CHEDDAR CHEESE SPREAD

The postwar period was the heyday of the cocktail party, and no get-together could be complete without a cheese concoction. "The cheese bowl is almost a necessity of modern entertaining," instructs Ruth Ellen Church. "Any and all kinds of cheese convert to dips and spreads very neatly. Very soft mixtures go into a bowl, to be surrounded with crackers, potato chips, vegetables like crisp cauliflower florets and carrots sticks, all meant for dipping and dunking. Heavier mixtures can be piled up in a bowl or molded into an attractive shape, and should be accompanied by a butter knife for spreading on crackers, rye bread or Melba toast." She further advises: "Have cheese at room temperature. Make your mixture a day ahead, to let the flavors blend and ripen." The author was particularly fond of this cheese bowl—"Maybe you'd better double the recipe," she writes.

1. Combine all the ingredients in a blender or food processor. Blend until smooth.

2. Scrape into a small bowl. Cover and refrigerate overnight. To serve, dip the bowl in hot water then unmold the spread on a decorative plate. Serve at room temperatures, accompanied by crackers and/or vegetables.

Mary Meade's Magic Recipes for the Electric Blender by Ruth Ellen Church

3 tablespoons Port or sherry

3 tablespoons heavy cream

¼ teaspoon paprika

Large pinch onion salt

½ pound very sharp Cheddar cheese, at room temperature, diced

Crackers or vegetables, for serving

MAKES ABOUT 1¼ CUPS

Scallop Cocktail

CHILLED SCALLOP COCKTAIL WITH RÉMOULADE SAUCE

Louis De Gouy drew on his French heritage to create this version of that all-American appetizer, the seafood cocktail. In the United States of the 1950s, fresh tarragon and chervil were practically unheard of. Even today, chervil, a delicate herb mildly redolent of anise and parsley, is difficult to track down. If fresh chervil is unavailable, add a little more parsley. Don't bother with dried chervil, as it has no flavor.

1½ pounds sea scallops

1 cup mayonnaise

3 teaspoons Dijon-style mustard

1½ cups shredded red cabbage

2 teaspoons lemon juice

Salt

Pepper

1 tablespoon finely chopped gherkins

1 teaspoon finely chopped capers

1 teaspoon chopped fresh parsley

1 teaspoon chopped fresh chervil

¼ teaspoon finely chopped fresh tarragon

½ teaspoon anchovy paste

SERVES 6 AS AN APPETIZER

1. Cook the scallops in their own juices in a large skillet over moderate heat, about 5 to 10 minutes, depending on size. They should be slightly rare at the center. Cool to room temperature. Stir together 2 tablespoons of the mayonnaise and 2 teaspoons of the mustard. Toss with the scallops and chill at least ½ hour.

2. Dress the cabbage with ¼ cup of the mayonnaise mixed with the lemon juice and salt and pepper to taste. Chill.

3. To make the sauce, stir together the remaining mayonnaise and mustard with the gherkins, capers, parsley, chervil, tarragon, and anchovy paste.

4. To assemble the cocktails, line 6 cocktail glasses with the red cabbage. (If it is too watery, drain.) Top each with ⅙ of the scallops and a dollop of the rémoulade sauce. (You may not need to use all the sauce.) Serve immediately.

The Cocktail Hour by Louis P. De Gouy

Cold Cucumber Soup
CHILLED CUCUMBER BEET SOUP

A lovely, refreshing soup that is vaguely like a cold borscht. As Helen Evans Brown notes, "This soup is shockingly, utterly, pink."

1. In a bowl, combine the cucumbers, garlic, beet, yogurt, parsley, and chives, and season with salt and pepper to taste. Cover and chill at least 1 hour. Stir before serving.

2. To serve, place an ice cube in the center of each soup bowl, spoon in the soup, and garnish with thin unpeeled slices of cucumber.

Patio Cook Book by Helen Evans Brown

2 medium cucumbers, peeled, seeded, and finely chopped (about 1½ cups), plus thin slices for garnish

1 garlic clove, minced

1 medium beet, cooked, peeled, and finely chopped (about ¾ cup)

3 cups plain yogurt

1½ teaspoons chopped fresh parsley

1½ teaspoons chopped fresh chives

Salt

Ground black pepper

SERVES 4

Chestnut and Squash Soup

Ruth Ellen Church writes that this soup is "Decidedly different, and decidedly delicious, too!" In the 1950s this creamy chestnut soup would definitely have turned heads. The squash is a delightful touch that makes this typically French recipe at least a little American. However, not willing to let good enough alone, the author recommends garnishing the soup with whipped cream. The choice is yours.

1 small butternut squash (about 1 pound)

½ pound chestnuts

1 tablespoon butter

¼ cup chopped onion

¼ cup chopped celery

¼ cup chopped carrot

4 cups beef broth

1 bay leaf

1 cup heavy or whipping cream

Salt

White pepper

1 teaspoon snipped chives, for garnish

SERVES 4

1. Preheat oven to 350°F.

2. Cut the squash in half lengthwise and scoop out the seeds. Wrap each piece with aluminum foil. Place on a baking sheet, cut side up, and bake until soft, about 1 hour. Scoop out the flesh and measure 1 cup.

3. Using a serrated knife, slit the skin of each chestnut. Bring about 3 cups of water to a rapid boil and add the chestnuts. Boil for 10 minutes. Drain the chestnuts and with the aid of a small paring knife remove both the exterior shell and the interior skin. (The hotter the chestnuts are, the easier they are to peel.)

4. Melt the butter in a medium saucepan over moderate heat. Add the onion, celery, and carrot and sauté until softened, about 5 minutes. Add the chestnuts, broth, and bay leaf. Bring to a boil and simmer until the chestnuts are very tender, about 20 to 30 minutes.

5. Remove the bay leaf. Ladle the soup mixture into a blender, add the squash, and purée. Pour back into the saucepan, add ½ cup of the cream, and bring to a simmer. Season with salt and pepper. (Add more broth if the soup seems to too thick.)

6. To serve, whip the remaining cream, ladle the soup into bowls, and top each with a dollop of whipped cream and a pinch of chives.

Mary Meade's Magic Recipes for the Electric Blender by Ruth Ellen Church

Tuna-Noodle Bake

4 oz. noodles, uncooked
1 can condensed cream of mushroom soup (10½ oz.)
⅔ cup water
½ teaspoon Worcestershire sauce
4 oz. American cheese, sliced
2 hard-cooked eggs, sliced
8 stuffed olives, sliced
1 can tuna fish (7 oz.)
sprig of parsley

1. Cook noodles according to directions on the package. Drain.

2. Heat mushroom soup and the water in a PYREX Flameware Saucepan, stirring until smooth. Add Worcestershire sauce and cheese. Continue cooking only until cheese is melted.

3. Reserve a few egg and olive slices for garnish. Add rest of egg slices, olive slices, and the tuna fish to noodles in a PYREX Open Baker. Pour mushroom sauce over noodle mixture and mix together lightly. Bake.

4. For serving, garnish with reserved egg and olive slices and a sprig of parsley.

Time: bake 30 minutes
Temperature: 375 F, moderate oven
Amount: 6 servings
Dish: PYREX 2-Quart Open Baker

Pyrex Prize Recipes

Stuffed Squab
SQUAB STUFFED WITH WILD RICE AND SHERRY

This "early gourmet revolution" dish comes from Chasen's restaurant in Los Angeles, which was a choice location for spotting motion picture and television celebrities. Boning the squab is a delicate procedure best left to an expert butcher. If you are unable to obtain the necessary assistance, stuff the squab as they are. If the squab are not boned, you will use only about half the filling. Heat the part you do not use and serve it on the side. If squab are hard to come by, use Cornish game hens. Unlike the squab, which should be served pink, make sure the hens are fully cooked through.

2 tablespoons butter
¼ cup finely chopped onion
2 tablespoons finely chopped celery
1 cup wild rice (about ¼ pound)
1 bay leaf
3 chicken livers
2 cups chicken broth
2 squab, boned and livers reserved
½ cup sherry
Salt
Pepper
2 teaspoons chopped fresh chives

SERVES 2

1. Heat 1 tablespoon of the butter in a small saucepan over moderate heat. Add the onion and celery and sauté until soft, about 5 minutes. Add the rice, bay leaf, and 1¾ cups of the chicken broth. Season with salt. Bring to a boil, cover, and simmer until the wild rice grains have burst, and the broth has been absorbed, about 1 hour.

2. In the meantime, heat the remaining 1 tablespoon butter in a small skillet over high heat. Add the chicken and reserved squab livers and sauté until lightly browned but still a little pink at the center, 3 to 4 minutes. Cool and chop coarsely. Stir into the wild rice along with ¼ cup of the sherry. Season with salt and pepper to taste.

3. Preheat oven to 450°F.

4. Stuff the squab with the rice mixture. Truss the squab, set in a small roasting pan, and roast until the breast meat is still a little pink, about 30 minutes. Remove from the pan. Set aside and keep warm.

5. Add the remaining ¼ cup broth and sherry to the pan juices. Boil until the juices have reduced to 3 tablespoons. Spoon the sauce over the squab and sprinkle with the chives. Serve with any additional stuffing on the side.

A Guide to Distinctive Dining compiled by Ruth V. Noble

Brazil Nut Stuffing

In the original recipe, the bread was crumbled one or two slices at a time in a blender. A food processor is much more efficient. The Brazil nuts were definitely a touch of the exotic.

Using a food processor, grind the bread to crumbs. In a bowl, toss with the nuts, broth, celery, onions, poultry seasoning, butter, and salt to taste.

Mary Meade's Magic Recipes for the Electric Blender by Ruth Ellen Church

15 slices stale white bread

2 cups coarsely chopped Brazil nuts

¼ cup chicken broth

2 celery stalks with tops, finely diced

2 medium onions, finely diced

1 teaspoon poultry seasoning

½ cup butter, melted

Salt

MAKES ENOUGH STUFFING FOR A 12- TO 15-POUND TURKEY OR TWO 7-POUND CHICKENS.

Asparagus and Bacon Salad

This is a variation of the spinach and bacon salad so beloved at the time.

2 pounds asparagus, cleaned

8 small romaine lettuce leaves

1 hard-boiled egg, finely chopped

¼ pound sliced bacon

2 tablespoons red wine vinegar

Freshly ground black pepper

Salt

SERVES 4

1. Steam the asparagus. Cool under cold running water, then drain. Arrange the lettuce leaves on a platter and lay the asparagus over them. Sprinkle with the egg.

2. Fry the bacon until very crisp. Crumble over the asparagus.

3. Pour off all but 2 tablespoons of the bacon drippings from the pan. Add the vinegar to the pan, bring to a boil, then pour over the asparagus. Season with pepper and just a touch of salt.

Patio Cook Book by Helen Evans Brown

Potato Salad with White Wine

Whenever fifties' cooks wanted a touch of the gourmet, they splashed a little wine into the dish. This salad is served warm.

1. Boil the potatoes until tender. Drain. While still warm, cut into ½-inch slices.

2. In a large serving bowl, toss the potatoes with the parsley, scallions, butter, wine, vinegar, and salt and pepper to taste. Serve warm.

Patio Cook Book by Helen Evans Brown

3 pounds red-skinned potatoes

¼ cup chopped fresh parsley

¼ cup chopped scallions

4 tablespoons butter, melted

½ cup dry white wine

2 tablespoons white wine vinegar

Salt

Freshly ground black pepper

SERVES 6 TO 8

Potato Griddle Scones

"A homey dish but one that goes beautifully with charcoal-broiled meat or fish," writes Helen Evans Brown. These scones are also terrific with breakfast.

2½ pounds starchy white potatoes, such as Russets, peeled and cut into 2-inch pieces

Salt

4 tablespoons butter, plus more for the griddle

½ pound mushrooms, finely chopped

1 tablespoon chopped fresh chives

½ cup flour

1 teaspoon baking powder

Pepper

MAKES ABOUT TWENTY 3-INCH SCONES

1. Boil the potatoes in lightly salted water to cover until tender. Drain well and mash. Measure 3 cups.

2. In the meantime, heat 2 tablespoons of the butter in a skillet over moderately high heat. Add the mushrooms and sauté until they no longer give off liquid and are quite dry, about 8 minutes. Stir into the mashed potatoes along with the chives and the remaining 2 tablespoons butter.

3. Sift together the flour and baking powder. Stir into the potatoes.

4. Roll the dough out on a well-floured board ½ inch thick. Cut in 3-inch rounds or squares.

5. Heat a griddle or large frying pan over moderate heat. Brush generously with butter. Cook the "scones" on both sides until light brown, about 8 to 10 minutes per side. Serve warm.

Patio Cook Book by Helen Evans Brown

Pecan Torte

The author exults, "Here's a triumphant ending for a patio meal. This is a moist and thoroughly satisfying nut cake." The author is rather fond of her icing, as well: "This frosting, and I say it without a particle of modesty, is perfect," she says.

1. Preheat oven to 350°F. Line three 8-inch cake pans with parchment or waxed paper. Butter the paper.

2. Sift together the flour, baking powder, and salt.

3. Beat the egg yolks with 1¼ cups of the sugar until light and lemon colored. Stir in the flour mixture, 2 tablespoons of the rum, and the nuts. Beat the egg whites until they form firm shiny peaks. Fold a third of the whites into the batter and then fold in the remainder.

4. Divide the batter evenly among the 3 pans. Smooth the tops. Set in the oven and bake until firm, about 25 minutes. Cool on racks and remove from pans.

5. About 3 hours before serving, whip the cream with the remaining 1 tablespoon sugar. Stir in the remaining 2 tablespoons rum. Divide the filling in half and use it to put together the 3 layers of the cake. Frost with Fabulous Frosting.

3 tablespoons flour

1 teaspoon baking powder

½ teaspoon salt

6 eggs, separated

1¼ cups plus 1 tablespoon sugar

4 tablespoons dark rum

3 cups (1 pound) finely chopped pecans

1 cup heavy or whipping cream

Fabulous Frosting (recipe follows)

SERVES 8 TO 10

Fabulous Frosting

CHOCOLATE SOUR CREAM FROSTING

1. Melt the chocolate in a bowl set over very hot (but not boiling) water. Stir until melted and smooth.

2. Stir the sour cream and salt into the chocolate until smooth.

Patio Cook Book by Helen Evans Brown

1 cup semisweet chocolate chips, or substitute 6 ounces semisweet chocolate, broken into small pieces

½ cup sour cream

Pinch salt

MAKES 1¼ CUPS FROSTING

Easter Chiffon Pie
LIME CHIFFON PIE

Lime-flavored gelatin gives a Fifties flavor and color to the chiffon filling. Bunny-shaped cookies give the pie that crowning touch. Present it to the kids after the Easter egg hunt—they'll love it.

PIE SHELL

½ cup sugar

4 tablespoons butter, slightly softened

1 egg

¼ cup milk

1¾ cups flour

1 teaspoon baking powder

½ teaspoon salt

½ teaspoon ground ginger

CHIFFON FILLING

3 eggs, separated

6 tablespoons sugar

Pinch salt

1 tablespoon grated lime rind

¼ cup lime juice

¼ cup lime-flavored gelatin

¼ teaspoon cream of tartar

ICING

1 ounce semisweet chocolate

SERVES 6

1. Preheat oven to 375°F. Lightly butter a 9-inch pie plate.

2. To make the pie shell, cream together the sugar, butter, and egg. Add the milk and blend well. Sift together the flour, baking powder, salt, and ginger and combine with the sugar mixture. Mix until smooth. Chill 1 hour.

3. On a floured surface roll out ⅔ of the dough into a 12-inch circle ⅛ inch thick. Transfer to the pie plate. Trim and make a fluted edge. Prick the bottom of the shell. Bake 12 to 15 minutes, until golden. Let cool.

4. Roll out the remaining dough on a floured surface. Use a cookie cutter to cut out 6 bunnies or other fancy shapes. Set on a cookie sheet and bake about 12 minutes, until golden. Reserve.

5. To make the chiffon filling, mix the egg yolks with 3 tablespoons of the sugar, the salt, rind and lime juice in a double boiler or in a metal bowl set over simmering water. Cook, stirring continually, until thick.

6. Stir the gelatin into ½ cup boiling water. Mix into the yolk mixture. Cool in the refrigerator until partially set, then beat until smooth.

7. Beat the egg whites with the cream of tartar until frothy. Gradually add the remaining 3 tablespoons sugar, beating until stiff and glossy. Fold into the egg-yolk mixture, then pour the filling into the cooled pie shell. Chill the pie until the filling is set, about 2 hours.

8. Melt the chocolate and spread the glaze on the cookies with a knife. Place the glazed cookies on the pie just before serving.

Pyrex Prize Recipes

Toll House Cookies
THE ORIGINAL CHOCOLATE CHIP COOKIE

Chocolate chip cookies may not have been invented in the fifties, but that is when they hit the big time. The story of the cookie, one of America's favorites, begins at the historic Toll House Inn near Whitman, Massachusetts. Sometime after 1930, Ruth Wakefield, the innkeeper's wife, added some chopped-up chocolate to a standard drop cookie recipe—and it worked. She dubbed it the Toll House cookie. The Nestlé Company found out about the recipe and received permission to print it on the back of their chocolate bars. Only some years later did they start making chocolate in the form of chips.

This particular recipe for the Toll House cookie that was actually served at the Toll House has almost twice the amount of chips as the standard recipe given on the back of Nestlé's chocolate morsel packages, something one would think a chocolate manufacturer would have preferred. Perhaps Mrs. Wakefield developed the richer version after she sold off the rights to the original.

1. Preheat oven to 375°F. Lightly butter 2 cookie sheets.

2. Cream together the butter and both sugars. Beat in the eggs, one by one, then the vanilla. Dissolve the baking soda in 1 tablespoon hot water. Stir into the butter mixture.

3. Sift together the flour and salt. Stir into the butter mixture. Finally, stir in the nuts and chocolate chips. Drop by level tablespoons on the prepared cookie sheets, leaving about 2 inches between each cookie. Bake 10 to 12 minutes until golden around the edges. Cool on wire racks.

A Guide to Distinctive Dining compiled by Ruth V. Noble

½ cup unsalted butter, softened

6 tablespoons dark brown sugar

6 tablespoons granulated sugar

1 egg

½ teaspoon vanilla extract

½ teaspoon baking soda

1¼ cups all-purpose flour

½ teaspoon salt

½ cup chopped walnuts

1 12-ounce package semisweet chocolate chips

MAKES 50 COOKIES

Peppermint Stick Sauce for Ice Cream

This thick, pink dessert sauce tastes and looks like a six-year-old's birthday party. The author suggests you serve it on chocolate ice cream. It is thoroughly silly, but fun.

2 peppermint sugar candy sticks (about 2½ ounces), broken into pieces

1 cup heavy cream

¼ cup milk

4 marshmallows, cut into 4 pieces

MAKES 1⅓ CUP SAUCE

1. Crush the peppermint candy in a blender.

2. Add the cream, milk, and marshmallows and blend until smooth. Add more milk if the sauce is too thick. Serve over ice cream.

Mary Meade's Magic Recipes for the Electric Blender by Ruth Ellen Church

Bibliography

For the Text

Camp, John. *Out of the Wilderness*. Middletown, CT: Wesleyan University Press, 1990.

Carson, Gerald. *Cornflake Crusade*. New York: Rinehart & Co., 1957.

Carson, Jane. *Colonial Virginia Cookery*. Williamsburg, VA: The Colonial Williamsburg Foundation, 1985.

Cherokee Heritage. Chattanooga, TN: Chattanooga Printing and Engraving, 1984.

Crump, Nancy Carter. *Hearthside Cooking*. McLean, VA: EPM Publications, 1986.

Degler, Carl N. *Out of Our Past*. New York: Harper & Row, 1984.

Diggins, John Patrick. *The Proud Decades: America in War and Peace*. New York: W.W. Norton, 1988.

Fussell, Betty. *I Hear America Cooking*. New York: Viking, 1986.

The Gallup Poll: Public Opinion 1935-1971. New York: Random House, 1972.

Genovese, Eugene D. *Roll, Jordan, Roll: The World the Slaves Made*. New York: Vintage, 1976.

Harriot, Thomas. *A Briefe and True Report of the New Found Land of Virginia* (facsimile edition of the 1590 Theodor de Bry edition). New York: Dover, 1972.

Harris, Jessica. *Iron Pots and Wooden Spoons*. New York: Atheneum, 1989.

Hawke, David Freeman. *Everyday Life in Early America*. New York: Harper & Row, 1988.

Hertzberg, Arthur. *The Jews in America*. New York: Simon and Schuster, 1989.

Hess, Karen. *The Carolina Rice Kitchen: The African Connection*. Columbia, SC: University of South Carolina Press, 1992.

Garraty, John A., ed. *Historical Viewpoints: Notable Articles from American Heritage*. New York: Harper & Row, 1987.

Hornblower, Malabar. *The Plimoth Plantation New England Cookery Book*. Boston: Harvard Common Press, 1990.

Keckley, Elizabeth. *Behind the Scenes*. New York: Oxford University Press, 1988. Originally published 1868.

Kimball, Marie. *Thomas Jefferson's Cook Book*. Richmond, VA: Garrett & Massie, 1949.

Levenstein, Harvey. *Paradox of Plenty*. New York: Oxford University Press, 1993.

— *Revolution at the Table*. New York: Oxford University Press, 1988.

Linck, Ernestine Sewell; Roach, Joyce Gibson. *Eats: A Folk History of Texas Foods*. Fort Worth, TX: Texas Christian University Press, 1989.

Mails, Thomas, E. *The Cherokee People*. Tulsa, OK: Council Oak Books, 1992.

Murrell, John. *A New Booke of Cookerie*. London: John Marriot, 1631.

Paige, Howard. *Aspects of Afro-American Cookery*. Southfield, MI: Aspects Publishing Co., 1987.

Parsons, William T. *The Pennsylvania Dutch: A Persistent Minority*. Boston: Twayne Publishers, 1976.

Perdue, Charles L., ed. *Pigsfoot Jelly & Persimmon Beer*. Santa Fe, NM: Ancient City Press, 1992.

Powell, Horace B. *The Original Has This Signature — W.K. Kellogg*. Englewood Cliffs, NJ: Prentice-Hall, 1956.

Root, Waverley and de Rochemont, Richard. *Eating in America*. Hopewell, NJ: Ecco Press, 1976.

Root, Waverley. *Food*. New York: Simon and Schuster, 1980.

Shapiro, Laura. *Perfection Salad*. New York: Farrar, Straus and Giroux, 1986.

Stoudt, John Joseph. *Sunbonnets and Shoofly Pies*. New York: A.S. Barnes, 1973.

Strasser, Susan. *Satisfaction Guaranteed: The Making of the American Mass Market*. New York: Pantheon Books, 1989.

Walker, Barbara M. *The Little House Cookbook*. New York: Harper and Row, 1979.

Whorf, Amy. "Potions for Pilgrims." *Country Living*. November 1988.

Wilder, Laura Ingalls. *Little House on the Prairie*. New York: Harper & Row, 1975. First published 1935.

—— *On the Banks of Plum Creek*. New York: HarperCollins, 1971. First published 1937.

—— *The First Four Years*. New York: HarperCollins, 1972.

—— *These Happy Golden Years*. New York: HarperCollins, 1971. First published 1943.

Wills, Margaret Sabo. "Founder of the Feast." *Country Living*. November 1988.

Wilson, Samuel M. "Pilgrims' Paradox." *Natural History*. November 1991.

For the Recipes

Best Wartime Recipes. Royal Baking Powder Co. New York, 1917.

Beverly Hills Woman's Club. *Fashions in Foods in Beverly Hills*. 3rd ed. Beverly Hills, CA: Beverly Hills Citizen, 1931.

Blake, Mary. *The Carnation Cook Book*. Milwaukee, WI: Carnation Co., 1941.

The Bread Basket. Standard Brands, 1942.

Brer Rabbit's Modern Recipes for the Modern Hostess. New Orleans: Penick & Forn, n.d. (probably 1920s but could be as late as 1940).

Brown, Helen Evans. *Patio Cook Book*. Los Angeles: The Ward Ritchie Press, 1951.

Carter, Susannah. *The Frugal Housewife: or, Complete Woman Cook*. Philadelphia: Matthew Carey, 1802.

Church, Ruth Ellen. *Mary Meade's Magic Recipes for the Electric Blender*. New York: Bobbs-Merrill, 1952 (revised 1956).

Cleveland Baking Powder Cookbook. New York, 1892.

Coleman, Arthur and Bobbie. *The Texas Cookbook*. New York: A.A. Wyn, 1949.

Colfax County Home Demonstration Clubs. *Favorite Recipes of Colfax County Club Women*. Colfax County, NM: self-published, 1946.

Colville, Jessie Henderson. *A Kentucky Woman's Handy Cook Book*. Jennings and Graham, 1912.

Dallas Chapter of the Association of Junior Leagues of America. *The Junior League of Dallas Cook Book*. 2nd ed. Dallas, TX: self-published, n.d.

De Gouy, Louis P. *The Cocktail Hour*. New York: Greenberg, 1951.

De Knight, Freda. *A Date with a Dish: A Cookbook of American Negro Recipes*. New York: Hermitage Press, 1948.

Dr. Price's Excellent Recipes for Delicious Desserts. New York: Price Flavoring Extract Co., c. 1880.

Estes, Rufus. *Good Things to Eat*. Chicago: self-published, 1911.

Eustis, Celestine. *Cooking in Old Creole Days*. New York: Derrydale Press, 1928. First edition, 1903.

Fergusson, Erna. *Mexican Cookbook*. Santa Fe, NM: Rydal Press, 1934.

Garfield Woman's Club. *Garfield Woman's Club Cook Book*. Garfield, UT: self-published, 1916.

Health in Every Shred. Niagara Falls, NY: The Shredded Wheat Co., c. 1925.

Hearn, Lafcadio. *Creole Cookbook*. New York: Will H. Coleman, 1885. Facsimile edition, Pelican 1967.

How Famous Chefs use Marshmallows. Chicago: Angelus-Campfire Co., 1930.

Indian Women's Club of Tulsa. *The Indian Cook Book*. Tulsa, OK: self-published, 1933.

Kent, Elizabeth. *True Gentlewoman's Delight*. 11th ed. London: 1659.

Kramer, Bertha F. *"Aunt Babette's" Cook Book*. 10th ed. Cincinnati and Chicago: Bloch Publishing and Printing, 1889.

Leiter, Mrs. Henry and Van Bergh, Sara. *The Flower City Cook Book*. Rochester, NY: The Du Bois Press, 1911.

Leslie, Eliza. *Miss Leslie's Complete Cookery: Directions for Cookery, in its Various Branches*. 59th ed. Philadelphia: Henry Carey Baird, 1863. First edition, 1837; last edition, 1851.

—— *The Indian Meal Book*. London: Elder & Co., 1846.

Levy, Esther. *Jewish Cookery Book*. Philadelphia: W.S. Turner, 1871. Facsimile edition, Arno Press, 1975.

Lincoln, D.A. *Russia Salve Cookbook*. Boston: Redding & Co., 1888.

Loeb, Mrs. Alfred. *The "Best by Test" Cook Book*. New York.

May, Robert. *The Accomplisht Cook or the Art & Mystery of Cookery*. London, 1685. First edition, 1660.

Meier, Lina. *The Art of German Cooking and Baking*. Milwaukee, 1922.

Mexican Cookery for American Homes. San Antonio, TX: Gebhardt's Chili Powder Co., 1935.

My Party Book of Tested Chocolate Recipes. General Foods, 1938.

National Council of Negro Women. *The Historical Cookbook of the American Negro*. 1958.

Neil, Marion Harris. *A Modern Manual of Cooking*. Cincinnati, OH: Procter & Gamble, 1923.

—— *The Story of Crisco*. 4th ed. Cincinnati, OH: Proctor & Gamble, 1914.

Noble, Ruth V., ed. *A Guide to Distinctive Dining: Recipes from Famous Restaurants of America*. Cambridge, MA: Berkshire Publishing, 1954.

Philadelphia Centennial Exhibition 1876, Women's Centennial Committees, *National Cookery Book*. Philadelphia, 1876.

The Picayune's Creole Cook Book. 4th ed. New Orleans: Picayune, 1910. First edition, 1901.

Pyrex Prize Recipes. New York: Greystone Press, 1953.

Randolph, Mary. *The Virginia Housewife*. Washington, DC: Davis and Force, 1824 and 1831 editions.

Rorer, Sarah Tyson. *How to Cook Vegetables*. 3rd ed. Philadelphia: W. Atlee Burpee & Co., 1892.

—— *McIlhenny's Tabasco Sauce Recipes*. Philadelphia: McIlhenny Co., 1913.

Sisterhood of the West End Synagogue. *The Practical Cookbook*. n.d. (probably c. 1920).

Smith, Jacqueline Harrison. *Famous Old Receipts: Used a hundred years and more in the kitchens of the North and South contributed by descendants*. 2nd ed. Philadelphia: John C. Winston Co., 1908.

Southwestern Cookery: Indian and Spanish Influences. New York: Promotory Press, 1974.

Thomas, Edith M. *Mary at the Farm and Book of Recipes*. 2nd ed. Harrisburg, PA: Evangelical Press, 1928. First edition 1915.

Tyree, Marion Cabell, ed., *Housekeeping in Old Virginia*. Louisville, KY: John P. Norton and Co., 1890. Preface dated 1877.

Ulmer, Mary and Beck, Samuel, ed. *Cherokee Cooklore*. Cherokee, NC: Museum of the Cherokee Indian, 1951.

The You and I Club. *The Sun-Flower Cook Book*. Lawrence, KS: self-published, n.d. (dedication in book dated 1888).

Young Ladies' Society, First Baptist Church, Rochester, N.Y., *Mother Hubbard's Cupboard*. Rochester: E.R. Andrews, 1880.

Woolley, Hannah. *The Queen-Like Closet*. 5th ed. London, 1684.

Illustration Credits

All the illustrations were drawn from the collections of The New York Public Library. At the end of each reference is the division where the piece is located.

Jacket: Detail of drawing by Jacques Le Moyne de Morgues, gouache on vellum, 1564. The Miriam and Ira D. Wallach Division of Art, Prints & Photographs. The drawing from which this detail is taken depicts the meeting of Huguenot sea captain René Goulaine de Laudonnière with Timucua Indian chief Athore at a marble column honoring the French king, Charles IX, and built by a previous French explorer on what is now Parris Island, South Carolina.

Page xxvi. Woman reading in kitchen. Chromolithograph by Louis Prang and Co. Print Division.

Page 8. The attack. Albumen photograph circa 1860. Dennis Stereograph Collection. Photography Division.

Page 10. Powhatan village. Theodor de Bry, Frankfurt, 1590. Rare Books and Manuscripts Division.

Page 13. Native Americans with harvest. Theodor de Bry, Frankfurt, 1590. Rare Books and Manuscripts Division.

Page 14. Sunflower. Woodcut from *The Herball* by John Gerard. London, John Norton, 1597. Arents Collection.

Page 20. Native Americans grilling fish. Theodor de Bry, Frankfurt, 1590, Rare Books and Manuscripts Division.

Page 26. Corn. Woodcut from *Neue Kreuterbuch* by Pietro Mattioli. Prague: Georgen Melantrich, 1563. Arents Collection.

Page 28. First Thanksgiving. Photomechanical reproduction after Ferris from *The Chronicles of America* edited by Allen Johnson. New Haven: Yale University Press, 1919. USLHG Division.

Page 32. Turkey. Hand-colored engraving by John James Audubon. Arents Collection.

Page 51. Pumpkin. Woodcut from *The Herball* by John Gerard. London, John Norton, 1597. Arents Collection.

Page 52. Reconstruction of a colonial kitchen. Silver gelatin photograph from *Pageant of America* Collection. Photography Division.

Page 54. Washington at Mount Vernon. Engraving by J. Rogers after M. Nevin, n.d. Print Division.

Page 59. Women at table. Wood engraving by Alexander Anderson, early nineteenth century. Print Division.

Page 72. Dressed turkey. Wood engraving by Alexander Anderson, early nineteenth century. Print Division.

Page 77. Chicken on table. Chromolithograph by Louis Prang and Co., late nineteenth century. Print Division.

Page 86. Girl at table. Wood engraving by Thomas Nast from *Thomas Nast's Christmas Drawings for the Human Race*. New York: Harper Brothers, 1890. Print Division.

Page 95. Lobster. Chromolithograph by Louis Prang and Co. Print Division.

Page 96. Uncle Sam with turkey. Wood engraving from Hotel San Remo menu, Thanksgiving Day, 1898, New York, New York. Buttolph Menu Collection, General Research Division.

Page 111. Woman and plum pudding. Chromolithograph by Louis Prang and Co. Print Division.

Page 113. Elves at fireplace. Engraving from H. C. Brown Palace Hotel menu, Christmas Day, 1892, Denver, Colorado. Buttolph Menu Collection, General Research Division.

Page 114. New Orleans. Engraving from *Picturesque America*. Print Collection.

Page 124. Peppers. Woodcut from *Neue Kreuterbuch* by Pietro Mattioli. Prague: Georgen Melantrich, 1563. Arents Collection.

Page 130. Terrapin. Wood engraving by Alexander Anderson, early nineteenth century. Print Division.

Page 142. Sod house, North Dakota. Albumen photography from *Pageant of America* Collection. Photography Division.

Page 147. Stove. Wood engraving from *Montgomery Ward Catalog*. Mail order catalog no. 83, August 15, 1914. Chicago, Montgomery Ward, 1914. The Science, Industry, and Business Library.

Page 160. Sheaf of wheat. Wood engraving by Alexander Anderson, early nineteenth century. Print Division.

Page 167. Breakfast menu, Pennsylvania Railroad. Steel engraving, The Admiralty Special, May 8, 1893. Buttolph Menu Collection, General Research Division.

Page 168. Cook. Stereograph, nineteenth century. Dennis Stereography Collection, Photography Division.

Page 175. Railroad dining car. Wood engraving from The Pennsylvania Railroad Menu, New York and Chicago Limited. 1882, Buttolph Menu Collection.

Page 176. Southern barbecue. Albumen photograph by B. W. Kilburn, 1896. Dennis Stereography Collection, Photography Division.

Page 181. Fish. Wood engraving from The Nantucket Restaurant menu, July 11, 1884, Nantucket, Massachusetts. Menu Collection, General Research Division.

Page 182. Crab with lighthouse. Wood engraving by Alexander Anderson, early nineteenth century. Print Division.

Page 188. Calas girl. Photomechanical reproduction from *Cooking in Old Creole Days* by Celestine Eustis. New York: R. H. Russell, 1903. General Research Division.

Page 194. Chicken market. 55 Hester Street, New York City, February 11, 1937. Silver gelatin photograph by Berenice Abbott. Javitz Collection, Photography Division.

Page 197. Man making speech. Wood engraving from *Banquet of American Institute of Mining Engineers*. Hotel Brunswick, New York, February 21, 1889. Menu Collection, General Research Division.

Page 214. Bakery lady. East Houston Street near Allen Street, New York City, 1948. Silver gelatin photograph by Edward Schwartz. Photography Division.

Page 218. Bread dough rising. Amana Society, Iowa, 1941. Silver gelatin photograph by Dorothea Lange. Javitz Collection, Photography Division.

Page 221. Aunt Sarah. Photomechanical reproduction from *Mary at the Farm* by Edith M. Thomas. Harrisburg, Pa.: Evangelical Press, 1928. USLHG Division.

Page 222. Farmhouse. Photomechanical reproduction from *Mary at the Farm* by Edith M. Thomas. Harrisburg, Pa.: Evangelical Press, 1928. USLHG Division.

Page 236. Woman making pies. Chromolithograph by Louis Prang and Co. Print Division.

Page 242. Pablo Beaumont, *Cronica de Mechoacan*. Manuscripts Division.

Page 246. Roundup. Wood engraving from *Harpers Weekly*, May 5, 1874. General Research Division.

Page 248. Mexican supper on military plaza, San Antonio. Albumen stereograph , circa 1890. Dennis Stereograph Collection.

Page 264. Two women with Crisco. Photomechanical reproduction from *The Story of Crisco* by Marion Harris Neil. Cincinnati, Ohio: Procter and Gamble Co., 1914. General Research Division.

Page 270. Shredded Wheat factories. Photomechanical reproduction from *Health in Every Shred*. The Shredded Wheat Company, 1925. General Research Division.

Page 272. Kitchen scene. Photomechanical reproduction from *Salads: How to make and dress them*. New York: E. R. Durkee and Company, 1907. General Research Division.

Page 286. Girl with brownies. Photomechanical reproduction from *The Story of Crisco* by Marion Harris Neil. Cincinnati, Ohio: Procter and Gamble Co., 1914. General Research Division.

Page 290. Photogravure from *How Famous Chefs Use Marshmallows*. Angelus Campfire Co., 1930. General Research Division.

Page 292. Kitchen scene. Photomechanical reproduction from *Ladies Home Journal*, October 1956, Vol. 73, no. 10. General Research Division.

Page 296. Jell-O mold. Photomechanical reproduction from *Ladies Home Journal*, October 1956, Vol. 73, no. 10. General Research Division.

Page 300. Couple with trays. Photomechanical reproduction from Air France menu, July 30, 1952. Menu Collection, General Research Division.

Index